A QUICK GUIDED TOUR

THROUGH THE
BIBLE

STEPHEN M. MILLER

HARVEST HOUSE PUBLISHERS
EUGENE, OREGON

Cover by Knail, Salem, Oregon

Published in association with the Steve Laube Agency, LLC, 5025 N. Central Ave., #635, Phoenix, Arizona 85012.

A QUICK GUIDED TOUR THROUGH THE BIBLE

Copyright © 2015 Stephen M. Miller
Published by Harvest House Publishers
Eugene, Oregon 97402
www.harvesthousepublishers.com

Library of Congress Cataloging-in-Publication Data
    Miller, Stephen M.
    A quick guided tour through the Bible / Stephen M. Miller.
        pages cm
    ISBN 978-0-7369-6075-5 (pbk.)
    ISBN 978-0-7369-6076-2 (eBook)
    1. Bible—Introductions. I. Title.
    BS475.3.M5545 2015
    220.6'1—dc23

                                            2014028422

Printed in China

15 16 17 18 19 20 21 22 23 / DS-JH / 10 9 8 7 6 5 4 3 2 1

INTRODUCTION

Hello there.
I wrote this book for you if you're…

- a Bible newbie

- a Christian who doesn't know the Bible especially well

- someone who isn't a Christian but who is curious about the Bible

When I decided what Bible highlights to cover and how to put them on a page, I was thinking about people who don't generally crack open a Bible. Some of my neighbors. Friends. Relatives.

I don't write in a bubble for imagined readers. I write for people I know, trying to introduce them to the Bible.

I'm not a preacher or a Bible scholar. I'm a news reporter who went to seminary. I cover the Bible beat.

I don't write to convert you. That's the Holy Spirit's beat, far as I can tell.

MEDITERRANEAN SEA

CANAAN

BEIRUT 100 FT 30 M

SIDON 50 FT 15 M

DAN 575 FT 175 M

MT. HERMON 9232 FT 281 M

DAMASC 2285 FT 696 M

TYRE 60 FT 18 M

HAZOR 713 FT 217 M

SEA OF GALILEE -700 FT -213 M

NAZARETH 1160 FT 354 M

MT. TABOR 1929 FT 588M

JEZREEL VALLEY

SAMARIA 1360 FT 415 M

SHECHEM (NABLUS) 1800 FT, 550 M

JABBOK RIVER

WEST BANK

SHILOH 2296 FT, 700 M

JORDAN RIVER

APHEK 100 FT 60 M

EBENEZER 390 FT, 119 M

JOPPA (TEL AVIV) 75 FT, 23 M

GIBEON 2555 FT 779 M

JERUSALEM 2445 FT 745 M

JERICHO -720 FT -220 M

ACACIA GROVE -700 FT, 213 M

EKRON 338 FT 103 M

BETH SHEMESH 840 FT, 256 M

BETHLEHEM 2450 FT, 747 M

ASHDOD 120 FT, 37 M

ASHKELON 120 FT 37 M

GATH 570 FT 174 M

LACHISH 845 FT 258 M

HEBRON 2916 FT 889 M

JUDEAN WILDERNESS

DEAD SEA -1294 FT -394 M

SEA LEVEL

JUDEAN HILLS

10 MILES (16 KM)

COASTAL PLAINS

JUDEAN FOOTHILLS

JORDAN VALLEY

ISRAEL

I don't write to win you over to my way of thinking about the puzzling Bible stories. That's the Bible prof's beat.

I write simply to report the Bible stories as accurately as I can and to fill in some of the most interesting background details that Bible experts uncover—facts as well as educated guesses that might help us all better understand why some of the Bible heroes and villains did what they did.

Here's an example of what I'm talking about.

It seems odd to some Bible newbies that a hard-nosed Roman governor like Pilate would buckle to local Jewish priests and order the crucifixion of Jesus after declaring him innocent. It doesn't add up.

But some Bible experts say Pilate caved because he was already on shaky ground with the emperor. A Jewish historian writing in the first century said the official in Rome who recommended Pilate for his job had gotten himself dead with good riddance. The emperor executed him and a bunch of his associates for plotting a coup. Pilate must have wondered if the emperor suspected him as well (see "Jesus's Last Week," page 174). Pilate didn't want the Jews complaining about him to the emperor.

I hope you enjoy reading the book—and that you learn a thing or two.

I enjoyed writing it. In fact, I have a great job. I get to study the Bible and what experts have to say about it. Then I get to pass that good news along to you.

I get paid for it too. Assuming you buy the book. It's a wonderful life.

Jesus calms the storm.

An angel stops Abraham from sacrificing his son Isaac.

A WORD OF THANKS

This is what some savvy publishers call a *complex book*.

What makes it complex is that the publishers have to deal with more than just words. They've got to grapple with photos, maps, and charts. And they've got to spread it all out on the pages in magazine style so it's gorgeous.

A job like that takes teamwork. I'd like to thank the team: Bob Hawkins, Terry Glaspey, Gene Skinner, Janelle Ho, and many others too numerous to name. God bless them every one.

Stephen M. Miller
StephenMillerBooks.com

CONTENTS

1

IN SEARCH OF THE BEGINNING

TIMELINE *(dates are approximate)*

5900 BC	Beer is brewed from barley in what is now Iraq.
5000 BC	The Stone Age ends; metal tools are made in Iraq.
4000 BC	Wine is made from grapes in the Middle East.
3500 BC	A Sumerian drawing in Iraq confirms the invention of the wheel.
2900 BC	A flood devastates the Sumer kingdom in south Iraq.
2200 BC	Pyramid-like ziggurats are built in Iraq with temples on top.
2025 BC	Abraham moves from Iraq to Israel.
1950 BC	Ur loses control of the city and region.
1920 BC	Jacob marries Leah and Rachel.

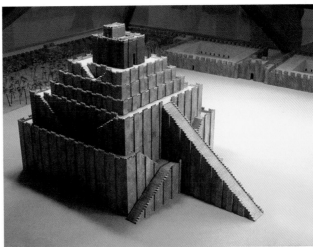

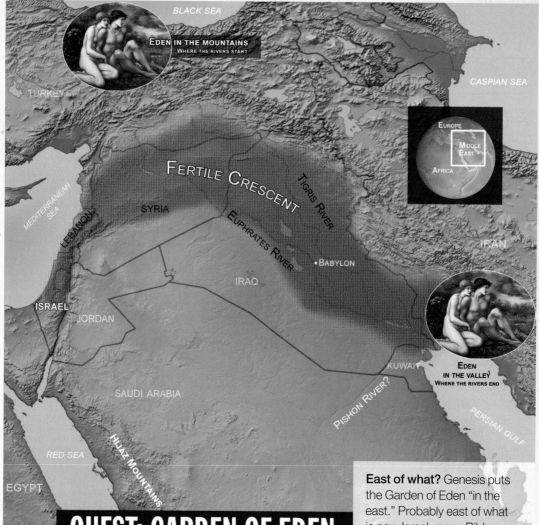

EDEN IN THE MOUNTAINS
WHERE THE RIVERS START

BLACK SEA

CASPIAN SEA

TURKEY

EUROPE
MIDDLE EAST
AFRICA

FERTILE CRESCENT

TIGRIS RIVER

MEDITERRANEAN SEA

SYRIA

EUPHRATES RIVER

•BABYLON

IRAN

LEBANON

ISRAEL

JORDAN

IRAQ

EDEN
IN THE VALLEY
WHERE THE RIVERS END

KUWAIT

SAUDI ARABIA

PISHON RIVER?

PERSIAN GULF

HIJAZ MOUNTAINS

RED SEA

EGYPT

QUEST: GARDEN OF EDEN
OASIS PARADISE OF THE MIDDLE EAST

The LORD God planted a garden in Eden in the east…A river watered the garden and then flowed out of Eden and divided into four branches… Pishon…Gihon…Tigris…Euphrates.

GENESIS 2:8-14

Eden never existed, some Christians speculate.

As far as they're concerned, sinking money into an expedition to find it would make as much sense as hiring a detective to track down a fairy godmother.

East of what? Genesis puts the Garden of Eden "in the east." Probably east of what is now Israel, many Bible experts guess, since the book was likely written by a Jew in Israel. Theories put the Garden in the ballpark of the Fertile Crescent, the river-fed land where archaeologists say civilization started in what is now Iraq. Genesis identifies four of the rivers, leading to one theory that God put the Garden at the source of the rivers in the mountains. Another theory puts Eden at the end of one of the rivers in an ancient river valley flooded by Ice Age melt and today known as the Persian Gulf.

It's not that these devoted Christians say the creation story is a fairy tale. Many of them would, however, call it a myth—but a myth with a message. A bit like a parable. They read a lot of symbolism into the story.

They say the writer's main goal was to paint word pictures to help folks understand that the Creator was God and not one of the other Middle Eastern gods that had been getting credit in earlier stories, such as the Epic of Gilgamesh, first written in about 2100 BC.

That Epic of Gilgamesh, which credits a goddess named Aruru for making a man from clay, came out of what is now Iraq. Middle Easterners had been telling that story for several centuries before Moses came along in either the 1400s or 1200s BC (scholars debate which). Moses is generally credited with writing the anonymous book of Genesis.

Most Christians, however, say they read the creation story as history—possibly God's account delivered personally to Moses. Some of these Christians say they wonder where the first humans lived: Adam and Eve in the mysterious Garden of Eden.

BIBLE CLUES POINTING TO EDEN

The Genesis writer teases readers with clues to Eden. There's a word clue (Eden) and four landmark clues (the names of four rivers).

That's not enough to pinpoint the Garden. But it does seem to get us in the neighborhood—at least in the right part of the world.

The word clue. Eden is a word that many scholars say might have come from Sumer, the world's first known empire. Homeland of Abraham, father of the Jews, Sumer was located in what is now south Iraq. In Sumerian lingo, the root word *edinu* refers to the fertile grazing pastures along the Iraqi river valley.

The word also shows up in ancient writings discovered in Syria. There, it describes a fertile land with lots of water.

The landmark clues. "In the east" (Genesis 2:8). East of what?

East of the writer and his intended readers, many Bible experts speculate. If that writer was Moses or just about any other Jew in early Old Testament times, and if the intended readers were the Jews of Israel, *east* could have been what is now Syria, Iraq, or Iran.

Historians say civilization began there, in the valley along the banks of the Tigris and Euphrates rivers. This stretch of land makes up part of a huge, green crescent on the ancient Middle Eastern map. Nickname: the Fertile Crescent.

"Pishon" (2:11). Flowing through a land "where gold is found," the Pishon River has been lost to history. One contender: Kuwait River. It's now just a sunbaked gully that runs diagonally from Saudi Arabia through Kuwait and empties into the Persian Gulf. Satellite pictures tracing the gully suggest it may have been an ancient river fed by streams from the Hijaz Mountains—mountains nicknamed the Cradle of Gold because they were the only major source of minable gold in the Arab world.

"Gihon" (2:13). Another mystery river, the Gihon "flowed around the entire land of Cush." In the Bible, Cush usually refers to what is now southern Egypt and Ethiopia. But in Genesis, many Bible experts say, this region was the land settled by descendants of "Cush…ancestor of Nimrod…He built his kingdom in the land of Babylonia" (Genesis 10:8,10). Babylon's empire grew up in what is now southern Iraq. That would put the river somewhere near the last two rivers mentioned.

"Tigris…Euphrates" (2:14). These are two

of the most famous rivers in the Middle East. They start in the hills of southern Turkey and flow southeast through Syria and Iraq before emptying into the Persian Gulf.

As the Genesis writer tells it, these four rivers were branches that broke off from the main river in Eden that "watered the garden" (2:10). That description has inspired lots of theories

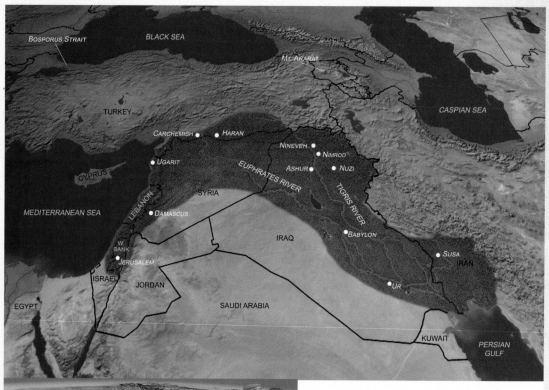

The Angry Eyebrow. That name doesn't sound as scholarly as the Fertile Crescent, the name an American archaeologist gave to the thousand-mile-wide (1600 km) stretch of land where human civilization began. Yet it captures the feel of the place over the long haul of 2000 years before Christ. Here is where the world's first empires rose and fell like dominoes, one after another: Sumerians, Assyrians, Babylonians, Persians, and Greeks. Most of the first cities grew up in the greenest stretch, an area scholars call Mesopotamia—a mouthful of syllables that comes from a Greek term meaning "between rivers." Many scholars include Egypt's Nile River Valley as an extended part of the Fertile Crescent.

about where the Garden of Eden may have been, including…

- *In the mountains.* Turkish mountains are the source of the Tigris and Euphrates Rivers. Perhaps the Pishon and Gihon are now long-lost, dried-up rivers that once flowed out of these mountains as well. Or maybe they are a couple of the other streams feeding into the river valley.

- *In the valley.* Perhaps the four rivers did not flow out of Eden, but into Eden. Maybe the Genesis writer flopped the description to hide the location of Eden. That's one theory. This theory puts the Garden of Eden underwater in what is now the Persian Gulf. As the theory goes, the Persian Gulf was once a river valley. As ice melted after the Ice Age, seawater flooded the Persian Valley, producing the Persian Gulf.

- *In Neverland.* Some Bible experts say it's a mistake to think of the river of Eden as a squiggly line on a map. Instead, they suggest, this river was the writer's way of describing God as the source of all life-giving water on earth. They say that may be why the writer of Revelation described heaven in a way that reads like a flashback to Eden: "The angel showed me the river of the water of life. It was shining like crystal and was flowing from the throne of God and of the Lamb down the middle of the street of the city. The tree of life was on each side of the river" (Revelation 22:1-2 NCV).

GOD'S CREATION TEMPLE

Some Bible experts who read the creation story as more metaphor than history say they see God creating the universe as a kind of temple. Creation's "worship center" includes…

A dome. "God made the dome and separated the waters that were under the dome from the waters that were above the dome" (Genesis 1:7 NRSV). The ancients seemed to think the sky was a hard dome. It was blue because there was water above the dome, which God sometimes released as rain.

A floor. "Let the dry land appear" (Genesis 1:9 NRSV).

Holy water. "He called the waters that were gathered together 'oceans'" (Genesis 1:10 NIRV). Jews would later call each large bronze basin of water in the temple courtyard a "sea" (1 Kings 7:23 NASB).

Supplies. "Let the land produce plants…Let the land produce all kinds of living creatures" (Genesis 1:11,24 NIRV).

Priests. "Let us make man in our likeness. Let them rule…over the whole earth" (Genesis 1:26 NIRV).

Holy day. "God blessed the seventh day and made it holy" (Genesis 2:3 NIRV).

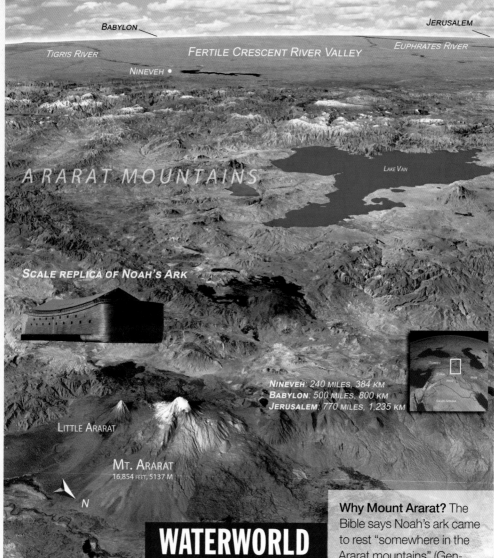

BABYLON

JERUSALEM

TIGRIS RIVER · FERTILE CRESCENT RIVER VALLEY · EUPHRATES RIVER

NINEVEH ·

ARARAT MOUNTAINS

LAKE VAN

SCALE REPLICA OF NOAH'S ARK

NINEVEH: 240 MILES, 384 KM
BABYLON: 500 MILES, 800 KM
JERUSALEM: 770 MILES, 1,235 KM

LITTLE ARARAT

MT. ARARAT
16,854 FEET, 5137 M

N

WATERWORLD

NOAH'S FLOOD— WORLDWIDE OR REGIONAL?

Water covered even the highest mountains on the earth, rising more than twenty-two feet [7 m] above the highest peaks.

GENESIS 7:19-20

Why Mount Ararat? The Bible says Noah's ark came to rest "somewhere in the Ararat mountains" (Genesis 8:4 CEV). Some Bible experts say Mount Ararat was the likely spot because it's the highest mountain in the range and because no other mountains appeared for two months. Supposed ark sightings on Mount Ararat remain unconfirmed.

Most Christians read the Bible story of Noah's flood like it's a news report—accurate in every detail. So say Gallup polls.

Other Christians—a minority—are puzzled by the story. They say the tale of a worldwide flood some 4000 years ago doesn't seem to have a shred of science to back it up.

FLOOD WARNING

The Genesis writer said that by ten generations into humanity, God was fed up. As far as God was concerned, these creatures who knew right from wrong couldn't seem to get anything right. A rotten excuse of a species, they stunk up creation like junkyard dogs at a garden wedding.

"The Lord said, 'I brought them into this world. I'm going to take them out'" (Genesis 6:7, author's paraphrase).

God planned a creation do-over. This time he wouldn't start humanity with a sinner like Adam. Instead, he would reboot the race with Noah, "the only person who lived right and obeyed God" (Genesis 6:9 CEV).

To wash away humanity's sins, God decided to wash away the sinners. As the Genesis writer reports it, God sent an extinction level event—a global flood.

To reseed the planet, God told Noah to build a barge with the storage capacity of about 370 railroad cars. Noah could have parked two arks side by side on a football field. They would have pushed beyond both end zones and into the front rows. They would have risen almost as high as the top of the goalposts. Ark specs: 150 yards long by 25 yards wide by 15 yards high (137 by 23 by 14 m).

Noah herded into the ark a pair of every air-breathing critter along with seven other humans, including his wife, his three sons, and their wives.

Rain fell. Underground water exploded in geysers. This water poured and gushed for 40 days, which some Bible experts say was a common expression meaning a long time.

From the time of the first raindrop to Noah's last day on the barge, more than a year had gone by. Only then did the passengers disembark.

READING THE STORY AS FACT

Many Christians say God reported this story to the writer. Jewish tradition tags the anonymous writer as Moses (1400s or 1200s BC—scholars disagree which).

These Christians insist that if God said water covered the planet, he ought to know. When they look at science, they say they start with the presumption that the writer got his facts right.

As a result, many theorize that the earth is just a few thousand years old. They base this on genealogies reported in Genesis and elsewhere in the Bible—as though these genealogies are complete and not just the headliners as some other Christians theorize.

Many "young-earth" Christians say Noah's flood gave the planet an instant facelift:

- splitting land masses into continents

- chiseling valleys

- shooting flatland prairies a mile high to become mountain ranges

READING THE STORY AS FICTION

So far, no geologist widely respected in the field has gone on record supporting these theories. Nearly all geologists insist that the earth is 4.54 billion years old and that there is no evidence of a worldwide flood in any millennia this side of carbon dating.

That's one reason why some Christians read the creation story for its message, not for its science. They don't have trouble believing there was a devastating flood in ancient times. But they say it makes more sense, given Geology 101, that the flood wiped out only the world as the ancients knew it—riverside cities in the Fertile Crescent, where human civilization started.

Mopping up. After the flood, Noah and his family leave the Ararat Mountains behind as they lead a caravan of critters to the chore of rebooting life on earth.

There is science to back that up.

Archaeologists confirm that floods wiped out entire cities in the Tigris and Euphrates River Valley, including one of the oldest cities—Ur, the New York City of its day and the hometown of Abraham (2100s BC). The flood, dated to about 3500 BC, buried Ur in a layer of mud up to 11 feet (3.5 m) thick.

Another massive flood about 4500 years ago churned a freshwater lake into the Black Sea. Rising ocean water fed by an Ice Age meltdown broke through a narrow wall of land, creating the Bosporus Strait (see the map of the Fertile Crescent on page 14). Like a busted dam allowing a mountain lake to flood the valley, the Bosporus Strait released enough ocean water to push the lakefront several miles back. Fossils of freshwater creatures show the limits of the ancient lake.

Some Christians say they read the entire flood story as a kind of parable intended to teach us not about our history but about the nature of God—specifically, that he doesn't tolerate sin. That's a minority opinion though.

2

IRAQI ABRAHAM ON THE MOVE

TIMELINE *(dates are approximate)*

2075 BC	Abraham's family moves to Haran.
2025 BC	Abraham moves to Canaan (Israel).
2000 BC	Abraham almost sacrifices Isaac.
1950 BC	Egypt invades what is now Israel.
1900 BC	Ur overrun by invaders

PERSIAN GULF

IRAN

• SUSA

• UR ABRAHAM'S HOME

UR DYNASTY
2050 BC

BAGHDAD • BABYLON •

TIGRIS RIVER

IRAQ

EUPHRATES RIVER

• MARI

N ◄

ABRAHAM'S FATHER, TERAH, LEAVES UR
AND MOVES THE FAMILY TO HARAN.

HARAN •
ABRAHAM'S SECOND HOMETOWN

BALIKH RIVER

TURKEY

600 MILES (966 KM)

ABRAHAM
IRAQI FATHER OF THE JEWS

The LORD had said to Abram, "Leave your native country, your relatives, and your father's family, and go to the land that I will show you. I will make you into a great nation."

GENESIS 12:1-2

The great northwest. Abraham's father, Terah, moves his family out of Ur and up the Euphrates River to the lush grazing fields of Haran, in what is now southern Turkey. Sometime later, Ur's regional empire collapses. Some scholars say they wonder if Terah saw it coming.

A city boy, Abraham grew up in what is now south Iraq in the riverside city of Ur—a throbbing, New York City kind of a town.

Why his dad, Terah, decided to pack up the family and move to the boonies of what is now Israel is anyone's guess. In distance and culture shock, it would have been a bit like a New Yorker today moving to Des Moines—1000 miles (1600 km) away.

Bible experts offer at least one intriguing guess. Terah may have been worried about the safety of his family.

Scholars base this guess partly on info gleaned from an ancient library of some 25,000 clay tablets found in the ruins of Mari, a city about halfway to Israel. Those records say that Abraham's hometown of Ur attracted so many immigrants from a desert tribe of troublesome nomads known as Amorites that the city got overrun. In time, Ur's leaders lost control of both the city and the outlying region. It all happened right around the time many say Terah moved—in the 2000s BC.

The chaos that followed opened the door to invaders from what is now Iran—Elamites from Persia.

For whatever reason, Terah and his family "headed for the land of Canaan, but they stopped at Haran and settled there" (Genesis 11:31).

Terah probably followed one of the main caravan routes that trailed northeast, upriver alongside the Euphrates. He couldn't go in any other direction.

- south: Persian Gulf
- east: Syrian Desert
- west: nasty Iranian invaders (Elamites)
- north: grazing pastures—no-brainer

Terah may have stopped along the way at Mari, the riverside city where archaeologists uncovered that ancient library about life at the time.

When Terah died, the Genesis storyteller says, God told Abraham to finish what his father had started. Go the last 400 miles (644 km) of the journey to what is now Israel.

"Abram was seventy-five years old when he left Haran. He took his wife, Sarai, his nephew

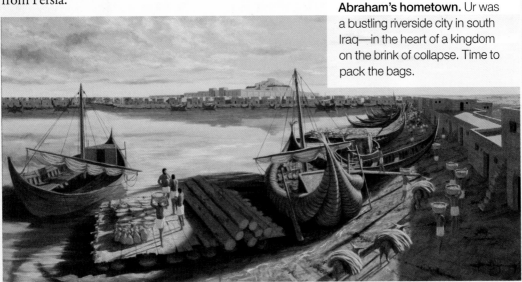

Abraham's hometown. Ur was a bustling riverside city in south Iraq—in the heart of a kingdom on the brink of collapse. Time to pack the bags.

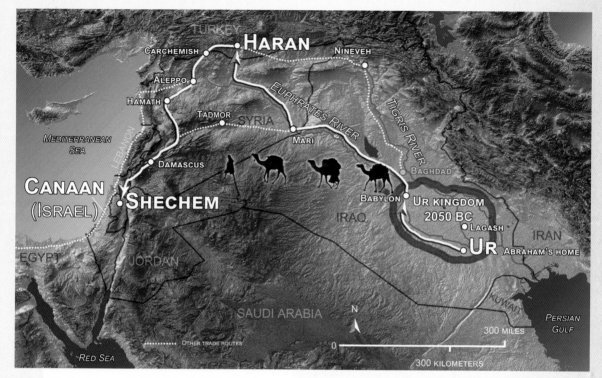

Homeland ahead. While Abraham is still living in Haran, God promises to give him the entire land of Canaan, in what is now Israel—and a lot of descendants. At age 75 and married to an infertile, 66-year-old woman, Abraham packs up and heads to Shechem—with more faith than common sense, it would seem.

Lot, and all his wealth—his livestock and all the people he had taken into his household at Haran—and headed for the land of Canaan" (Genesis 12:4-5).

If he followed one of the main caravan routes to the village the Bible identifies as Shechem, in the center of what is now Israel, he traveled along Syria's western border, through the towns of Carchemish, Aleppo, Hamath, and Damascus.

ABE'S CONTRACT WITH GOD

God made a deal with Abraham, as the Genesis writer tells it—a *covenant*, many Bible versions call it. A binding contract.

This agreement was written in the style of ancient contracts between masters and their subjects. The masters spelled out the rules. If the subjects obeyed, they got the blessings listed on the contract, usually including protection. If they disobeyed, they got the nasty consequences listed on the contract, sometimes including a free trip into the next world.

- *Abraham's contract obligation.* "Every male among you must be circumcised" (Genesis 17:10 NCV). Why circumcision, the writer never says. But this procedure certainly puts the focus on a body part essential to what God says will happen.

Drought resistant.
A Middle Eastern drought forces Abraham to temporarily leave what is now Israel. He drives his flocks south to the region's only reliable source of water: the Nile River. Fed by run-off of Central Africa's hills, the Nile—longest river in the world—flows north more than 4000 miles (about 6600 km). That's the distance from New York City to Los Angeles and most of the way back again.

Image labels:

MEDITERRANEAN SEA
NILE RIVER DELTA
GIZA
MEMPHIS CAIRO
LOWER EGYPT
DOWN RIVER
BENI HASAN
HIEROGLYPHS ABOUT REFUGEES, POSSIBLY JEWS OF ABRAHAM'S ERA
RIVER FLOWS NORTH FROM CENTRAL AFRICAN MOUNTAINS
NILE RIVER VALLEY
UPPER EGYPT
UP RIVER
LUXOR THEBES
6-9 MILES WIDE (10-15 KM)
DROUGHT-RESISTANT NILE RIVER VALLEY CUTS A FERTILE PATH THROUGH OTHERWISE BARREN EGYPTIAN DESERT
ASWAN DAM

MEDITERRANEAN SEA
LEBANON
SYRIA
SHECHEM (NABLUS)
GAZA STRIP
W. BANK
NILE DELTA
PRIMO GRAZING FIELDS
GOSHEN
ISRAEL
EGYPT
JORDAN
NILE RIVER
SINAI PENINSULA
RED SEA

- *God's contract promise.* "I promise that you will be the father of many nations. That's why I now change your name from Abram to Abraham [a Hebrew word that sounds like "father of many nations"]. I will give you a lot of descendants…I will give the whole land of Canaan to your family forever" (Genesis 17:5-8 CEV).

Many Arabs consider Abraham the father of their people through his first son, Ishmael. Hagar, the servant of Abraham's infertile wife, served as the surrogate birth mother.

Many Jews consider Abraham the father of their race through Isaac, the son he had with his wife Sarah.

MEDITERRANEAN SEA

SYRIA

LEBANON

DAMASCUS

DAN

MT. HERMON

ISRAEL

SEA OF GALILEE

INVADERS FROM IRAQ PLUNDER
THE JORDAN RIVER VALLEY
AND HEAD HOME.
ABRAHAM'S MILITIA
CATCHES THEM AT DAN.

SHECHEM
(NABLUS)

JORDAN RIVER VALLEY

JERUSALEM

ABRAHAM'S MILITIA
CHASES INVADERS.

DEAD SEA

HEBRON
ABRAHAM'S HOME

JORDAN

SODOM? (BAB EDH-DHRA)
LOT'S HOME

EVAPORATION PONDS
ONCE SODOM VALLEY?

MT. SODOM

GOMORRAH? (NUMEIRA)

130 MILES (209 KM) TO THE BATTLEGROUND

N

KIDNAPPED: LOT AND FAMILY
UNCLE ABRAHAM TO THE RESCUE

*Enemies took everything of value from Sodom and
Gomorrah, including their food supplies. They also
captured Abram's nephew Lot, who lived in Sodom.*

GENESIS 14:11-12 CEV

Search and rescue. Invaders from what is now Iraq overrun Sodom and other cities of the Jordan River Valley, capturing Lot and other locals. Abraham, living in the hills of Hebron, mobilizes his servants into a militia. His men catch up with the enemy at Dan and run them all the way to north of Damascus, freeing Lot and the other captives. Routes of the armies are uncertain.

Drought drove Abraham to Egypt, where the king loaded him up with gifts of livestock and slaves—perhaps including Hagar, who would become the mother of his first child, Ishmael.

By the time he returned home to what is now Israel, Abraham's flocks and herds had grown so massive that a single pasture couldn't sustain them all. He decided to split his extended family in half. His nephew Lot would lead the other clan.

Abraham gave Lot first choice of the land. Lot chose the fertile Jordan River Valley, laced in green fields nourished by the region's largest river. That left Abraham with the ridge of highlands that ran parallel to the river through the center of what is now Israel.

Lot settled in Sodom, which many Bible experts speculate was in a fertile valley that is now flooded under the southern shallows of the Dead Sea. Israelis today harvest minerals from rows of evaporation ponds they've created there.

Lot wasn't the only one attracted to those lush pastures and their cities. So were neighboring kings, including King Kedorlaomer of Elam, in what is now Iraq. He ran the region for a dozen years like a bully stealing lunch money. When the locals rebelled, he invaded and crushed them. He plundered their cities and kidnapped their people as slaves—including Lot and his family.

One of Lot's servants escaped and rushed to Abraham, who mobilized a militia of 318 of his servants. Abraham's men caught up with the invaders at Dan, a village on Israel's northern border. Abraham's militia attacked at night, overran the enemy, and chased them more than 40 miles (60 km)—beyond Damascus. The militiamen freed Lot and all the other captives. They also reclaimed the plunder the invaders stole.

ABRAHAM'S TEST
CHOP UP YOUR SON AND BURN HIM

Then God said, "Take your only son, Isaac, the son you love, and go to the land of Moriah. Kill him there and offer him as a whole burnt offering on one of the mountains I will tell you about."

GENESIS 22:2 NCV

Stop. The moment Abraham takes the knife to kill his son, he's stopped by a celestial being—perhaps God himself, some scholars say.

God is not the good guy in this story—not as many Bible newcomers read it. To some he comes across more horrible than holy.

That's because he asks old Abraham to slaughter his son Isaac and sacrifice him as a burnt offering. When worshippers offered "whole burnt offerings," they usually killed the animal quickly with a knife to the throat. Then they chopped it into manageable pieces and burned all of it on an altar.

As horrifying as that sounds, Abraham agreed to do it even though God seemed to be breaking his promise. God had vowed to give Abraham a nation of descendants through Isaac—the Jewish nation, in "an agreement that continues forever" (Genesis 17:19 NCV).

Kinda hard to do with Isaac chopped up and fried like a Happy Meal. According to one New Testament writer, Abraham figured God could reanimate Isaac, piecing him back together like a shattered Humpty Dumpty (Hebrews 11:17-19).

Camped at Beersheba, in what is now southern Israel, Abraham led his son on a three-day walk to a hilltop called Moriah. Jewish tradition places that in Jerusalem, about a 50-mile (80 km) walk on meandering trails north of Beersheba. Hundreds of years later, "Solomon began to build the Temple of the LORD in Jerusalem on Mount Moriah" (2 Chronicles 3:1).

At the hilltop, Abraham tied his son, laid him on a stone-pile altar, and reached for his knife.

Suddenly, a celestial being appeared—"the angel of the LORD," which many scholars say was God himself.

MT. HERMON 9232 FT 2814 M

SEA OF GALILEE

JORDAN RIVER VALLEY

SHECHEM
ABRAHAM ENTERS PROMISED LAND
BUILDS ALTAR FOR SACRIFICE

MOUNT MORIAH
(JERUSALEM)
ABRAHAM ALMOST SACRIFICES
HIS SON ISAAC

DEAD SEA

THE BIBLE DOESN'T SAY HOW OLD ISAAC WAS.
ONE JEWISH TRADITION SAYS HE WAS 37,
AND THAT HIS 127-YEAR-OLD MOTHER DIED OF SHOCK
WHEN SHE HEARD THAT ABRAHAM PLANNED TO SACRIFICE HIM.

HEBRON
ONE OF ABRAHAM'S EARLY CAMPS
AND WHERE HE BOUGHT A FAMILY BURIAL CAVE

POSSIBLE ROUTE TO MOUNT MORIAH
50 MILES (80 KM)

BEERSHEBA
ABRAHAM'S CAMP

N

"'Don't lay a hand on the boy!' the angel said. 'Do not hurt him in any way, for now I know that you truly fear God. You have not withheld from me even your son, your only son'" (Genesis 22:12).

Many Christian Bible experts say this wasn't a test as much as a foreshadowing of what God did later in sacrificing his only Son in Jerusalem. Reading Abraham's torturous experience helps us get a sense of what it may have been like for God to sacrifice Jesus.

On the other hand, some Jewish scholars say the gut-wrenching story is intended to help us see why God forbids human sacrifice. No parent should have to suffer what Abraham went through.

FATHER OF THREE RELIGIONS

Jews, Christians, and Muslims all revere Abraham—for different reasons.

- *First Jew.* Jews consider him as the founder of their race and their faith.

- *Foreshadowing Jesus.* Christians see Abraham's willingness to sacrifice his son Isaac as a foreshadowing of God sacrificing his Son 2000 years later.

- *First Muslim.* Muslims consider Abraham the first *Muslim*, an Arabic word that means "one who submits to God." Muslim sacred scripture calls their faith "the religion of Abraham" (Quran 2:135).

SCORCHED EARTH

HUNTING FOR SODOM AND GOMORRAH

Firestorm. Lot and his two daughters escape the fires in Sodom. Lot's wife, however, apparently pauses long enough to get caught in the explosive spray of salt and other minerals.

The LORD rained down fire and burning sulfur from the sky on Sodom and Gomorrah. He utterly destroyed them, along with the other cities and villages of the plain, wiping out all the people and every bit of vegetation.

GENESIS 19:24-25

Sodom and Gomorrah, along with other doomed "cities of the plain" (Genesis 13:12), grew up in a once-green valley that's now part of the Dead Sea. So says one popular theory.

This rocky badlands is rich in natural gas, salt, sulfur, and other minerals. Israelis drill and mine there. They've turned the Dead Sea's southern shallows into a massive evaporation bed where the desert sun vaporizes the water, leaving minerals behind.

The Genesis writer said God himself visited the twin sin cities and confirmed what he had been told: "Their sin is very serious" (Genesis 18:20 GWT).

God sent two angels to save Lot and his family by leading them out of town at dawn, just before God unleashed a firestorm that wiped out all the cities of the plain.

How he did it remains a mystery. But all the chemical elements mentioned in the story are still in the area—a quake-prone region that rests on a massive break in the earth's crust. Here's one possible chain of events, according to some Bible experts.

- An earthquake rips open pockets of natural gas.
- Lightning or an early-morning oil lamp ignites the gas.
- A massive explosion sprays salt, sulfur, and other burning minerals sky-high.
- Lot's wife gets caught in the fallout.
- Part of the plain drops into a sinkhole.
- Seawater rushes in, flooding the plain.

THE SOUTHERN SHALLOWS OF THE DEAD SEA

Search for toasted cities. Sodom and Gomorrah sank their roots into "the fertile plains of the Jordan Valley" (Genesis 13:10). That seems to place them along the banks of the Jordan River, north of the Dead Sea. But some scholars say the continuation of that valley to south of the Dead Sea was once fertile too, fed by rainwater that drained into the lowest valley on earth. Contenders for Sodom and Gomorrah include the scorched ruins of Bab edh-Dhra and Numeria. These are just two of several burned-out ancient cities with traces of sulfur that were discovered in the area—possibly the region the Genesis writer called the "cities of the plain."

MEDITERRANEAN SEA

MT. HERMON

SEA OF GALILEE

SYRIA

JORDAN RIVER VALLEY

CANAAN (ISRAEL)

DEAD SEA
1,294 FEET BELOW SEA LEVEL
394 M

JORDAN

BAB EDH-DHRA
• (SODOM?)

SODOM VALLEY?

EVAPORATION PONDS
FOR HARVESTING MINERALS

• NUMERIA
(GOMORRAH?)

MT. SODOM •

Jacob feeds Esau
a bowl of soup.

JACOB RUNS FOR HIS LIFE
BROTHER ESAU VOWS TO KILL HIM

*Esau hated his brother Jacob because he had stolen the blessing
that was supposed to be his. So he said to himself, "Just
as soon as my father dies, I'll kill Jacob."*

GENESIS 27:41 CEV

A lying son and a sneaky snake of a little brother—that's Abraham's grandson Jacob, the man
who would eventually father 12 sons whose families would grow into the 12 tribes of Israel.
But for now, this future father of the Jewish nation had to put some distance between himself
and his moments-older twin brother, Esau. Young Jacob had cheated Esau out of his...

- *Inheritance.* When Esau was famished after hunting, Jacob sold him a bowl of soup in
trade for Esau's "rights as the firstborn son" (Genesis 25:31). The oldest son got twice as
much as any of his brothers. The story makes Jacob look exploitive and Esau look dumber
than a bag of beans.

- *Father's deathbed blessing.* When old and nearly blind Isaac thought he was dying, he
wanted to give his oldest son, Esau, a special blessing. This blessing was a bit like a confident prayer that people believed had power to make things happen. Isaac wanted to bless

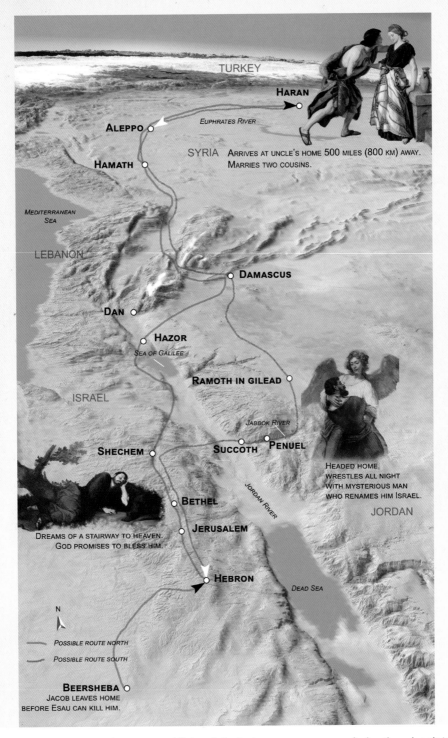

TURKEY

HARAN

ALEPPO

EUPHRATES RIVER

SYRIA   ARRIVES AT UNCLE'S HOME 500 MILES (800 KM) AWAY.
MARRIES TWO COUSINS.

HAMATH

*MEDITERRANEAN
SEA*

LEBANON

DAMASCUS

DAN

HAZOR

SEA OF GALILEE

RAMOTH IN GILEAD

ISRAEL

JABBOK RIVER

SHECHEM

SUCCOTH   PENUEL

HEADED HOME,
WRESTLES ALL NIGHT
WITH MYSTERIOUS MAN
WHO RENAMES HIM ISRAEL.

BETHEL

JORDAN RIVER

JORDAN

JERUSALEM

DREAMS OF A STAIRWAY TO HEAVEN.
GOD PROMISES TO BLESS HIM.

HEBRON

DEAD SEA

N

— POSSIBLE ROUTE NORTH
— POSSIBLE ROUTE SOUTH

BEERSHEBA
JACOB LEAVES HOME
BEFORE ESAU CAN KILL HIM.

Safe house. When Esau threatens to kill Jacob for being a poor excuse of a brother, Jacob takes his mom's advice and runs to her brother's house in what is now Haran, Turkey—some 500 meandering miles (800 km) north. God promises to bless the runaway. Jacob returns to a happy reunion: Esau greets him with tears and a hug.

Jacob's dad got a Turkey of a wife too.
Jacob wasn't the first descendant of Abraham to go wife shopping in what is now Turkey. That's where his dad, Isaac, got his wife, Rebekah. Abraham sent a servant there to find a wife for 40-year-old Isaac.

Esau with success and with power over his brother. But Jacob and his mother, Rebekah, teamed up to trick Isaac into thinking Jacob was Esau. Jacob got the special blessing. Once spoken, the sacred words could not be unsaid.

Rebekah overheard Esau vow to kill his younger twin brother. So she sent Jacob back to her childhood hometown—Haran, a city in what is now southern Turkey. Abraham had lived in Haran for many years before moving to what is now Israel.

Jacob fell in love with his cousin Rachel—daughter of his mom's brother, Laban. Since Jacob arrived in Haran apparently with no assets but his brain, he agreed to work as a shepherd for Laban for seven years if he could marry Rachel.

Uncle Laban pulled a "Jacob" by cheating his nephew. Laban subbed in another daughter under the wedding veil. It wasn't until morning that Jacob realized he was married to Leah, a lady not described as a looker. "Rachel was beautiful," but "Leah was older...her eyes didn't sparkle" (Genesis 29:16-17 CEV). It sounds like the writer was trying to be kind, describing "hog homely" as painlessly as possible.

Laban justified his underhanded, under-the-veil bait and switch by saying it was custom to marry off the oldest daughter first. Not custom, apparently, to tell the groom the custom ahead of time.

Laban offered to let Jacob marry Rachel in a week if Jacob agreed to work another seven years.

Deal.

Jacob fathered a dozen sons and one daughter with these two wives and two surrogate mothers—Bilhah and Zilpah, second-class slave-wives who worked as servants for Rachel and Leah.

When Jacob's 14-year deal was up, Laban gave him seed critters to start his own flocks—"all the sheep and goats that are speckled or spotted, along with all the black sheep" (Genesis 30:32). In time, Jacob got rich.

Some 20 years after Jacob left his home in what is now Israel, he took the risk of moving his family and flocks back. By then, Esau had calmed down. "Esau ran to meet him and embraced him, threw his arms around his neck, and kissed him. And they both wept" (Genesis 33:4). Happy reunion.

3

ISRAEL VISITS EGYPT—FOR 430 YEARS

TIMELINE *(dates are approximate)*

1900 BC	Joseph is sold into slavery.
1875 BC	Drought forces Jews into Egypt.
1860 BC	Joseph dies; Jews are enslaved later.
1800 BC	The Epic of Gilgamesh is compiled (Iraqi stories of the creation and flood).
1756 BC	Egypt's 200-year-long twelfth dynasty of kings ends.

Pharaoh Senusret III
(1874–1855 BC)

FOR SALE: LITTLE BRO JOE

BIG BROTHERS SELL HIM TO SLAVE TRADERS

Joseph's brothers...sold him to the Ishmaelite traders for eight ounces of silver. Then the traders took him to Egypt.

GENESIS 37:28 NIRV

Small change. Joseph's ten older brothers sell him to a passing caravan of slave traders for half a pound (228 g) of silver. That's what a roll and a half of quarters weigh—more exactly, 56 quarters, or $14. Divided among the ten brothers, that would have been a buck and a quarter each.

Jacob had a love child with his favorite wife, Rachel. As the favorite son, Joseph was doomed to wear a bull's-eye—to become a target for his older brothers.

Jacob fathered ten sons before Joseph came along. But they were all from Leah, the woman he got tricked into marrying, or from the surrogate-mother slaves, Zilpah and Bilhah. Joseph came along many years later. Everyone thought Rachel was infertile.

In a way, Joseph wore his bull's-eye literally—"a spectacularly colorful robe with long sleeves" (Genesis 37:3 TVB).

Bible translations of the vague Hebrew word describing the robe can look like they come from a guessing game: long sleeves, colorful fabric, striped fabric. But any way you cut that cloth,

EGYPT

CAIRO

GOSHEN
Rameses

**JOSEPH BEGINS LIFE IN EGYPT
AS A SLAVE AND ENDS UP
A TOP OFFICIAL**

Red Sea Gulf of Suez

SINAI PENINSULA

MEDITERRANEAN SEA

BEERSHEBA

HEBRON
CAMP OF JACOB'S FAMILY

JERUSALEM
BETHEL

DEAD SEA

ISRAEL

SHECHEM
JOSEPH'S BROTHERS
MOVE FLOCK FROM SHECHEM TO DOTHAN
FOR BETTER GRAZING PASTURE

DOTHAN JOSEPH'S BROTHERS SELL HIM TO SLAVE TRADERS

JORDAN RIVER

CARAVAN OF TRADERS FROM GILEAD HEAD TO EGYPT,
MEETING JOSEPH'S BROTHERS TENDING THEIR FLOCK

JORDAN

N

GILEAD

SEA OF GALILEE

it's looking nothing like the sleeveless, tattered tunics and the ragged wool coats that ancient pictures slap on shepherds of the Middle East.

Joseph didn't do himself any favors by "always telling his father all sorts of bad things about his brothers" (Genesis 37:2 CEV). Tattletale.

He was a bragger too. When he had a dream that the sun, the moon, and 11 stars bowed to him, he couldn't keep his mouth shut. He told everyone. That even ticked off Jacob: "His father became angry and said, 'What's that supposed to mean? Are your mother and I and your brothers all going to come and bow down in front of you?'" (Genesis 37:10 CEV).

Twenty-year trip. On orders from his dad, Joseph heads north out of their camp in Hebron to check on his ten older brothers, who hate the guts out of him. The brothers are moving their livestock to fresh grazing pastures. Joseph catches up with them in Dothan. They sell him to traders carrying salves and perfumes from Gilead to markets in Egypt. The brothers keep Joseph's fancy robe, dip it in animal blood, and take it back to their father, where they tell him they found it on the trail. Jacob presumes an animal killed his favorite son. Famine will drive Jacob's brothers to Egypt in 20 years, where they hope to buy grain from the drought-resistant Nile River Valley. They're in for a surprise family reunion.

In fact, that's exactly what would happen. But not for another 20 years or so.

In the meantime, aging Jacob sent his 17-year-old favorite son out to check on his big brothers, who were grazing their flocks in Dothan, a city some 60 miles (100 km) north of their home in Hebron. That made it about a three-day walk. Far enough away from Papa Jacob for the big brothers to tear into little bro Joe.

They tossed him into a dry cistern—a pit for storing rainwater. While they were bantering around ideas about how to get rid of him, a caravan of Ishmaelite traders came along. They were descendants of Abraham's first son, Ishmael, who is often considered father of the Arab people.

Loaded with salves, perfumes, and spices from Gilead, on Jordan's side of the Jordan River, they were headed south to Egypt, a seller's market for everything from salves to slaves. Egyptians started writing a lot about slaves during Egypt's twelfth dynasty of rulers (about 1938–1756 BC)—when many scholars say Joseph's brothers sold him into slavery there.

PRETTY BOY MEETS MRS. COUGAR

In Egypt, a married woman took a liking to enslaved Joseph, "a very handsome and well-built young man" (Genesis 39:6).

This lady was the wife of Joseph's master, Potipher, captain of the king's palace guard.

"Come and sleep with me," she said to Joseph, probably with no plans to sleep.

"My master trusts me with everything in his entire household," Joseph answered. "How could I do such a wicked thing?" (Genesis 39:8-9).

The cougar wife said she would show him how.

She continued to stalk him, purring her invitations day after day.

Eventually, she clawed him into her arms. He wormed his way loose and ran off, leaving her holding nothing but the cloak he was wearing.

She cried rape.

A good thing.

Joseph ended up in prison, where fellow prisoners discovered he had the gift of interpreting dreams. Word got back to the king. He called on Joseph to interpret two bizarre dreams of his:

- Seven gaunt cows ate seven fat cows.
- Seven dried-up heads of grain ate seven fat heads of grain.

Joseph said the dreams meant Egypt would have seven years of bumper crops that would get eaten up by seven years of drought. He advised the king to stockpile as much grain as possible.

The king was so impressed that he gave the job to Joseph—a made-for position that had the former slave reporting directly to the king.

A job promotion.

SEVEN-YEAR DRY SPELL

EGYPT: JEWISH HOME AWAY FROM HOME

Jacob set out for Egypt with all his possessions…altogether, there were seventy members of Jacob's family in the land of Egypt.

GENESIS 46:1,27

Joseph saves Egypt. Seven years of drought, personified in this painting, can't get past Joseph. He saw them coming in a pair of dreams he interpreted for the king. Wisely, as it turns out, the king put him in charge of stockpiling bumper crops of grain before the drought hit.

Drought hammered the Middle East, just as Joseph had predicted. He may have been about 40 years old by then. That would explain why his brothers didn't recognize him when they came down to Egypt, shopping for grain.

Joseph was 17 when they sold him. "He was thirty years old when he began serving in the court of Pharaoh, the king of Egypt" (Genesis 41:46). If the seven years of predicted bumper crops started right away, that would put him at age 37 just as the seven years of drought started. Jacob's family endured two years of drought before Jacob sent his sons down to Egypt to buy grain (Genesis 45:6).

Jacob sent all ten of Joseph's older brothers on the monthlong trip down to Egypt—which was perhaps the only place in the region that still had grain for sale.

Joseph recognized them right away. But he hid his identity and probed to find out if they were sorry for what they had done to him and if they treated his little brother Benjamin with the same disdain they had shown him.

His probing went like this: He accused them of being spies, and he held one of them hostage until they brought Benjamin to him. When Joseph finally agreed to sell them grain, he had one of his servants stuff his silver cup into one of Benjamin's grain sacks. Then he accused Benjamin of stealing the cup, and he threatened to sell him into slavery.

When Joseph overheard his older brothers accusing themselves of deserving this because of what they had done to Joseph years ago, and when the second-oldest brother, Judah, offered to take Benjamin's place as a slave, Joseph knew his brothers had changed.

"'I am Joseph!' he said to his brothers. 'Is my father still alive?'" (Genesis 45:3).

He assured his shocked-speechless brothers that he had forgiven them. "Don't blame yourselves for selling me. God was behind it. God sent me here ahead of you to save lives" (Genesis 45:5 MSG).

Someone rushed news to the king that Joseph was celebrating a reunion with his brothers. The king told Joseph to have his entire extended family move to Egypt. "I will give them the best land in Egypt, and they can eat and enjoy everything that grows on it" (Genesis 45:18 CEV).

They came and they stayed—"for 430 years" (Exodus 12:40).

Somewhere along the line, a not-so-hospitable king decided to enslave the Jewish race.

It would take Moses to free them.

One-month move. Jacob and his family may have taken about a month to travel the 200 miles (320 km) from their camp in Hebron to the primo grazing fields of the Nile Delta's east side—a region known as Goshen.

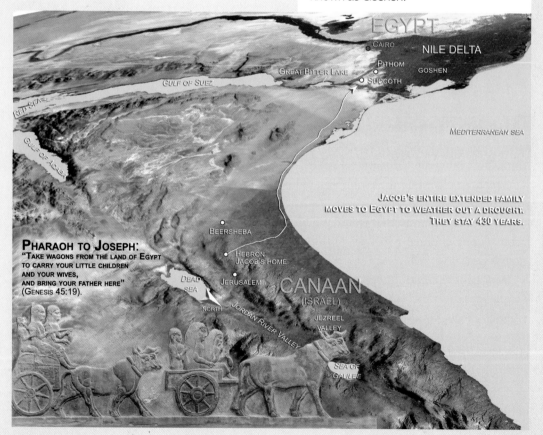

EGYPT

CAIRO
PITHOM
GREAT BITTER LAKE
SUCCOTH
GOSHEN

NILE DELTA

GULF OF SUEZ

RED SEA

GULF OF AQABA

MEDITERRANEAN SEA

JACOB'S ENTIRE EXTENDED FAMILY MOVES TO EGYPT TO WEATHER OUT A DROUGHT. THEY STAY 430 YEARS.

BEERSHEBA

PHARAOH TO JOSEPH:
"TAKE WAGONS FROM THE LAND OF EGYPT TO CARRY YOUR LITTLE CHILDREN AND YOUR WIVES, AND BRING YOUR FATHER HERE" (GENESIS 45:19).

HEBRON
JACOB'S HOME

DEAD SEA

JERUSALEM

CANAAN
(ISRAEL)

NORTH

JORDAN RIVER VALLEY

JEZREEL VALLEY

SEA OF GALILEE

4

MOSES LEADS THE EXODUS HOME

TIMELINE *(dates are approximate)*

1539 BC	Pharaoh Ahmose starts a 250-year dynasty of kings.
1468 BC	Pharaoh Thutmoses III defeats the Hittites in Canaan (Israel).
1446 BC	Moses leads the Jews to freedom.
1270 BC	Rameses II builds the city of Rameses.
1267 BC	Alternate date of Moses and the Exodus.
1200 BC	Iron replaces bronze as the go-to metal.

Rock-a-bye baby. Newborn Moses gets the royal treatment from a princess in Egypt. The king had ordered newborn Jewish boys tossed in the Nile for population control. But his daughter, the princess, couldn't resist adopting Moses after she saw him abandoned near her bathing spot. Someone had tossed him into the Nile as ordered but had given him a flotation device—a basket waterproofed with tar.

TEN PLAGUES OF EGYPT
A LONG WINTER IN THE SOUTHLAND

The LORD, the God of the Hebrews, says: Let my people go, so they
can worship me. If you don't, I will send more plagues on you.

EXODUS 9:13-14

An adopted prince in Egypt—that was Moses, the man God chose to free the Jewish race from slavery.

At age 40, as the Bible reports it, Moses went out to see how the Egyptians treated his fellow Jews. When he saw an Egyptian foreman beating one of the slaves, Moses killed the Egyptian. Word got back to the king. He apparently saw this as a challenge to his authority over the slaves because the foreman was acting on his orders.

The king ordered Moses killed.

Moses fled east across the Sinai Peninsula into what is now Saudi Arabia, then called Midian. There he met a herder with seven daughters. Moses married one of them and spent the next 40 years helping his father-in-law as a shepherd.

That's exactly what he was doing when the Bible says God appeared to him as a voice speaking from "a blazing fire from the middle of a bush" (Exodus 3:2).

FROM ONE GOD TO ANOTHER

On orders from God, 80-year-old Moses tag teamed with his older brother, Aaron, to deliver God's message to the current pharaoh, king of Egypt. "This is what the LORD, the God of Israel, says: Let my people go so they may hold a festival in my honor in the wilderness" (Exodus 5:1).

The king was not impressed.

For one, he was considered a god himself—the son of Ra, powerful sun god in a blazing desert land. For another, the king may well have concluded that Israel's God was a wimp because God had allowed everyone who worshipped him to become slaves.

As the Bible tells it, God decided to prove him wrong.

Many Bible experts theorize that God did it in a way that proved he is stronger than any god of Egypt, the king included. He did this with ten plagues—a string of events that has become one of the most famous in Bible history.

Most of these Bible experts say that because the plagues targeted objects under the control of powerful Egyptian gods, they see these plagues as a battle of the gods.

Some scientists in various specialties, such as marine life and infectious diseases, have speculated that many of the plagues may have followed a cycle of natural disasters with each disaster pulling the trigger on the next.

As one theory goes, it started with a swamp toxin filtering into the Nile River during the annual autumn flood season. This set off a string of environmental catastrophes that ended in springtime.

PLAGUE	EGYPTIAN GOD	NATURAL DISASTER
1. Nile River turns red	Hapi, god of Nile	Swamp toxins wash into Nile during autumn flood.
2. frog infestation	Heqet, goddess pictured with a frog head	Frogs flee the poisoned river.
3. gnats	Thoth, god of magic who can't help Egypt's magicians duplicate this miracle	Gnats breed in pools of receding floodwater.
4. flies	Ptah, creator god who can't control flies	Stable flies lay eggs in wet, decaying straw, frogs, and wood.
5. sick livestock	Hathor, goddess pictured with cow horns	Livestock are killed by anthrax from toxic water.
6. blisters	Isis, goddess of health	Diseases carried by stable flies cause the blisters.
7. hail	Shu, god of air	A crop is wiped out—harvest begins in February.
8. locusts	Min, god of farming	Locusts are common in the desert regions, where predators are few.
9. three-day darkness	Ra (or Re), sun god	Lingering sandstorms, common in springtime, block the sun.
10. death of oldest sons	Pharaoh, son of Ra	Oldest sons get extra portion of food from contaminated harvest.

Incoming. Marine Corporal Alicia M. Garcia captures a wave of sand about to swallow a military camp in Iraq. In Egypt, hot spring winds that blast in from Africa's Sahara Desert are called *Khamsin*, Arabic for "Fifty." These blistering winds can come and go anytime during the spring, usually beginning in April and stretching over a couple of months. They sometimes fill the air with sand that can block the sun for days. Some wonder if that was the ninth plague to hit Egypt—three days of darkness.

CUE THE WIND

WHICH SEA PARTED FOR THE JEWS?

The LORD opened up a path through the water with a strong east wind…So the people of Israel walked through the middle of the sea on dry ground, with walls of water on each side!

EXODUS 14:21-22

Fish bait. Pharaoh's army drowns in the Red Sea while trying to catch Moses and the fleeing Jewish refugees. The Bible says everyone in the Egyptian army who entered the water drowned. But it stops short of reporting that the king himself died.

Ten plagues weren't enough for the king of Egypt. He needed eleven—the drowning of his army. The tenth plague had taken the life of his oldest son and the firstborn of every Egyptian family. That horrified him so much that he ordered the Jews to leave his country. But after they left, he had second thoughts: "What have we done, letting Israel, our slave labor, go free?" (Exodus 14:5 MSG).

His army, with the chariot corps and the cavalry, catches up with the Jews, who were "camping by the sea, beside Pi-hahiroth, in front of Baal-zephon" (Exodus 14:9 NASB)—two locations lost to history, though some top scholars speculate they were references to temples near the city of Succoth, about a three-day walk north of the Red Sea.

The Bible writer says a pillar of fire that had been leading the Jews moved to protect their rear flank, blocking the advance of the Egyptians.

Overnight, a powerful wind blowing from the east, in what is now Saudi Arabia, cut a path through the water. It allowed the Jews to escape the next morning.

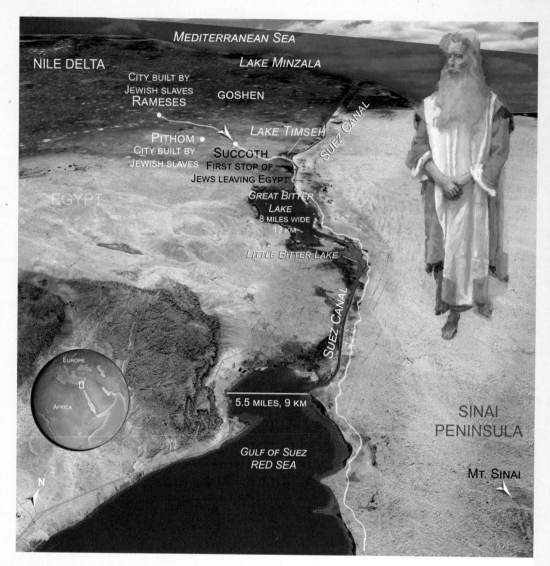

MEDITERRANEAN SEA

NILE DELTA

LAKE MINZALA

CITY BUILT BY
JEWISH SLAVES
RAMESES

GOSHEN

EGYPT

PITHOM •
CITY BUILT BY
JEWISH SLAVES

LAKE TIMSEH

SUCCOTH
FIRST STOP OF
JEWS LEAVING EGYPT

SUEZ CANAL

*GREAT BITTER
LAKE*
8 MILES WIDE
13 KM

LITTLE BITTER LAKE

SUEZ CANAL

EUROPE

AFRICA

5.5 MILES, 9 KM

SINAI
PENINSULA

GULF OF SUEZ
RED SEA

MT. SINAI

N

When the Egyptians tried to follow, the water collapsed on them "and covered all the chariots and charioteers—the entire army of Pharaoh. Of all the Egyptians who had chased the Israelites into the sea, not a single one survived" (Exodus 14:28).

That's the end of the Egyptian threat. They don't show up again during the Jews' 40-year journey home.

Getting out of town. It's anyone's guess what route Moses took to lead the Jews out of Egypt—or what sea they crossed. Bible experts say the original Hebrew language calls it the Reed Sea, not necessarily the Red Sea. The Jews would have passed lots of reed-framed lakes, lagoons, and marshes on Egypt's eastern frontier at the edge of the Sinai badlands.

SINAI BADLANDS AHEAD
MOSES TAKES JEWS ON THE SCENIC ROUTE

God did not lead them on the road through the Philistine country, though that was the shortest way... God led them through the desert toward the Red Sea.

EXODUS 13:17-18 NCV

Rock pie. A view of the Red Sea from the South Sinai can be stunning—for those who like their water on the rocks. On a map, the Sinai Peninsula looks like a slice of pie wedged between Israel and the green part of Egypt. On the ground, it's mostly rock pie. If landscape could have kids, this kid would have been the love child of Mars and the Dakota badlands.

It was a week's walk to the Promised Land. Not 40 years.

A lone traveler walking from the northeastern edge of Egyptian civilization, which is where the Bible says Moses and the Jews were, in Succoth, could have walked a fairly straight shot to what is now Israel's southern border—some 150 miles (240 km) away. Walking 20 miles (32 km) a day, that's about eight days.

The Bible says God didn't want Moses and the Jews going that way: "If they have to go into battle, they might change their minds. They might return to Egypt" (Exodus 13:17 NIRV).

Archaeologists have confirmed that the coastal route—the most popular caravan trail to Egypt—was heavily fortified with military outposts along the pathway.

Fear of having to fight off the Philistine army was not the real reason God sent the Jews on a meandering route into the Sinai badlands, according to some Bible experts. That may have been the explanation that would have made sense to Moses and the Jewish refugees at the time.

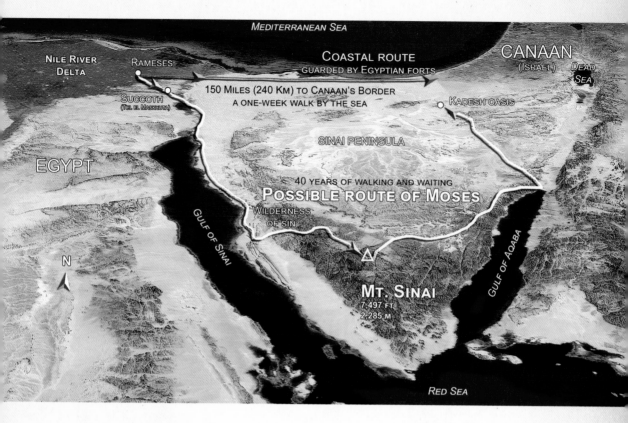

MEDITERRANEAN SEA

NILE RIVER
DELTA

RAMESES

COASTAL ROUTE
GUARDED BY EGYPTIAN FORTS

CANAAN
(ISRAEL)

DEAD
SEA

150 MILES (240 KM) TO CANAAN'S BORDER
A ONE-WEEK WALK BY THE SEA

SUCCOTH
(TEL EL MASKHUTA)

KADESH OASIS

SINAI PENINSULA

EGYPT

40 YEARS OF WALKING AND WAITING
POSSIBLE ROUTE OF MOSES

WILDERNESS
OF SIN

N

GULF OF SINAI

GULF OF AQABA

MT. SINAI
7,497 FT
2,285 M

RED SEA

But some scholars say the real reason comes out later, after everyone sees what happens on this meandering trail.

- God parts the water for the Jews.
- God drowns the Egyptian army in the same water.

The real reason for the odd route to the Promised Land, as some scholars see it: "This will bring honor to me, and the Egyptians will know that I am the LORD" (Exodus 14:4 NCV). Jews will know it too.

High and dry. After invading Egypt, Napoleon nearly drowned in the Red Sea. He was traveling along the north shore of the Gulf of Suez when a surge of rising tidewater knocked him off his horse.

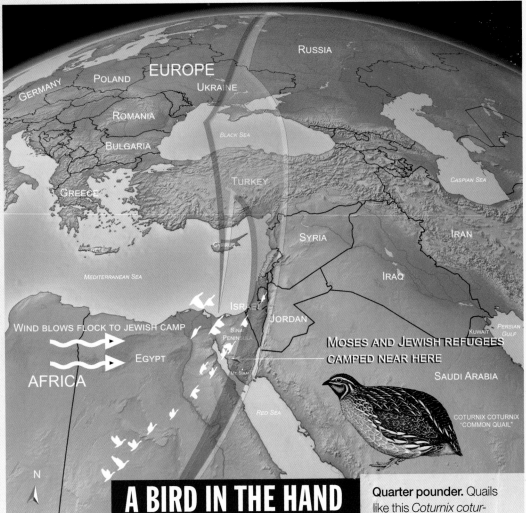

RUSSIA

EUROPE

GERMANY POLAND

UKRAINE

ROMANIA

BLACK SEA

BULGARIA

TURKEY

CASPIAN SEA

GREECE

SYRIA

IRAN

CYPRUS

MEDITERRANEAN SEA

ISRAEL

JORDAN

IRAQ

WIND BLOWS FLOCK TO JEWISH CAMP

SINAI
PENINSULA

KUWAIT

PERSIAN
GULF

EGYPT

MT. SINAI

MOSES AND JEWISH REFUGEES
CAMPED NEAR HERE

AFRICA

SAUDI ARABIA

RED SEA

COTURNIX COTURNIX
"COMMON QUAIL"

N

A BIRD IN THE HAND
GOD FLIES IN FAST FOOD

*The LORD sent a wind that brought quail from
the sea and let them fall all around the camp.
For miles in every direction there were quail
flying about three feet above the ground.*

NUMBERS 11:31

T he Sinai badlands is a great place to complain. There's hardly
anything there but rocks, which poses a problem at mealtime.
About six weeks after the exodus from Egypt and about
halfway to the traditional site of Mount Sinai, the refugees

Quarter pounder. Quails
like this *Coturnix coturnix* migrate from Africa to
Europe every spring to
escape the North African
heat. Ancient art shows
Egyptians using nothing
more than their hands to
catch exhausted quail (see
page 48). The birds weigh
in at about a quarter-pound
(113 g), and they stretch
about half the length of a
footlong hot dog (15 cm).
They make for a tasty meal
if you pluck the feathers.

started complaining. "We wish the LORD had killed us in Egypt. When we lived there, we could at least sit down and eat all the bread and meat we wanted. But you have brought us out here into this desert, where we are going to starve" (Exodus 16:3 CEV).

God serves up some food, as the Bible reports it. First course: manna. Second course: quail.

MANNA FROM HEAVEN

When we say *manna*, we're talking Hebrew, and we're asking a question: "What is it?"

Bible experts still have no idea what manna was. The Bible describes it as white flakes that covered the ground every morning except on Saturday, the Jewish Sabbath day of rest. Jews crushed the flakes into flour to make flat loaves of sweet bread. "It tasted like bread baked with olive oil" (Numbers 11:8 NCV).

One guess is that manna was bug poop—sweet secretions of the plant-sucking mealybug. Sweet balls dry into white flakes that herders in the area call manna. They use it to sweeten their tea.

But there are problems with that theory. First, it would have taken wagonloads of bug poop to feed this crowd. Second, those bugs work their magic only in May and June. The Bible says God provided the manna year-round.

QUAIL HUNTING BY HAND

For a little protein added to the diet, God sent a wind to blow migrating birds off their path and into the laps of the Jews. Almost literally. The Bible says the Jews plucked the

Ancient Egyptians catching quail by hand.

MANNA BUGS?

Plant-sucking mealy bugs excrete sweet juices sometimes called honeydew. The juice dries into white flakes that stick to them and the plants they nibble on. Herders sometimes scrape off the flakes and use it to sweeten their tea. Some speculate that the Bible story about manna comes from what is essentially bug poop. Those two red spots on the big bug are not eyeballs. Wrong end.

exhausted birds as if they were picking tomatoes. Gathered them up by the bushels.

Ancient Egyptian pictures show Egyptians catching quail by hand too. The quail in those pictures look a lot like the *Coturnix coturnix*—aka the common quail—a stubby quarter-pounder to go.

A migrating bird, the European quail spends the winter in Africa. But when summer heats up the continent, the flocks migrate back to Europe for milder weather.

That timeline puts the flocks on track to migrate past the Sinai Peninsula about the time Moses and the Jews were making their springtime escape from Egypt—sometime around May. The Jews left Egypt on Passover, a springtime holiday about the time of Easter.

After a long flight and fighting a strong wind, the birds were lumbering low and slow if they were flying at all. Exhausted, they were perfect for plucking.

Today, hunters in Mediterranean countries still go after these tasty birds. Estimated population of these European quail: more than five million.

UNDERCOVER JEWS
MOSES SENDS A DOZEN SPIES AHEAD

The LORD said to Moses, "Choose a leader from each tribe and send them into Canaan to explore the land I am giving you."
NUMBERS 13:1-2 CEV

Sculpture in Petah Tikva, Israel, commemorating the Jewish scouts Joshua and Caleb

Camping for a year at the foot of Mount Sinai gives Moses time to organize the Jews into a nation. He structures them around their extended family groups—12 tribes. Each tribe came from a different son or grandson of Jacob, the man who moved his family to Egypt some 400 years earlier.

At God's order, the Jews break camp and move north toward their Promised Land—today known as Israel.

Following a mysterious pillar of light, Moses and the refugees travel north to an oasis just beyond the southern border of modern-day Israel. From there, Moses sends a dozen spies north to scout out the land.

"After exploring the land for forty days, the men returned to Moses, Aaron, and the whole community of Israel at Kadesh in the wilderness of Paran" (Numbers 13:25-26).

The scouts brought a mixed report. Joshua and Caleb gave their minority opinion: "Let's go at once to take the land…We can certainly conquer it!" (Numbers 13:30).

The majority opinion of the ten other scouts was not quite as optimistic. "The people living there are powerful, and their towns are large and fortified. We even saw giants there…Next to them we felt like grasshoppers" (Numbers 13:28,33).

Terrified at that report, the Jews refused to go any farther. In God they did not trust.

God sentenced them to 40 years in the badlands. The chickenhearted generation would live out the rest of their lives there, possibly camping at the Kadesh oasis for most of that time.

The only two adults of the chicken generation who would step foot in the Promised Land would be Joshua and Caleb.

LEBO-HAMATH

SYRIA

DAMASCUS

MT. HERMON

MEDITERRANEAN SEA

HAZOR

SEA OF GALILEE

JORDAN

SHECHEM

JERICHO

JERUSALEM

DEAD SEA

HEBRON

ISRAEL
(CANAAN)

ARAD

BEERSHEBA

ROUTE OF SCOUTS IS UNKNOWN
OTHER THAN THEIR VISITS TO
HEBRON AND LEBO-HAMATH
ABOUT 300 MILES (480 KM)
NORTH OF THEIR KADESH OASIS CAMP

N

WILDERNESS OF ZIN

KADESH OASIS
CAMP OF THE JEWS

WILDERNESS OF PARAN

EGYPT

Scout's honor. With grapes in tow from a late-summer reconnaissance mission into what is now Israel, Jewish scouts report that the land God promised the Jews is nothing like the barren Sinai they've endured for 40 years. Yet only two of the dozen scouts Moses sent give a favorable report—one that would honor God. The majority opinion from the other ten is that this land will be impossible to conquer. Too many walled cities. Too many giants. What towns the scouts visited, other than Hebron and Lebo-hamath, is anyone's guess. The Bible doesn't say.

MEDITERRANEAN SEA

SYRIA

LEBANON

MT HERMON
9232 FT
2814 M

• DAMASCUS

DAN

SEA OF
GALILEE

BASHAN

GILEAD

✗ BATTLE AT ENDREI
KING OG OF BASHAN DEFEATED

CANAAN

JORDAN RIVER

MT. NEBO
2631 FT
802 M

AMMON

JERICHO •

DEAD
SEA

MOSES DIES

✗ BATTLE AT JAHAZ
KING SIHON OF AMORITES DEFEATED

ISRAEL

MOAB

JORDAN

KADESH OASIS
JEWISH CAMP

PUNON
BATTLE AVOIDED

E D O M

AARON DIES • MT. HOR?
JABAL AN NABI HARUN
5689 FT
1734 M

EZION-GEBER

GULF
OF
AQABA

M I D I A N

SLINGER
LOW-TECH ARTILLERY

N

SLOW AS MOSES
TAKING THE SCENIC ROUTE AGAIN

The people of Israel set out from Mount Hor, taking the road to the Red Sea to go around the land of Edom. But the people grew impatient with the long journey.

NUMBERS 21:4

Tracking Moses. No one is sure what route Moses and his fellow Jewish refugees took when they finally left the Kadesh oasis. Perhaps hoping to avoid another fight with southland Canaanites, they turned east toward what is now Jordan. And to avoid a fight with Edom's militia, the Jews bypassed this kingdom of distant relatives who descended from Esau, Jacob's brother. Sadly, the Jews couldn't bypass all the hostiles. Eventually they had to fight. They won all their battles in what are now parts of Jordan and Syria, and they took the land.

When God sentenced the Jews to 40 years in the Sinai badlands for failing to trust him enough to invade the Promised Land, Moses was 80 years old.

He was 120 years old by the time the Jews completed their sentence. By then, almost every adult who had left Egypt 40 years earlier was dead and buried. Moses and his big brother, Aaron, would soon die too.

God did, however, allow Moses to lead the Jews to the eastern border of the Promised Land.

Again, Moses took the scenic route.

The Bible doesn't say why he didn't simply go north, directly into what is now Israel. Perhaps he didn't want to face the southland hill people again. Forty years earlier, when some of the Jews tried to ignore God's sentence and invade the Promised Land, the local hill people weren't particularly hospitable. "Amalekites and Canaanites who lived in that hill country came down. They attacked the people of Israel. They won the battle over them" (Numbers 14:45 NIRV).

Moses could have taken the Jews west and invaded from the coastal land. But Philistines may have been settling in there at the time, and they were formidable fighters, as the Jews would discover later.

For whatever reason, Moses decided to swing around to what is now Israel's eastern border, into what is now Jordan. They would invade from across the Jordan River Valley. The shortest route there was through the nation of Edom—distant relatives. The people of Edom descended from Isaac's son Esau. The Jews descended from Esau's brother, Jacob.

Moses sent ambassadors to ask Edom's king for permission to pass through.

Jewish relatives were not welcome. "Stay out of my land, or I will meet you with an army!" (Numbers 20:18).

The Jews turned south, back toward the Red Sea. Aaron died along the way and was buried at Mount Hor.

If Moses wanted to get into Israel without a fight, he should have dug a tunnel.

Several armies attacked the Jews along the way. But the Jews, led by Joshua, seemed invincible.

MOSES, DEAD IN JORDAN

Moses never makes it into what is now Israel. The Bible doesn't say why, exactly. It says only that Moses did something that offended God. "Because you did not trust me enough to demonstrate my holiness to the people of Israel, you will not lead them into the land I am giving them!" (Numbers 20:12).

At least Moses got to see the place from a distance. "Moses went up to Mount Nebo from the plains of Moab and climbed Pisgah Peak, which is across from Jericho. And the LORD showed him the whole land" (Deuteronomy 34:1).

Some ancient copies of the Bible say, "He buried him," suggesting God buried Moses "in a valley...no one knows the exact place" (Deuteronomy 34:6). Other ancient copies read, "They buried him," suggesting the people who were with him when he died.

CURSES

Desperate to stop the advancing horde of Jewish refugees, one king hired a magical mercenary to put a hex on them. Many people in ancient times believed that words spoken as a blessing or a curse had the power to make things happen, for better or worse.

Balak, king of Moab, a nation in what is now Jordan, wanted "better" for his people and "worse" for the Jews.

He sent riders several hundred miles north to bring back a famous sorcerer who lived near the Euphrates River in what is now Syria.

The sorcerer, Balaam, agreed to come. Along the way his donkey stopped for no apparent reason. When Balaam beat the donkey, it spoke: "What have I done to you that deserves your beating me three times?" (Numbers 22:28).

Suddenly, the renowned seer was able to see what his dumb donkey had seen all along: an angel with a sword blocking their path.

The angel convinced Balaam not to curse the Jews, but to curse the Moabites instead. "Someday, a king of Israel will appear like a star. He will wipe out you Moabites" (Numbers 24:17 CEV).

Centuries later, many Jews said King David fulfilled that prediction.

First class. Donkeys were the preferred mode of travel in Bible times. Reliable. Able to maneuver rugged land. Strong enough to carry about 200 pounds (91 kg). In one case, as the Bible tells it, a donkey could talk.

They crushed the attacking armies, overran the defenseless cities, and claimed the lands east of the Jordan River as part of their Promised Land. Two and a half tribes settled there— "Reuben, Gad, and half the tribe of Manasseh" (Numbers 34:14).

5

TAKING BACK THE PROMISED LAND

TIMELINE *(dates are approximate)*

1550 BC	Jericho is destroyed (or 1400—date debated).
1400 BC	Jews invade the Promised Land (or 1200s—date debated).
1345 BC	A sculptor crafts bust of Egyptian Queen Nefertiti.
1230 BC	Jews destroy the Canaanite city of Hazor.
1200 BC	Camel saddles start to appear.
1193 BC	Troy falls in the Trojan War.
1180 BC	Philistines try to invade Egypt but fail.

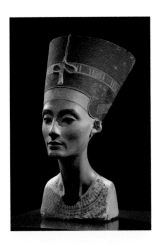

Queen Nefertiti

Trojan horse

CROSSING THE JORDAN RIVER IN FLOOD SEASON

The water of the Jordan was going over its banks... The priests came to the river. Their feet touched the water's edge. Right away the water that was coming down the river stopped flowing. It piled up far away at a town called Adam.

JOSHUA 3:15-16 NIRV

No big deal crossing the Jordan. It's a poor excuse for a river. On a good day, it splashes no wider than a bus is long, no deeper than a bus is high—some 30 yards (27 m) wide by 10 feet (3 m) deep.

In early Bible times, before bridges, the two spies Joshua sent to scout out Jericho would have had little trouble crossing the stream even though it was springtime—"the harvest season, and the Jordan was overflowing its banks" (Joshua 3:15).*

Desert dwellers who couldn't swim? No problem.

The spies may have found one of the paths that locals used to cross at a shallow sandbar, known as a ford. Perhaps there was a rope to hang on to as they waded across. In case of an emergency, a wineskin will work as a flotation device.

After Joshua's scouts got back from Jericho with happy news that the Canaanite residents were terrified of them, the Jews broke camp and made their move. They left Acacia Grove, also known in some Bible translations as Shittim—a name no one but the pastor's kid wants to read out loud in church.

The Jews walked about six miles (9 km) along the banks of the river before camping again. Joshua told them what would happen next: "Priests will carry the Ark of the LORD...As soon as their feet touch the water, the flow of water will be cut off upstream, and the river will stand up like a wall" (Joshua 3:13).

That's what happened, the Bible says.

It doesn't take a biblical lit professor to see the theological link to God parting the water for Moses and the Exodus Jews a generation earlier. God seemed to be saying, once again, that nothing on earth could stop him from taking his people home.

---

* Farmers harvest flax and barley as early as February and April.

Mediterranean Sea

Mt. Hermon

Sea of Galilee

ARABIAN TECTONIC PLATE

AFRICAN TECTONIC PLATE

Adam
(Damiya, Jordan)

Gilgal?

Jericho

Jordan River

Possible route of the Jews

N

Dead Sea

EARTHQUAKES STILL DAM THE JORDAN

In 1927, an earthquake did what the Bible says God did in Joshua's day. At the same place too—the city of Adam.

The Jordan River Valley marks a fault line separating a pair of tectonic plates moving in the same direction at different speeds. When one plate grinds into the other…earthquake.

The quake of 1927 shook loose the 150-foot-high (46 m) clay cliffs near the ruins of what many say was ancient Adam. This site, upriver of Jericho some 20 miles (32 km) in the Arab country of Jordan, is known today by its similar-sounding Arabic name: Damiya.

The quake dammed the river for 21 hours.

Quakes have spawned landslides that dammed the Jordan River many other times in recorded history—1956, 1906, 1834, 1546, and 1267.

JERICHO SPEED BUMP

GETTING PAST THE WORLD'S OLDEST WALLED CITY

When the people heard the sound of the rams' horns [blown by the priests], they shouted as loud as they could. Suddenly, the walls of Jericho collapsed, and the Israelites charged straight into the town and captured it.

JOSHUA 6:20

Downtown ghost town. A bump at the edge of an oasis is all that remains of ancient Jericho (foreground), photographed in 1931. That's the decade archaeologist John Garstang begin excavating the site, concluding that Jericho was burned and its double walls torn down in about 1400 BC. Archaeologist Kathleen Kenyon, digging in the 1950s, disagreed and said the city fell 150 years earlier—making it a ghost town by the time Joshua arrived. Kenyon's opinion is the one most archaeologists support today, though not everyone agrees. This photo looks southeast toward the Jordan River Valley and the Dead Sea, distant right.

Surrounded by double walls, the ridgetop city of Jericho would have looked impregnable...until the walls fell down.

Busting these walls was quite the feat since Jericho is estimated at 7000 years old when Joshua and his militia arrived—the oldest walled city in the world as far as archaeologists have been able to tell so far.

Jericho crowned the top of a 10-acre knoll—a mound about 75 feet (23 m) high and 350 yards long by 150 yards wide (320 by 137 m). That's a bump in the earth about the size of ten football fields. The city was protected

PROFILE OF MIDDLE EASTERN MAN
FROM JOSHUA'S TIME

MT. HERMON

SEA OF GALILEE

JORDAN RIVER

JABBOK RIVER

AI
KHIRBAT AT TALL

KHIRBET AL MAFJIR
JEWISH BASE CAMP
ELEVATION -700 FT (-213 M)

GILGAL

JERICHO
OASIS 'CITY OF PALMS'

ACACIA GROVE

GIBEON
ELEVATION 255 FT (779 M)

JERUSALEM

DEAD
SEA

N

Uphill battle. As nighttime fell, Joshua's militia started their all-night climb, dressed in battle gear, to Gibeon—about 20 miles away (36 km) and nearly three-quarters of a mile (1 km) higher than their base camp at Gilgal in the Jordan River Valley. Gilgal was "just east of Jericho," exact location uncertain. Current best guess: a ruin called Khirbet al Mafjir.

by a mud brick wall at the top of the knoll and another at the bottom.

As the Bible writer tells it, once the Jews reached Jericho, six miles (10 km) west of the Jordan River, they camped outside the city. Once a day for six days, the Jewish militia marched completely around the city, following their priests who carried the Ark of the Covenant—Israel's most sacred relic. It was a gold-covered wooden chest containing the Ten Commandments.

On day seven, they marched around the city seven times. Then the priests blew their rams' horns while the soldiers shouted. The walls collapsed.

It may not be that the militia found the perfect note for shattering mud bricks the way a soprano's high C can explode a crystal goblet.

More likely, some Bible experts speculate, this was a miracle of timing. God may have brought down the walls with aftershocks from an earlier earthquake (see "Earthquakes Still Dam the Jordan," page 57). Other students of the Bible say they think it was entirely a God thing—supernatural, pure and simple.

Joshua ordered his Jewish militia to kill everyone and everything in Jericho as a way of devoting the entire city to God. The only exception was Rahab and her family. Rahab was a prostitute who had helped Jewish spies escape after they nearly got caught scouting Jericho before the attack.

JOSHUA: "SUN STOP"
ONE ODD PRAYER BEFORE BATTLE

Surprise. In a dawn attack, Joshua's militia routes a coalition of five armies laying siege to Gibeon, a city allied with the Jews.

The sun and the moon stopped and stood still until Israel defeated its enemies.

JOSHUA 10:13 CEV

After an all-night forced march up into enemy hill country, Joshua prayed one of the weirdest prayers in the Bible. Strange, too, that he prayed it on behalf of a Canaanite city he had come to protect. Moses, before dying, had told Joshua to annihilate every Canaanite city.

The bizarre story starts when a delegation of foreign ambassadors arrives in Joshua's camp at Gilgal, somewhere in the Jordan River Valley, "just east of Jericho" (Joshua 4:19). The delegates were wearing tattered clothes and toting moldy bread. They said they came from a distant country, hoping to make a peace treaty with God's people.

Liars.

They came from a Canaanite city a day's walk away—Gibeon.

Joshua didn't discover their lie until he had already sealed the peace treaty. By then, he felt obligated to honor the contract.

Gibeon's neighboring kingdom-cities were not pleased that Gibeon aligned itself with the invaders. A coalition of five angry neighbor cities marched on Gibeon and surrounded the walled city in a siege.

Gibeon managed to get a messenger through to Joshua.

A loyal ally, "Joshua and his army marched all night from Gilgal for a surprise attack," (Joshua 10:9 NCV). The march was uphill, about a quarter mile (½ km) above their base camp and 20 miles (32 km) away.

Arriving at daybreak, Joshua prayed the odd prayer that the writer quotes as poetry and attributes to the long-lost Book of Jashar (Joshua 10:13 NCV).

Some students of the Bible say they read the story literally and believe that the sun and moon actually appeared to stop in the sky. Perhaps Joshua was afraid the enemy would escape after sundown, so he prayed for a longer day.

Others say they wonder if we should grant the writer a poetic license, given the fact that the apparent movement of the sun and moon are caused by the earth's rotation at about 1000 miles an hour (1600 km/h). If the earth stopped, they argue, everyone would have gotten whiplash. Or blasted off into outer space at Mach 1.

A popular theory for understanding Joshua's prayer hangs on the Hebrew word for "stop," *daman*. Some Bible scholars say the word can mean either "stop moving" or simply "stop," as in stop shining.

Think cloud cover.

As the theory goes, perhaps Joshua was worried that after an all-night forced march, his men would wilt under a blazing sun.

If cloud cover is what he wanted, he got his wish.

Shocked to wake up to Joshua's surprise attack, the coalition army scattered.

They could run, but in the open air of the Judean highlands, they could not hide. "The LORD threw large hailstones on them from the sky and killed them. More people were killed by the hailstones than by the Israelites' swords" (Joshua 10:11 NCV).

OPERATION HIGH GROUND

JOSHUA'S STRATEGY FOR KILLING CANAANITES

Joshua captured the whole land—the mountains, the Negev, the foothills, and the slopes.

JOSHUA 10:40 GWT

War zone: Judean hills. Walking a trail through the Judean highlands is something Joshua and his militia did a lot. Hills like these were Joshua's preferred battlefields. This is where lightly armed soldiers, like his Jewish militia, could outmaneuver heavily armed warriors reinforced with cavalry and chariots.

Joshua had 40 years in the wilderness to perfect his strategy for conquering the Promised Land. Forty years before the invasion, Moses included him among the dozen scouts sent on a mission to explore the defenses of what is now Israel. That might explain why Joshua was able to defeat the armies of 31 kings with his ragtag band of lightly armed refugees. He knew his militia would face heavily armed warriors defending walled cities, some with the added defense of cavalry and a chariot corps boasting state-of-the-art iron hardware—the fear-factor equivalent of an infantryman today facing a tank.

Joshua's strategy:

- Avoid the flat coastal plains where large armies, cavalry, and chariots have the advantage.
- Head for the hills, where a lightly armed strike force can maneuver easily but heavily armed warriors can't.

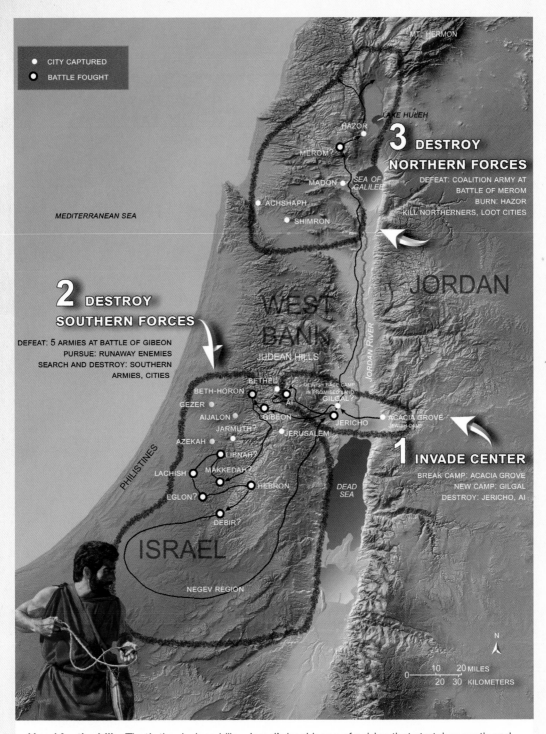

- CITY CAPTURED
- BATTLE FOUGHT

MT. HERMON

LAKE HULEH

HAZOR

MEROM?

3 **DESTROY
NORTHERN FORCES**

MADON

SEA OF
GALILEE

DEFEAT: COALITION ARMY AT
BATTLE OF MEROM
BURN: HAZOR
KILL NORTHERNERS, LOOT CITIES

ACHSHAPH

SHIMRON

MEDITERRANEAN SEA

JORDAN

WEST
BANK

JUDEAN HILLS

Jordan River

2 **DESTROY
SOUTHERN FORCES**

DEFEAT: 5 ARMIES AT BATTLE OF GIBEON
PURSUE: RUNAWAY ENEMIES
SEARCH AND DESTROY: SOUTHERN
ARMIES, CITIES

BETHEL

BETH-HORON

JEWISH BASE CAMP
IN PROMISED LAND

AI

GILGAL?

GEZER

AIJALON

GIBEON

ACACIA GROVE
Jewish camp

JARMUTH?

JERICHO

JERUSALEM

AZEKAH

1 **INVADE CENTER**

PHILISTINES

LIBNAH?

MAKKEDAH?

LACHISH

BREAK CAMP: ACACIA GROVE
NEW CAMP: GILGAL
DESTROY: JERICHO, AI

EGLON?

HEBRON

DEAD
SEA

DEBIR?

ISRAEL

NEGEV REGION

N

0   10   20 MILES
     20   30 KILOMETERS

Head for the hills. That's the Judean hills—Israel's backbone of a ridge that stretches north and south through what was then central Canaan. This is where Joshua's lightly armed strike force could outmaneuver Canaanite chariots and soldiers weighed down with heavy battle gear.

Taking Back the Promised Land

ONE NATION, A DOZEN TRIBES
CARVING UP THE PROMISED LAND

Tribes of Israel received land in Canaan...by means of sacred lots.

JOSHUA 14:1-2

Joshua's conquest was no quickie, it would seem from clues in the Bible. It may have taken many years.

That would explain why, when it came time to divvy up the land, God told Joshua, "You are growing old, and much land remains to be conquered" (Joshua 13:1).

Joshua disbanded his army and divided the land among the tribes, commissioning each tribe to finish mopping up resistance in their own territories.

Jewish priests bless the congregation with a traditional hand gesture. They hold their hands in a way that represents an opening through which the glory of God can shine on the people.

Easier said than done for some tribes.

The tiny tribe of Dan, for example, drew the short straw. They ended up with a tiny plug of land mostly on the coast, where the warlike Philistines were digging in and building fortified cities. Dan's tribe eventually moved to the north, settling at the foot of Mount Hermon.

When Joshua divided the territory, he honored the promise Moses had given earlier, allowing the tribes of Reuben, Gad, and the half-tribe of Manasseh to settle east of the Jordan River in what are now the Arab countries of Jordan and Syria.

As for the nine and a half tribes that settled west of the river, in what is now Israel, Joshua used sacred lots to determine which tribes got what sections of land. Bible experts aren't sure how the lots worked, but many guess the lots were marked stones that provided yes and no answers—a bit like flipping a coin.

Joshua died "at the age of 110" (Joshua 24:29).

For the first time in the history of the two-generation-old nation of Israel, the people had no leader. Family elders led each tribe, and a high priest ran the tent worship center at Shiloh, a city near the middle of the country.

SYRIA

LEBANON   MT. HERMON

Rebob
Abdon   KADESH
ASHER   NAPHTALI   GOLAN HEIGHTS
                                  EAST MANASSEH
Mishal
Nahalal   Rimmon   Kartan   SEA OF GALILEE   Ashtaroth
          ZEBULUN   Yarmuk River   GOLAN
          Daberath   Hammath
          Helkath   Tabor
Yokneam   Kishon   Nazareth   RAMOTH
          ISSACHAR
Taanach   En-gannim

MEDITERRANEAN   Ibleam
SEA
                                  Jabbok River
          WEST MANASSEH
                    SHECHEM   Mahanaim
                                        Jazer
                    ▲ SHILOH
                    WORSHIP CENTER   GAD   Mephaath
          Gath-rimmon   Kibzaim
Eltekeh   EPHRAIM
          Gezer   BENJAMIN
Gibbethon   Gibeon Geba Almon
          DAN   Aijalon   Anathoth   Heshbon   BEZER
          Beth-shemesh
               Jerusalem
                                        REUBEN   Kedemoth
          Libnah   DEAD
ISRAEL   HEBRON   SEA
          JUDAH
WEST BANK   Jahaz   JORDAN
          Debir   Holon   Juttah
                                        Arnon River
          Jattir   Eshtemoa
Ashan
     SIMEON   6 CITIES OF REFUGE ●
                         48 CITIES OF THE LEVITE PRIESTS ◦
                              Some locations uncertain

JUDAH

N
W E
S
0   10   20 MILES
    20   30 KILOMETERS

Putting Israel on the map. Joshua assigns each of Israel's 12 tribes a plug of land in what is now Israel, Palestinian territory, and parts of Jordan and Syria. He scatters a thirteenth tribe—Levi, an extended family of priests and other worship leaders—assigning them 48 cities throughout the land. He also set up half a dozen cities of refuge where people accused of murder could get a fair trial, protected from "relatives seeking revenge for the person who was killed" (Joshua 20:3).

N

MEDITERRANEAN SEA

MT. HERMON

SEA OF GALILEE

BATTLE OF APHEK

APHEK
CAMP OF PHILISTINES

EBENEZER
Jewish army brings the Ark of the Covenant from Shiloh to their camp at Ebenezer.

EKRON
(TEL MIQNE)
Ekron doesn't want it because "it will kill us all" (1 Samuel 5:11)

KIRIATH-JEARIM
(TEL QIRYAT YEARIM)

SHILOH
(KHIRBAT SAYLUN)

GILGAL?

ASHKELON
When Philistines put the Ark in their temple the statue of their god Dagon falls face to the ground "in front of the Ark" (1 Samuel 5:3).

GATH
(TEL ZAFIT)
When the Ark comes to Gath a plague of tumors comes with it.

BETH SHEMESH
70 Philistines die when they look inside the Ark.

Jews store Ark here for "twenty years" (1 Samuel 7:2)

JERUSALEM
King David later moves Ark to Jerusalem capital.

JERICHO

JUDEAN HILLS

DEAD SEA

WAR TROPHY

PHILISTINE RAIDERS OF THE LOST ARK

"Let's bring the Ark here from Shiloh," they said. "If we carry it into battle with us, the Lord will be among us and he will surely save us from our enemies."

1 Samuel 4:3 TLB

Ark on tour. Desperate to win a losing battle, Jewish soldiers camped at Ebenezer call on divine reinforcements—the sacred Ark of the Covenant kept at the Jewish worship center in Shiloh, about twenty miles (36 km) east. Jews lose the battle and the Ark to the Philistine army, staged at Aphek, about two and a half miles away (4 km). Philistines take their war trophy on tour. A plague follows it to each town. Some scholars say the disease sounds like the bubonic plague.

A magic war box is what the sacred Ark of the Covenant became to some Jews after the time of Joshua.

When they found themselves losing a battle to the Philistines near the western foothills, they decided to rush the Ark to the front lines.

The Ark, Israel's most sacred relic, was a gold-covered chest that held the Ten Commandments. Carried by priests, it had led the march of refugee ancestors out of Egypt. And at God's order, priests sometimes carried it to the edge of the battle, as they did when the Jews conquered Jericho.

This time, however, the Jews did not consult God. They took it upon themselves to bring the chest into battle, as if the power came from the chest and not necessarily from God. "Let's bring the Ark of the Covenant of the LORD from Shiloh. If we carry it into battle with us, it will save us from our enemies" (1 Samuel 4:3).

The chest was a wonderful motivator. For the Jews and for the Philistines.

When it arrived in camp, the Jews cheered so loud that the Bible writer says, "It made the ground shake!" (1 Samuel 4:5).

Terrified Philistine warriors fought all the harder, fearing that they were battling soldiers empowered by gods—and that if they lost, their families would become slaves to the Jews.

The Philistines won the battle, killed the priests, and took the Ark as a war trophy. Some Bible scholars speculate that the Philistines pushed farther into Jewish territory and possibly even destroyed the worship center in Shiloh.

The Philistines took the Ark on tour, probably to show that they and their gods were more powerful than the Jews and their God.

It didn't work out so well for them.

When they put the Ark on display beside the statue of their chief god, Dagon, in the temple at the city of Ashdod, Philistine priests woke up the next morning to discover Dagon's statue had somehow fallen on its face beside the Ark.

Wherever they sent the Ark on tour, a plague of tumors followed. For seven months.

Some Bible experts guess that the disease was the tumor-producing bubonic plague, carried by rats. When the Philistines finally returned the Ark to the Jews, they sent it back with a second chest containing "five gold tumors and five gold rats" (1 Samuel 6:4).

One for each of the major Philistine city-kingdoms.

MEDITERRANEAN SEA

SHAMGAR

JEPHTHAH
From Gilead, he overpowered Ammon trying to take back their homeland from Jews.

ELON
TOLA JAIR
Ashur NAPHTALI BETH-ANATH?
RIMMON? HAZOR EAST MANASSEH
ABDON ZEBULUN SEA OF GALILEE
ISSACHAR GILEAD
OPHRAH?
EHUD WEST MANASSEH SHAMIR?
IBZAN PIRATHON? SHECHEM
OTHNIEL EPHRAIM BETHEL GAD
DAN BENJAMIN AMMON
ZORAH JERUSALEM JERICHO
JUDAH BETHLEHEM REUBEN
DEBIR DEAD SEA
ISRAEL

GIDEON
From Israel's best farmland, he raised an army and drove off invaders from Midian who raided farms at harvesttime.

SIMEON MOAB

JUDAH
NEGEV EDOM

N

DEBORAH
Lived in Ephraim but commanded an army that fought off a chariot corps from Hazor, a city kingdom north of the Sea of Galilee.

SAMSON
From Zorah, he waged a one-man war against Philistines living nearby on the coast. He killed 1,000 with a donkey's jawbone.

A DOZEN JEWISH HEROES
JUDGES ON THE WARPATH

When the people of Israel cried out to the LORD for help, the LORD raised up a rescuer to save them.

JUDGES 3:9

Heroes in the neighborhood. Israel's dozen deliverers in the book of Judges weren't kings or strongmen who ruled over all 12 tribes. They were locals who fought local threats.

Israel's judges weren't judges in the way we think of judges. At least not most of them.

Judge Deborah was an exception. She tried legal cases. A wife and a prophet, she "held court under the Palm of Deborah between Ramah and Bethel in the hill country of Ephraim, and the Israelites went up to her to have their disputes decided" (Judges 4:5 NIV).

Her claim to fame, however, was commanding a Jewish militia that routed an invading chariot corps at the foot of Mount Tabor in northern Israel.

Bible students call Deborah and 11 other Jewish leaders *judges* from the Hebrew word *shofet*, which is actually a broader word. It can mean a judge who tries cases. But it can also mean a

JUDGE	HOME TURF	CLAIM TO FAME
Othniel 3:7-11	Debir	defeats an invading king from what is now Syria
Ehud 3:12-30	Jericho area	assassinates the oppressive king of Moab in what is now Jordan and then leads a successful revolt
Shamgar 3:31	Beth-anath	kills 600 Philistines with an ox herder's stick
Deborah 4:1–5:31	tribe of Ephraim	leads an army of foot soldiers that defeats an invading chariot corps from the city of Hazor
Gideon 6:1–8:35	farmland in northern tribes	drives off invaders from Midian in what is now Jordan or Saudi Arabia
Tola 10:1-2	tribe of Issachar but linked to Shamir	a minor judge and a descendant of Dodo, which seems like a sad claim to fame for a hero
Jair 10:3-5	Gilead region	has 30 sons who own 30 towns in the rich grazing land of Gilead in what is now Jordan
Jephthah 10:6–12:7	Gilead	defeats Ammonites in what is now Jordan and then sacrifices his daughter to honor a stupid vow
Ibzan 12:8-10	Bethlehem	has 30 sons and 30 daughters
Elon 12:11-12	tribe of Zebulun	unknown
Abdon 12:13-15	Pirathon, possibly in tribe of Ephraim	has 40 sons and 30 grandsons, all of whom ride donkeys, suggesting a time of prosperity and peace
Samson 13:1–16:31	Zorah in tribe of Dan	wages a one-man war against the Philistines, killing 1000 with a donkey's jawbone

ruler or a leader of some sort. That describes all of the dozen, including the son of a hooker, Jephthah, and a left-handed assassin named Ehud.

The book of Judges is a sad tale that runs in circles, like a dog chasing its tail. Here's how the tale spins.

- The Jews sin, often by worshipping idols.
- God punishes them by allowing a foreign country to oppress them.
- The Jews pray for God to deliver them.
- God sends a deliverer who rescues the people, resulting in anywhere from 6 to 80 years of peace.
- The Jews go back to sinning.

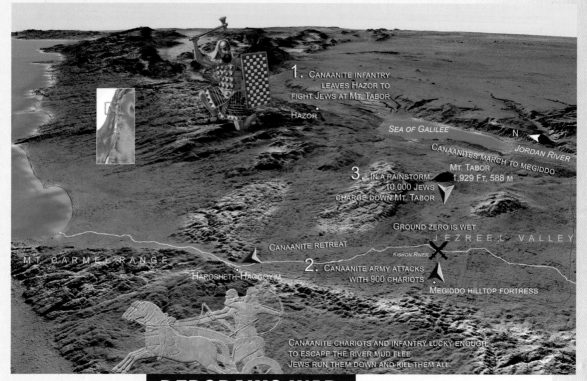

1. CANAANITE INFANTRY LEAVES HAZOR TO FIGHT JEWS AT MT. TABOR

HAZOR

SEA OF GALILEE

JORDAN RIVER

N

CANAANITES MARCH TO MEGIDDO

MT. TABOR 1,929 FT, 588 M

3. IN A RAINSTORM, 10,000 JEWS CHARGE DOWN MT. TABOR

GROUND ZERO IS WET

JEZREEL VALLEY

CANAANITE RETREAT

KISHON RIVER

MT CARMEL RANGE

HAROSHETH-HAGGOYIM

2. CANAANITE ARMY ATTACKS WITH 900 CHARIOTS

MEGIDDO HILLTOP FORTRESS

CANAANITE CHARIOTS AND INFANTRY LUCKY ENOUGH TO ESCAPE THE RIVER MUD FLEE. JEWS RUN THEM DOWN AND KILL THEM ALL.

DEBORAH'S WAR
BATTLE OF MOUNT TABOR

Deborah said to Barak, "Charge! This very day GOD has given you victory over Sisera. Isn't GOD marching before you?"

JUDGES 4:14 MSG

When this lady yelled "charge!" she wasn't shopping. She was about to make a killing.

Deborah was a prophetess—one of several mentioned in the Bible, along with Miriam and Huldah. Perhaps because folks realized she had a connection to God, "the people of Israel would come to her to settle their arguments" (Judges 4:5 NCV).

She held court under what became known as the Palm Tree of Deborah. It grew somewhere between the cities of Ramah and Bethel in the hill country of Ephraim's tribe.

She'll take the high ground.
Like Joshua, Deborah takes her attitude to altitude. She musters her 10,000-man militia from Israel's northern tribes onto Mount Tabor. It's a great strategy because Canaanite chariots can't maneuver those steep slopes. Jabin, a Canaanite who has been making life tough on northern Jews, orders his army to attack, reinforced by 900 chariots. A rainstorm floods the Kishon River, churning the Jezreel Valley battlefield into a mud pit. Some chariots that manage to escape race back to their base at Harosheth-haggoyim.

That put Deborah in the middle of the country, far from the Canaanite king who had raided the northern tribes for 20 years.

The king's name and city come as a surprise: King Jabin of Hazor. Many years earlier, Joshua's militia had supposedly killed "King Jabin of Hazor" and "burned the city" (Joshua 11:1,11). Bible experts say this new story suggests King Jabin's dynasty lived on through a son, and Canaanite survivors of Joshua's attack rebuilt the city. Scholars also say this story shows that the Jews struggled to conquer the land and hold it—and that the conquest was a process that took centuries.

Deborah sent for Barak, a military commander who lived in Naphtali, the very tribe responsible for conquering the territory that included Hazor. She said she had a message for him from God. Barak was to call up 10,000 militiamen from the neighboring northland tribes of Zebulun and Naphtali. Some Bible experts say the word for "thousand" can mean units—as in ten military units.

Deborah told him to stage his troops on the slopes of Mount Tabor, and God would give him victory.

Barak apparently didn't want to bet his life on this prophecy unless the prophet was willing to bet her life on it too. He insisted Deborah go into battle with him.

Deborah was not happy. Maybe she thought chivalry had died. Or maybe she thought Barak was dissing her role as a prophet, doubting her connection to God.

She said she'd go, but she added, "You will receive no honor...the LORD's victory over Sisera [the enemy commander] will be at the hands of a woman" (Judges 4:9).

When King Jabin found out the Jews had staged their militia on Mount Tabor, he sent his army there, reinforced with 900 iron chariots.

The Bible story and the song Deborah sang after the battle suggest that Jabin's invasion force got caught in a rainstorm while marching alongside the Kishon River Valley.

Their iron chariots sank in the mud.

Deborah ordered her militia to charge down the hill and engage the enemy. Some invaders were already dead, caught in the flood. "The Kishon River swept them away" (Judges 5:21).

Sisera, the Canaanite general, ran for his life—right into the tent of the woman Deborah predicted would get the glory for Israel's victory. She was Jael, the wife of a herder whose family had been on friendly terms with King Jabin.

Perhaps Jael knew a loser when she saw one—and an opportunity to get on the good side of the winning team.

With traditional Middle Eastern hospitality, she welcomed him, offering him a place to rest. She gave him milk (which, by the way, is a sedative) and a cover to sleep under.

Then, with nontraditional Middle Eastern hospitality, she made sure he would rest in peace. She got a hammer and a tent peg and "drove the tent peg through his temple and into the ground, and so he died" (Judges 4:21).

GIDEON'S LITTLE ARMY
HERO FROM A HOLE IN THE GROUND

Camel corps. Palestine's camel corps lines up for inspection in Beersheba in 1940, when the British Empire ran what was called the British Mandate for Palestine. Gideon's story provides history's first report of using camels in warfare. They can sprint 40 miles an hour (64 km), allowing Midianite raiders to show up almost out of nowhere.

When Gideon's three hundred men blew their trumpets, the LORD made all the Midianites fight each other with their swords!

JUDGES 7:22 NCV

If ever an angel made a wisecrack preserved in the holy Bible, it was the angel who recruited Gideon to lead a Jewish strike force against invading raiders.

At the time, Gideon was hiding from the raiders in a hole in the ground.

It was harvest season. Gideon was beating stalks of wheat to knock the grain kernels loose, and he was doing it in a winepress pit "to hide the grain from the Midianites" (Judges 6:11).

That's when the angel—apparently in the form of a human—suddenly showed up, sat under a nearby tree, and called down to Gideon hiding in the hole. "Mighty hero, the LORD is with you!" (verse 12).

Sarcastic though it may sound, it turns out to be the truth.

Midianites were descendants of Abraham's son Midian, born to the woman Abraham married after Sarah died. That means Isaac, father of the Jews, was Midian's big brother. But according to the Bible, their kids and their kids' kids where nothing close to kissing cousins.

Midianite folks were mostly herders and traders. That might explain why they and some of their allies raided Israel's best farmland for seven years—until Gideon stopped them.

The Bible says God allowed the invaders to raid Israel as punishment for Israel's sin. But when the people cried out to God, repenting and asking for deliverance, God's messenger tapped Gideon for the job.

Gideon didn't want the job.

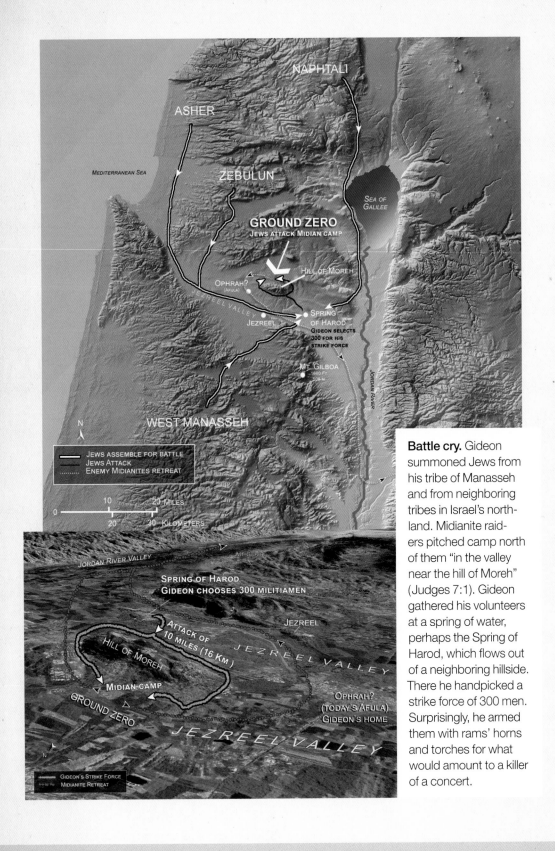

NAPHTALI

ASHER

MEDITERRANEAN SEA

ZEBULUN

SEA OF GALILEE

GROUND ZERO
Jews attack Midian camp

HILL OF MOREH

OPHRAH?
(AFULA)

JEZREEL VALLEY

JEZREEL

SPRING OF HAROD
Gideon selects 300 for his strike force

MT. GILBOA
1660 FT
506 M.

JORDAN RIVER

WEST MANASSEH

Jews assemble for battle
Jews attack
Enemy Midianites retreat

10   20 MILES
0
20   30 KILOMETERS

JORDAN RIVER VALLEY   MT. GILBOA

SPRING OF HAROD
GIDEON CHOOSES 300 MILITIAMEN

JEZREEL

ATTACK OF 10 MILES (16 KM)

HILL OF MOREH   JEZREEL VALLEY

MIDIAN CAMP

GROUND ZERO

OPHRAH?
(TODAY'S AFULA)
GIDEON'S HOME

JEZREEL VALLEY

GIDEON'S STRIKE FORCE
MIDIANITE RETREAT

Battle cry. Gideon summoned Jews from his tribe of Manasseh and from neighboring tribes in Israel's north-land. Midianite raiders pitched camp north of them "in the valley near the hill of Moreh" (Judges 7:1). Gideon gathered his volunteers at a spring of water, perhaps the Spring of Harod, which flows out of a neighboring hillside. There he handpicked a strike force of 300 men. Surprisingly, he armed them with rams' horns and torches for what would amount to a killer of a concert.

He needed a little convincing that the job offer was from God himself. So, in a way, he fleeced God. He asked the messenger of God to prove himself with a fleece.

- *Morning number one.* He left the fleece outside overnight, asking that it would be wet with dew the next morning while the ground would be dry. Done.

- *Morning number two.* He left the fleece outside overnight again, asking this time that it would be dry the next morning while the ground would be wet with dew. Done.

The people of Midian formed an alliance with other people east of the Jordan River, in what is now the Arab country of Jordan. They invaded the Jezreel Valley, where Gideon lived.

Gideon formed an alliance of his own, mobilizing 32,000 militiamen from the northern Jewish tribes of Manasseh, Asher, Zebulun, and Naphtali.

The 135,000 invaders outnumbered the Jews more than four to one (Judges 8:10).

God decided those odds weren't bad enough. He preferred something closer to forty-five to one against the Jews—possibly to reinforce the idea that the coming victory wasn't because of manpower, but because of God's power.

Three hundred Jews against 135,000 ancestors of the people who became Arabs.

Gideon, however, overpowered the invaders with shock and awe.

He divided his strike force into three groups, surrounding the invader camp. He equipped each of his men with a ram's horn and a clay jar that hid a lit torch. Late that night, just after the changing of the guard, Gideon led his unit of 100 men to the very edge of the invader camp.

There, he gave the signal. He broke his clay jar, exposing the lit torch, and blew the trumpet blast on his ram's horn.

His men did the same.

In the tar black of night, the invaded invaders thought the enemy was already in their camp. "The LORD made the enemy soldiers pull out their swords and start fighting each other" (Judges 7:22 CEV).

Those who survived fled, living to die another day. Gideon sent a message to the tribe of Ephraim, mobilizing troops that cut off some of the retreating invaders as they tried to cross the sandbar-like shallow fords of the Jordan River. Some 15,000 other warriors escaped, but "Gideon chased them down and captured all their warriors" (Judges 8:12).

Gideon's spring. Author Stephen M. Miller scoops a handful of water from the Spring of Harod in the area where Gideon ordered 10,000 volunteers to get a drink. Most "drank with their mouths in the stream" (Judges 7:6). Only 300 scooped up the water and drank from their hands. That bought them a ticket to the battle.

HIRED HELP: BAD-BOY HERO

JEPHTHAH, THE JUDGE WHO KILLED HIS DAUGHTER

Jephthah made a vow to the LORD. He said… "I will give to the LORD whatever comes out of my house to meet me when I return in triumph"… When Jephthah returned home to Mizpah, his daughter came out.

JUDGES 11:30-31,34

Dead meat. Jephthah's virgin daughter greets her father with music and dancing when he returns safely home from war. Big mistake. He kills her for it, cuts her up, and burns her body parts on a pile of wood. He didn't want to, but he felt compelled.

Who did this guy think would come out of his house to greet him when he returned home from war as the conquering general? The family goat?

His only child came out. His virgin daughter.

In fairness to Jephthah, he had suffered through a twisted childhood that may have warped his parenting skills.

The son of a hooker, he grew up in the home of his father and stepmother in Gilead—a hilly territory east of the Jordan River in what is now the Arab country of Jordan.

Jephthah's brothers—legit sons of their dad and his wife—kicked him out of the family so they wouldn't have to share the family estate with him. Perhaps Jephthah's only ally in the family—his dad—had died.

To survive on his own, Jephthah formed his own family—"a band of worthless rebels" (Judges 11:3).

War broke out in Jephthah's part of Israel. Three centuries earlier, when Jewish refugees of the Exodus left Egypt and returned to what is now Israel, they had to fight their way through what is now Jordan. That's because the locals, leery of such a large swath of strangers entering their land, greeted them with men holding sharp objects bigger than scissors. One such army—the Ammonites—attacked them. The Jews won the battle and confiscated most of the Ammonite land.

Now, after all this time, the Ammonites wanted it back. Again they attacked the Jews.

Jewish tribal leaders hired Jephthah—who already had a small, ragtag army—to recruit and lead a militia to push back the Ammonite invaders.

His pay: He would rule Jews in the region as a kind of uncrowned king.

Done deal.

Jephthah sent ambassadors to reason with the king of Ammon, reminding him that the Jews won the land fair and square as spoils of a war they didn't start.

"It was the LORD, the God of Israel, who took away the land from the Amorites and gave it to Israel," Jephthah argued. "You keep whatever your god Chemosh gives you, and we will keep whatever the LORD our God gives us" (Judges 11:23-24).

No deal.

Jephthah raised an army from his tribe of Manasseh and the region of Gilead.

Going into battle, he vowed that if God let him win the war, he would sacrifice as a burnt offering whatever greeted him when he came home.

A burnt offering got its throat cut, and its corpse was chopped into pieces and burned on a woodpile.

Cue the virgin, who "came out to meet him, playing on a tambourine and dancing for joy" (Judges 11:34).

Had Jephthah known Jewish law, he probably wouldn't have killed her. He had a way out.

- Human sacrifice was illegal. "God hates it all with a passion" (Deuteronomy 12:31 MSG).

- He could have paid the fee. "If any of you makes a special vow to give a person to the LORD, you may give money instead of the person'" (Leviticus 27:1-2 GWT). The amount was four ounces of silver—about the weight of half a roll of quarters.

Jephthah gave the person.

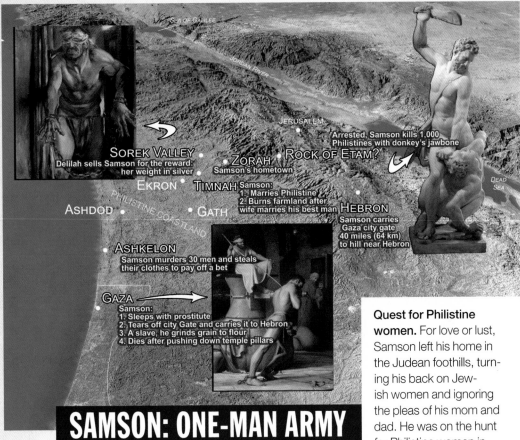

SEA OF GALILEE

JORDAN RIVER

JERUSALEM

Arrested, Samson kills 1,000
Philistines with donkey's jawbone

SOREK VALLEY
Delilah sells Samson for the reward:
her weight in silver

ZORAH
Samson's hometown

ROCK OF ETAM?

DEAD
SEA

EKRON

TIMNAH

Samson:
1. Marries Philistine
2. Burns farmland after
wife marries his best man

HEBRON
Samson carries
Gaza city gate
40 miles (64 km)
to hill near Hebron

ASHDOD

GATH

PHILISTINE COASTLAND

ASHKELON
Samson murders 30 men and steals
their clothes to pay off a bet

GAZA
Samson:
1. Sleeps with prostitute
2. Tears off city Gate and carries it to Hebron
3. A slave, he grinds grain to flour
4. Dies after pushing down temple pillars

SAMSON: ONE-MAN ARMY
JUICED ON TESTOSTERONE

*Samson found the jawbone of a dead donkey, took
it, and killed a thousand men with it!*

JUDGES 15:15 NCV

Quest for Philistine women. For love or lust, Samson left his home in the Judean foothills, turning his back on Jewish women and ignoring the pleas of his mom and dad. He was on the hunt for Philistine women in greener pastures of the Mediterranean coast. He found three: a wife, a hooker, and the world's worst girlfriend—Delilah. Each romantic encounter drew blood (Philistines', mostly).

For a hero sent from God, Samson was a jerk of a jock.

That comes as a surprise. After all, before he was born an angel told his mom—who had been infertile—that she'd have a son who would "begin to save Israel from the power of the Philistines" (Judges 13:5 NIRV).

Reading Samson's story, folks might expect another charismatic warrior, like Gideon, who rallied the Jews to fight a just war, defending the rights of Israel.

Instead, they get a one-man wrecking ball who chases Philistine women in his spare time. Samson decided to marry one.

Some would call that fraternizing with the enemy. The Bible writer called it God's will. "The LORD was at work in this" (Judges 14:4).

Philistines were the top dogs of Canaan. Jews lived with their tails tucked under—very much in danger of becoming assimilated into Philistine culture, many scholars say.

Cue Samson to drive a wedge of distrust and hatred between Philistines and Jews.

- *He murders 30 Philistines.* He bet 30 Philistine men at his wedding that they couldn't solve a riddle. When they got the answer from his bride by threatening to kill her, Samson was forced to pay up—one set of clothes for each man. He got them off the bodies of 30 men he killed in the Philistine city of Ashkelon.

- *He burns Philistine crops.* When Samson cools off and goes back to get his bride, her dad says he gave her to the best man. Livid, Samson tied torches to the tails of 300 foxes and set them loose in fields during the wheat harvest. Fires spread to vineyards, which took three to five years to replace and become productive. Olive orchards too. They took forty to fifty years to reach peak production.

- *Philistines burn his bride.* She's actually Samson's ex. But that's close enough for the angry Philistines. They torched her and her father.

- *Samson retaliates.* "He attacked the Philistines with great fury and killed many of them" (Judges 15:8).

- *Philistines invade Israel on a manhunt.* In the only selfless act in his story, Samson surrendered himself to Jews so they could turn him over to the Philistines.

- *Samson kills 1000 Philistines.* Once in Philistine custody, Samson breaks free of his ropes and kills the Philistines with a dead donkey's jawbone.

- *Samson tears off the city gate of Gaza.* Philistines wait to jump him when he comes out of the home of a Philistine prostitute in Gaza. But he rips off the city gate and carries it 40 miles (64 km), dumping it on a hill near the Jewish town of Hebron.

- *Philistines enslave him.* Philistine city leaders—perhaps from all five major cities—each offer a reward for Samson. They each promise his Philistine girlfriend, Delilah, 28 pounds (12.7 kg) of silver—combined for perhaps more than her weight in silver. Deal. She coaxed out of Samson the secret of his strength and then arranged a haircut. Philistines blinded him and turned him into a slave who grinds grain into flour.

- *Samson kills thousands in a suicide attack.* To brag on their god, Philistines parade Samson as a war trophy in their crowded temple. Samson dislodges two of the support pillars. "He killed more people when he died than he had during his entire lifetime" (Judges 16:30).

After that long bout with Samson, Philistines decide to keep the Jews at a distance. No more getting cozy.

About a generation later, King David crushed the Philistine army. Eventually, the once-dominant Philistines vanish, assimilated into other Middle Eastern nations—Arab as well as Jewish.

What remains of them is the modern version of their name—Palestine. It's from the Greek word for "Philistines," *Palaistine.*

Some Palestinians live in an area once controlled by the Philistines: Gaza and the Gaza Strip.

6

ISRAEL'S FIRST KINGS

TIMELINE *(dates are approximate)*

1050 BC	High Priest Eli dies; Samuel leads Israel.
1025 BC	Samuel anoints Saul king.
1010 BC	The Hebrew alphabet appears, based on Phoenician (Lebanon).
1010–970 BC	Israel's favorite hero, David, rules as king.
1000 BC	David captures Jerusalem and declares it Israel's capital.
966–959 BC	King Solomon builds Jerusalem temple, which lasts 400 years.

KING SAUL THE TALL
PROMOTED FROM DONKEY HERDER

Saul was the most handsome man in Israel—head and shoulders taller than anyone else in the land.

1 SAMUEL 9:2

Saul's comfort zone. Donkeys were the SUVs of Bible times—a preferred way of getting people and their stuff from one place to another. They weren't usually something poor folks could afford. Saul raised them for a living as the son of a rich donkey herder. Given what happened at his coronation as Israel's first king, it seems he would have preferred herding donkeys rather than people.

On a donkey hunt, out looking for his dad's herd of lost donkeys—that's where Saul was when he found out God had picked him to become Israel's first king.

Saul and the servant traveling with him, unable to find the lost donkeys, decided to see if the prophet Samuel could help them, since they knew Samuel had unique powers from God.

To Saul's shock, Samuel anointed him by pouring a jar of olive oil over his head and telling him, "The LORD has appointed you to be the ruler over Israel" (1 Samuel 10:1).

Saul didn't seem interested in the job. When Samuel called the tribal leaders together to introduce them to their king and to offer sacrifices uniting the tribes under the authority of God's chosen leader, Saul hid. Not just anywhere. He seemed to go to his happy place—among the donkeys and the supplies they carried. "He is hiding behind the baggage" (1 Samuel 10:22 CEV).

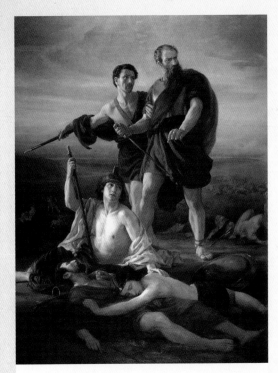

Dead dynasty. Saul and three of his sons die in a battle against an overwhelming force of Philistines. Another son of Saul's takes over—Ishbosheth, the nervous sort. He leads only part of the kingdom and for only a short time. That's because southern Jews of Judah proclaim David king. Northland tribes soon follow after a couple of Ishbosheth's commanders assassinate him.

WARRIOR KING

Reluctant though Saul may have been to serve as king, when the first crisis erupted, he quickly shifted gears from herder-farmer to commander in chief.

Saul got an urgent message that Ammonites, Arabs in what is now Jordan, had surrounded the Jewish city of Jabesh-gilead. The Jews offered to surrender. King Nahash of Ammon replied, "All right...but only on one condition. I will gouge out the right eye of every one of you as a disgrace to all Israel" (1 Samuel 11:2).

Saul quickly mobilized a force of more than 300,000 men and caught the Ammonites by surprise, slaughtering many of their soldiers and scattering the rest.

Following this victory, Saul decided to take on other enemies on the border, including the Philistines, who had managed to capture some of the Jewish highlands years earlier.

Philistines were no pushover. Skirmishes, raids, and battles continued throughout Saul's 40-year reign. War-weary, perhaps, Saul began to struggle with depression. He also had other reasons to feel bummed.

- *Goodbye throne.* Samuel told him, "Your kingly rule is already falling to pieces. GOD is out looking for your replacement right now" (1 Samuel 13:14 MSG). The reason: Saul had disobeyed God by offering a prebattle sacrifice that only priests were supposed to offer.

- *Goodbye Samuel.* Saul lost his only link to God—the prophet Samuel. Because God had rejected Saul, "Samuel never went to meet with Saul again, but he mourned constantly for him" (1 Samuel 15:35).

- *Hello David.* This young shepherd from Bethlehem soared to the top of the Jewish popularity polls after killing Goliath, the Philistine champion warrior, in mortal combat.

Saul became insanely jealous of David, who had to run for his life and live as a refugee among the Philistines. In Saul's final years, he fixated on killing David—perhaps even misdirecting his military assets toward the hunt for David and away from the Philistine threat.

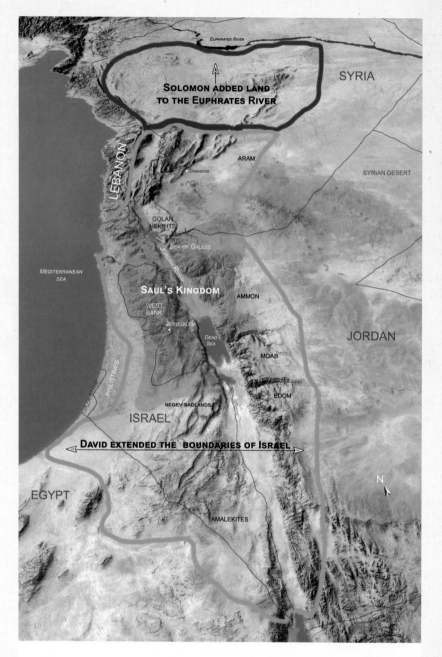

EUPHRATES RIVER

SYRIA

SOLOMON ADDED LAND
TO THE EUPHRATES RIVER

ARAM

SYRIAN DESERT

DAMASCUS

LEBANON

GOLAN
HEIGHTS

SEA OF GALILEE

Jordan River

MEDITERRANEAN
SEA

SAUL'S KINGDOM

AMMON

WEST
BANK

JERUSALEM

DEAD
SEA

JORDAN

MOAB

PHILISTINES

EDOM

NEGEV BADLANDS

ISRAEL

DAVID EXTENDED THE BOUNDARIES OF ISRAEL

N

EGYPT

AMALEKITES

Starting small. Israel's first king, Saul, managed to hold the highland territory, where most Jews settled after the exodus out of Egypt. Kings two and three—David and his son Solomon—each managed to extend Israel's domination of neighboring nations well into what are now the Arab countries of Syria, Jordan, and Egypt. Some saw this as a fulfillment of God's promise to Abraham, father of the Jews: "I have given this land to your descendants, all the way from the border of Egypt to the great Euphrates River" (Genesis 15:18). That's roughly double the size of modern Israel.

2. Plays harp to calm troubled King Saul.

6. Captures Jerusalem and makes it his capital.

1. David grows up as a shepherd.

3. Kills Goliath with a sling.

4. Hides from King Saul who is trying to kill him.

5. Tribe of Judah declares David king. Northern tribes soon do the same.

MEDITERRANEAN SEA
SEA OF GALILEE
JORDAN RIVER
JUDEAN HILLS
GIBEAH
ASHDOD
EKRON (TEL MIQNE)
JERUSALEM
GATH (TEL ZAFIT)
BETHLEHEM
VALLEY OF ELAH
ASHKELON
HEBRON
DEAD SEA
EN-GEDI
GAZA
PHILISTINES

SAUL FIRED, DAVID HIRED

DONKEY HERDER REPLACED BY SHEEP HERDER

Samuel took the flask of olive oil and anointed David… The LORD's Spirit came over David and stayed with him from that day on.

1 SAMUEL 16:13 GWT

God fired King Saul. But like a canned employee tying himself to the desk, Saul refused to give up his throne.

The prophet Samuel mourned for Israel's first king. He felt terrible and may have even blamed himself because he recruited Saul on God's behalf. The Bible says God chose Saul, but Samuel introduced this donkey herder as God's pick and then anointed him king. As Israel's lead prophet, Samuel also served as the king's spiritual guide.

"You have mourned long enough for Saul," God finally told the prophet. "I have rejected him as king of Israel, so fill your flask with olive oil and go to Bethlehem. Find a man named Jesse who lives there, for I have selected one of his sons to be my king" (1 Samuel 16:1).

Jesse and his seven oldest sons welcome elderly Samuel without having any idea why he came.

Samuel spots Eliab, the tallest and best-looking of Jesse's crew. Saul was tall and handsome too, so Samuel figures he has found his man.

Nope. "People judge others by what they look like," God somehow tells Samuel, perhaps in a vision or in a vivid thought. "But I judge people by what is in their hearts" (1 Samuel 16:7 CEV).

In fact, none of the seven sons pass muster. Samuel asks if Jesse has any more.

Jesse sends for David, his youngest. David has been out watching the sheep and goats while the big boys did grown-up stuff with their important guest. That important guest ends up anointing young David as the future king of Israel.

The Bible writer doesn't say if Samuel kept this a secret even from David, figuring that if Saul found out about it, he would have killed the entire family. But some consider it a fair bet.

Still, the anointing ritual was a common way of crowning kings, so it could have served as a clue to David—especially later, when he reflected back on how he became king.

In the meantime, anointing someone with olive oil in this hot, dry climate was also a way of giving them a refreshing treat or of making them feel welcome.

SING SAUL A SAD SONG

From the moment Samuel anointed David, God's Spirit seemed to surround the young man with blessing and success—maybe even sunshine and whistling. Many Jews in Bible times interpreted consistent good fortune as God's reward to deserving souls. In David's case, as the Bible reports it, they would have been right.

Saul, on the other hand, ran on empty: "The Spirit of the LORD had left Saul" (1 Samuel 16:14 CEV).

Depressed and afraid of what would happen to him, he wasn't up for whistling. If he wanted a song, he had to buy it.

That's what he did.

He bought the music of the person who still had the song of heaven inside him.

"Whenever the bad depression from God tormented Saul, David got out his harp and played. That would calm Saul down, and he would feel better as the moodiness lifted" (1 Samuel 16:23 MSG).

All of that would change once David became a hero.

After that, David might as well have been a yodeler trying to sooth someone's hangover.

David, the Goliath killer—suddenly more popular than the king—became just one more reason Saul felt bummed.

"Saul, who was fiddling with his spear, suddenly hurled it at David, intending to pin him to the wall" (1 Samuel 18:10-11 TLB).

Missed. Twice.

David was quick. He would need to be for all the battles he would have to fight. And especially for his first battle, against the Philistine's champion warrior.

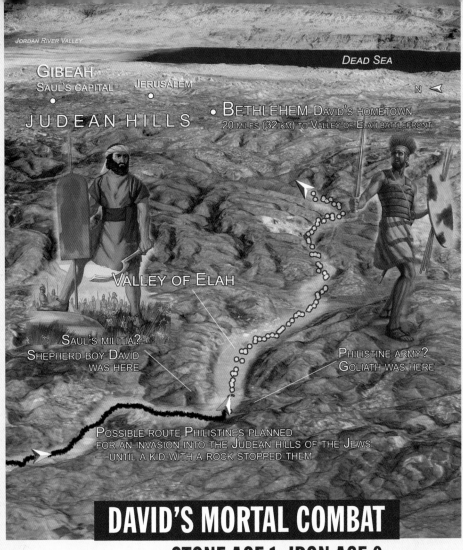

JORDAN RIVER VALLEY

DEAD SEA

GIBEAH
SAUL'S CAPITAL

JERUSALEM

N

JUDEAN HILLS

BETHLEHEM DAVID'S HOMETOWN
20 MILES (32 KM) TO VALLEY OF ELAH BATTLEFRONT

VALLEY OF ELAH

SAUL'S MILITIA?
SHEPHERD BOY DAVID
WAS HERE

PHILISTINE ARMY?
GOLIATH WAS HERE

POSSIBLE ROUTE PHILISTINES PLANNED
FOR AN INVASION INTO THE JUDEAN HILLS OF THE JEWS
—UNTIL A KID WITH A ROCK STOPPED THEM

DAVID'S MORTAL COMBAT
STONE AGE 1, IRON AGE 0

*A giant nearly ten feet tall stepped out from the Philistine line
into the open, Goliath from Gath…His spear was like a fence
rail—the spear tip alone weighed over fifteen pounds [7 kg].*

1 SAMUEL 17:4,7 MSG

The Philistine army boldly marched into the Jewish foothills of Judah along a wide valley that
leads up into the highlands, where most Jews lived peacefully in their scattered villages.

Saul called up his militia. He led them to a hillside across the valley from the Philistine camp.
Think blockade.

Instead of attacking the Jews, the Philistines sent out Goliath, their champion warrior. He
had a mouth on him, and he used it to trash talk the Jews 40 days in a row and to challenge

their best fighter to mortal combat. Winner take all—the losing side promises to surrender. Pinky swear.

Goliath was almost seven feet (2 m) tall. Perhaps over nine (2.8 m). And he was dressed to kill:

- bronze helmet
- 125-pound (57 kg) bronze coat of mail
- bronze leg armor
- bronze javelin
- spear, fence-post thick, tipped with the Philistine secret weapon—iron, the weight of a 15-pound bowling ball (7 kg)
- sword, possibly iron—"There is nothing like it!" (1 Samuel 21:9).

- shield in front of him, carried by another soldier

King Saul offered a hefty reward to any soldier courageous enough to fight Goliath—lots of money, no taxes for the rest of his life, and Saul's daughter as wife.

No deal. Rich, tax-free, and married to the princess would be no fun for a dead man.

Then David showed up, delivering grain and bread to three of his brothers in Saul's militia. The kid seemed to have the swagger of someone not particularly acquainted with failure—someone who knew he was blessed by God.

He volunteered to take out Goliath, just as he had taken out a lion and a bear that tried

Invader highway. Philistines choose the broad Valley of Elah as their marching path into the Judean hills, where the Jews live. They set up their base camp on a hillside by the valley's entrance. Saul mobilizes his militia and camps on a hill directly across the valley from the Philistines. This photo is taken from what many say are the ruins of Azekah. The Bible writer says both armies camped near Azekah, perhaps on the hills tagged here.

to kill his sheep. To David, Goliath was just one more critter that needed killing. For that reason, some scholars see a little irony in the line Goliath belched when he saw David coming: "Am I a dog that you come after me with a stick?" (1 Samuel 17:43 MSG).

Pretty much.

David loaded a rock into his sling, swirled it above his head to gain momentum, and then drove the rock like a bullet into Goliath's exposed forehead. Dead dog.

If not killed by the rock, Goliath was finished by his own sword. David used it to take a little off the top, decapitating Goliath.

The Philistines did not honor the pinky swear. Instead of surrendering, they ran for their lives back to their nearest walled cities in Gath and Ekron—Jews chasing them all the way.

Sling stones, with modern sling
From the main gate

POOR MAN'S ARTILLERY

Covering 100 yards (91 m) in three seconds or less, a rock fired from a sling can drop an enemy long before he can get close enough to hit a target with his javelin, another long-range weapon. Effective range of the ancient javelin based on recent tests: 15-20 yards or meters. Slings, fired in a high arch, can reach about 400 yards or meters. The Guinness Record is 1565 feet, 3 inches (477.10 m). Effective range for a single target is about 100 yards (91 m) or less. David exploited this advantage as a skilled slinger. He loaded a rock into the pocket of his sling, swirled the sling around his head several times to build momentum, and then released one end of the sling. The rock became a stone bullet that struck Goliath in the head. He collapsed, face in the dirt.

SINAI PENINSULA

MEDITERRANEAN SEA

TEL AVIV

● HEBRON
WHERE JEWS CROWN DAVID
KING OF JUDAH

JERUSALEM
FUTURE CAPITAL
OF DAVID

BETHLEHEM ●
DAVID'S HOMETOWN

● GIBEAH
CAPITAL OF DEPRESSED
KING SAUL

EN-GEDI OASIS
ONE OF DAVID'S HIDEOUTS
30 MILES (48 KM) FROM SAUL IN GIBEAH

DEAD SEA

QUMRAN ●
DEAD SEA SCROLLS FOUND HERE

JERICHO

N

JORDAN RIVER VALLEY

SYRIA

ISRAEL   JORDAN

FUGITIVE DAVE
SHEPHERD ON THE LAM

*Saul sent men to David's house to stake it out and
then, first thing in the morning, to kill him.*

1 SAMUEL 19:11 MSG

Music messed with King Saul's head.

He needed the humming strum of harp music to calm him down when "he began to
rave in his house like a madman" (1 Samuel 18:10). But music sometimes ticked him off too. One
song in particular—"Saul has killed his thousands, and David his ten thousands!" (1 Samuel 18:7).

Women started singing that song after young David killed the Philistine champion warrior,
Goliath.

"From that time on Saul kept a jealous eye on David" (1 Samuel 18:9). To put it mildly. Saul
tried many times to get David dead.

- *Shish kebab.* Saul tried to spear him while David played a harp to soothe the troubled
  king—twice (1 Samuel 18:11).

- *Mission impossible.* Saul said David could marry the princess, Michel, but first he had to
  show his bravery by killing 100 Philistines and bringing their foreskins as proof that he did

the job—scalps, at a lower altitude. Saul hoped David would get killed in the process. David came back with 200 low-blow scalps.

- *Assassination attempt 1.* "Saul now urged his servants and his son Jonathan to assassinate David" (1 Samuel 19:1). Jonathan, David's good friend, talked Saul out of it.

- *Assassination attempt 2.* Saul sent soldiers to watch David's house and kill him when he came out. David's wife warned him and helped him escape through a window. He remained a fugitive from Saul for the rest of Saul's life.

On the run, David stayed first with the prophet Samuel, who earlier had secretly anointed him Israel's future king. Word got back to Saul, and the manhunt was on.

David got his parents out of Bethlehem, moving them to Moab, a kingdom in what is now the Arab country of Jordan.

David fled to the "cave of Adullam" (1 Samuel 22:1) in the Valley of Elah, where he had killed Goliath. His brothers joined him. So did other relatives and strangers too—"men who were in trouble or in debt or who were just discontented—until David was the captain of about 400 men" (1 Samuel 22:2). Two hundred more joined him later.

When David moved his 600 men to the caves of En-gedi, Saul led 3000 of his best soldiers there.

In perhaps Saul's most embarrassing moment ever, he made the mistake of stepping into the wrong cave to use it as a restroom facility. Worse than accidentally stepping into the women's restroom, he was onstage—with David and his men watching him like an audience.

David's hideout. A spring-fed waterfall helps nourish the En-gedi oasis. The waterfall and pond lie hidden in an unlikely spot—deep in a crevice of the Judean badlands, near the Dead Sea. Caves along the face of the cliffs made it a wonderful hideout for David and his men on the run from King Saul. Even when Saul searched the area, he couldn't find them. But they found him.

Saul's one-man show became interactive when David snuck up close enough to cut off a piece of Saul's robe. After Saul left and had walked some distance away, David yelled at him and held up the piece of cloth—proof that David could have killed Saul but didn't.

King Saul went home humiliated, but the truce was short-lived.

David moved his men and their families into Philistine territory—to Goliath's hometown of Gath. Philistines were happy to now have on their side the man who killed their champion. But David only pretended to join the Philistines. Under their protection, he attacked villages hostile to the Jewish people, killing everyone so no witnesses could report back to the Philistines.

When King Saul died in battle against the Philistines, Jews in David's tribe of Judah gathered at the city of Hebron, where David was living at the time. There they declared him king of the large tribe that dominated most of what is now southern Israel.

Northern tribes crowned Ishbosheth, one of Saul's surviving sons. But two years later, a couple of the king's own soldiers assassinated him, and the northern tribes declared David their king as well.

At age 30, David was king of Israel.

OPERATION MOLE
DAVID CAPTURES JERUSALEM

A king needs a capital. David ruled from Hebron for seven years. But to Jews in the northland tribes, that probably looked like David was playing favorites—ruling from a city in his own tribe of Judah.

David made a wonderful choice that would unify the tribes. He picked a neutral city. It didn't belong to any of the tribes. It was the last Canaanite stronghold in the Jewish highlands along the border of the Judah and Benjamin tribes: the ridgetop city we now call Jerusalem. It was Jebus back then, inhabited by a race of people called the Jebusites.

They were a confident bunch, perched on the peak of a steep ridge and surrounded by walls.

When they saw David and his army below, they taunted them, "You'll never get in here! Even the blind and lame could keep you out!" (2 Samuel 5:6).

David knew the area. He had grown up in Bethlehem, about six miles (10 km) south, and had probably grazed his flocks this far north. He knew that the city got its water from a spring outside the walls, at the base of the ridge. They didn't have to go outside the city to get the water though. There was a shaft inside the city that led all the way down to a cave, where the spring collected its water into a pool. They simply dropped their bucket down a 52-foot (16 m) shaft into the pool and pulled it up as if they were drawing water from a well.

David gave his men an incentive to climb the shaft: "Whoever is first to attack the Jebusites will become the commander of my armies!" (1 Chronicles 11:6).

His sister's son, Joab, won that privilege. Perhaps Joab led a small strike force up the shaft and into the city at night and then opened up the city gates for David's army. But that's just a guess. The Bible doesn't say what happened except that David and his men captured the city.

"David made the fortress his home, and that is why it is called the City of David" (1 Chronicles 11:7).

Ship To:

Lawrence Friestad
901 W 7TH ST
MCCOOK, NE 69001-3044

Order ID: 102-1174379-9218635

Thank you for buying from ma_jim on Amazon Marketplace.

Shipping Address:	Order Date: Jan 22, 2016
Lawrence Friestad	Shipping Service: Standard
901 W 7TH ST	Buyer Name: Lawrence Friestad
MCCOOK, NE 69001-3044	Seller Name: ma_jim

Quantity	Product Details
1	**A Quick Guided Tour Through the Bible: Experience the Story from Genesis to Revelation [Paperback] [2015] Miller, Stephen M.** **SKU:** NN-SOHH-8QZV **ASIN:** 0736960759 **Listing ID:** 1215P3V57WV **Order Item ID:** 66367135775810 **Condition:** New **Comments:** New, Ship Daily

COUP: KICKING DAD OFF THE THRONE
DAVID'S SON DECLARES HIMSELF KING

Absalom sent undercover agents to all the tribes of Israel with the message, "When you hear the blast of the ram's horn trumpet, that's your signal: Shout, 'Absalom is king in Hebron!'"

2 SAMUEL 15:10 MSG

Bad hair day. Five pounds (2.3 kg) of hair might look pretty blowing in the wind. But it snagged Absalom onto an oak tree at a really bad time: while he was riding his mule fast as all get-out from a lost battle. When enemy soldiers arrived, they realized he wasn't just another nut hanging on the tree.

Incestuous rape festers into a coup. Crown Prince Amnon, King David's oldest son and the next in line to become king, rapes his own half-sister, Tamar. Same father, different mothers.

Humiliated, Tamar moves out of the palace housing for

virgin daughters of the king. She moves in with her full brother, Absalom, who is livid. Not only did his older brother turn Tamar into damaged goods (as far as the Bible reports, she never got married), but the crown prince also dissed his younger brother by treating his sister this way.

When David found out about the rape, he got angry. But he did nothing.

Absalom wasn't about to do nothing. Two years later he invited his older brother to the annual sheep-shearing—a festive time when herders harvested their annual crop of wool for a happy payday.

Absalom got his brother drunk, had him assassinated, and then left the country to live with his mother's dad, the King of Geshur, in what is now the Golan Heights.

After three years of self-imposed exile, Absalom returned home. David refused to see him for another two years.

Absalom royally hated his father by this time.

The people loved Absalom. What's not to love about a man who has the chutzpah to kill the sleazy crown prince who raped his own sister?

Besides, Absalom was "the most handsome man in all Israel" (2 Samuel 14:25). Humble too, in a showboating sort of a way. "When people tried to bow before him, Absalom wouldn't let them. Instead, he took them by the hand and embraced them" (2 Samuel 15:5).

Absalom put together the pieces of a coup and went to Hebron—the city where his father, David, was declared king. There Absalom declared himself the new king of Israel.

As Absalom prepared to march on Jerusalem, David took the threat seriously—he fled. But he left behind an adviser who pretended to pledge allegiance to the new king. Instead, he gave Absalom terrible advice: Take the time to build a massive army "as numerous as the sand on the seashore" (2 Samuel 17:11).

That advice worked to David's advantage. It gave him time to rally the seasoned army he had used to extend and secure Israel's borders.

The two armies clashed in the forest of Ephraim—perhaps near where David had fled, in what is now the Arab country of Jordan. David had withdrawn to the city of Mahanaim, somewhere in the tribal area of Gad, east of the Jordan River. That city may have been the temporary capital of Israel after Philistines killed King Saul and probably overran many Jewish settlements in what is now Israel. That's also the city to which Saul's general retreated with Saul's son and with what was left of the Jewish army (2 Samuel 2:8).

David's army defeated Absalom's army.

Absalom tried to escape on his mule. But his mop-like head of hair snagged the branch of an oak tree, yanking him off his mule and leaving him hanging in the air like a bull's-eye.

David's top general, Joab, stabbed him to death—against David's orders.

David never seemed to forgive his nephew Joab for doing that. Old and dying, David would tell his son and successor, Solomon, "Don't let him grow old and go to his grave in peace" (1 Kings 2:6).

Solomon didn't.

Joab ran from the king-approved assassin—rushing to the worship center for sanctuary and grabbing hold of the altar.

Solomon's man killed him there.

SOLOMON: KINGDOM BUILDER

WHEN "BUILDER'S GRADE" DIDN'T MEAN CHEAP

I am planning to build a Temple to honor the name of the LORD my God...please command that cedars from Lebanon be cut for me.

1 KINGS 5:5-6

Israel's Lego temple. Noise-free construction is what Solomon ordered for the first Jewish temple. Builders constructed a limestone temple 30 yards long, 10 yards wide, and 15 yards high (27 by 9 by 14 m)—about the size of a big barn. And they did it with "no sound of hammer, ax, or any other iron tool at the building site" (1 Kings 6:7). Possible reason for the odd order: The building site on the peak of Jerusalem's ridge was already sacred. Jews sacrificed there at a tent worship center.

Solomon's claim to fame is a temple—a relatively small one compared to some vast temple complexes in Middle Eastern towns, such as Nineveh in what is now Iraq and Thebes in Egypt. But Solomon's temple was unique.

- It was the first Jewish temple. Before that, they worshipped in a tent.
- It survived 400 years. Invaders from what is now Iraq tore it down in 586 BC.
- Builders pieced it together a bit like they would a prefab house—with no noise of tools on-site.

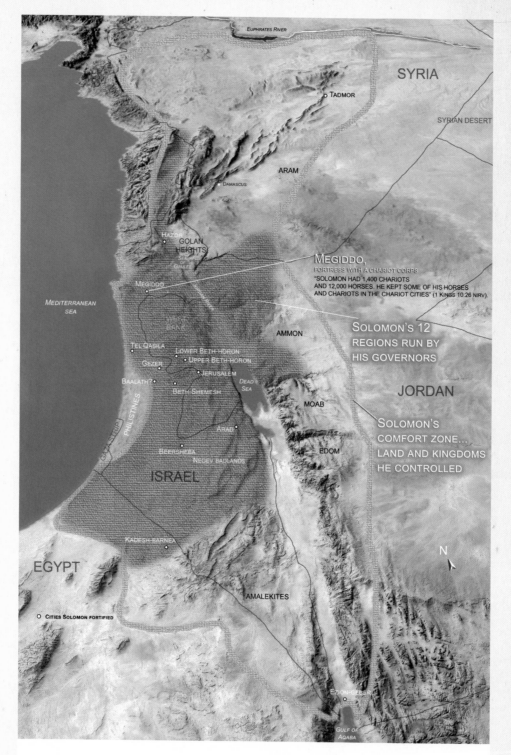

EUPHRATES RIVER

SYRIA

TADMOR

SYRIAN DESERT

ARAM

DAMASCUS

HAZOR

GOLAN HEIGHTS

SEA OF GALILEE

MEGIDDO

MEGIDDO, FORTRESS WITH A CHARIOT CORPS
"SOLOMON HAD 1,400 CHARIOTS AND 12,000 HORSES. HE KEPT SOME OF HIS HORSES AND CHARIOTS IN THE CHARIOT CITIES" (1 KINGS 10:26 NIRV).

MEDITERRANEAN SEA

WEST BANK

AMMON

SOLOMON'S 12 REGIONS RUN BY HIS GOVERNORS

TEL QASILA

LOWER BETH-HORON

UPPER BETH-HORON

GEZER

JERUSALEM

BAALATH?

DEAD SEA

BETH-SHEMESH

JORDAN

MOAB

SOLOMON'S COMFORT ZONE... LAND AND KINGDOMS HE CONTROLLED

GAZA STRIP

PHILISTINES

ARAD

EDOM

BEERSHEBA

NEGEV BADLANDS

ISRAEL

KADESH-BARNEA

N

EGYPT

AMALEKITES

○ CITIES SOLOMON FORTIFIED

EZION-GEBER

GULF OF AQABA

Keeping the peace. With the money King Solomon saved from not having to fight wars, he built up his cities. He started in Jerusalem with construction of the first Jewish temple. Then he added a palace complex in Jerusalem. After that, he fortified cities in strategic locations throughout his zone of influence, which extended well beyond Israel, engulfing neighboring kingdoms in what are now Syria, Jordan, and Egypt.

A LOVER, NOT A FIGHTER

There's a reason Solomon got to build this temple and his father, David, didn't. In a word, blood. Old and dying David explained it this way to his son.

> I wanted to build a temple for worshiping the LORD my God. But the LORD spoke his word to me… "You cannot build a temple for worship to me, because you have killed many people. But, you will have a son, a man of peace… Solomon will build a temple for worship to me" (1 Chronicles 22:7-10 NCV).

David used war to build his kingdom, expanding it to about triple the size of King Saul's zone of control. Solomon used love and marriage to build his even more, pushing north to the Euphrates River and picking up "servant kingdoms" deep into what is now Syria.

Bible writers report that Solomon married 1000 women. Oddly enough, given what his home life may have been like with all those wives, that's how he kept the peace with his neighbors. He didn't kill them. He married them.

Peace treaties at that time were sometimes sealed by royal marriages. When Solomon wanted to secure his southern border, he married "the daughter of the king of Egypt" (1 Kings 11:1 NCV).

What king is going to attack his daughter's new country? He'll likely do just the opposite—give good stuff to his new son-in-law. This particular Egyptian king may have been Siamun (978–960 BC). He invaded Philistine territory on what is now Israel's coast. Then he captured their city of Gezer and "gave it as a wedding present to his daughter, who married Solomon" (1 Kings 9:16 NCV).

Mazel tov.

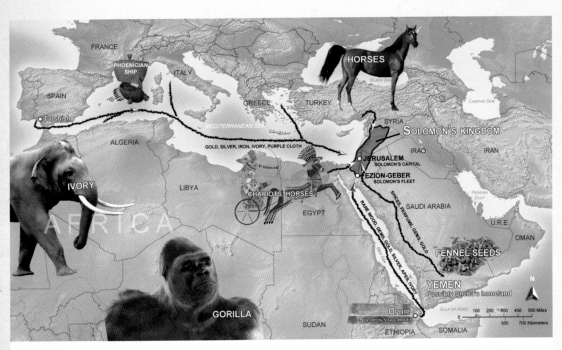

Going international. Solomon hired Phoenicians to build and man a fleet of merchant ships so he could export Israel's trade goods—wine, olive oil, grain—in return for gold, silver, and exotic surprises from perfumes to peacocks.

ISRAEL'S BEST GENERATION

With peace secured, Solomon didn't have to worry about raising money for springtime wars year after year.

With the money he raised, he built his kingdom like no Jewish king in Israel's history. This was Israel's finest hour if economics and national pride were any measure. Solomon raised money by…

- collecting tolls from caravans passing through Israel, the best land bridge between all nations north and south

- earning profits from royal monopolies, approved franchises, and payments by servant nations

- developing international trade

In trade alone, "each year Solomon received about 25 tons of gold" (1 Kings 10:14). That's about the weight of a dozen Cadillacs.

With all this money, he went on a building frenzy. He constructed the lavish, gold-paneled Jerusalem temple and his palace complex and then turned more than a dozen cities into battle-resistant fortresses.

For workers, he drafted men the way wartime countries draft soldiers—about 200,000 for the seven-year temple project alone, including "80,000 quarry workers in the hill country" (1 Kings 5:15).

By the end of Solomon's reign, Israel was a jewel of a nation—peaceful, prosperous, and admired by rulers such as the queen of Sheba from the distant edge of the Middle East.

SHEBA: SHOPPING QUEEN
A LONG WALK TO THE MALL

The queen of Sheba heard of Solomon's fame...she came to test him with hard questions.

1 KINGS 10:1

King Solomon's mall. The queen of Sheba arrives in Jerusalem with a huge caravan of what appear to be gifts and trade goods: "gold, great quantities of spices, and precious jewels" (1 Kings 10:10). She will leave Jerusalem with "whatever she asked for, besides all the customary gifts" (verse 13).

It's curious that the Bible writer didn't bother to report what "hard questions" the queen of Sheba asked King Solomon.

How about this one?

"What can I buy for 9000 pounds (4000 kg) of gold?"

That's a lot of gold to carry the 1500 miles (2400 km) many Bible experts guess the queen of Sheba had to come, presuming she lived in what is now the Arab country of Yemen at the far end of the Red Sea. It would take a caravan of about two dozen camels to carry that much gold, which weighed about as much as 50 well-fed adults.

Given the context of the story, sandwiched between reports of Solomon's successful business in international trade, some Bible experts guess that the real reason for the queen's visit to Jerusalem wasn't about religion or education—it was about business.

Bypassing tribal leaders. Bedouin herders at the turn of the 1900s take a break in what is now Israel. Leaders of Israel's 12 tribes could have done the same in Solomon's day. He cut them out of the loop. He divided the country into a dozen regions, slicing right through the 12 tribal boundaries. Then he appointed his own men as governors who reported to him. Solomon took seriously his father's last words of advice: "Take charge!...GOD, my God, is with you in this" (1 Chronicles 28:20 MSG).

Before telling the story of the queen's visit, the writer reports that Solomon built a fleet of ships that sailed the full extent of the Red Sea, all the way down to what is now Yemen. And immediately after telling the story of the queen's visit, he reports Solomon's long list of exotic imports, including "gold, silver, ivory, apes, and peacocks" (1 Kings 10:22).

Yet many Bible experts agree that there's more to the story than shopping.

Middle Eastern history is full of stories about pairs of rulers going toe-to-toe in battles of wits and wealth to determine who is the wisest and richest of the two.

If this is partly what the queen wanted to do in Israel, Solomon won that battle. And God got the glory for it.

The queen told Solomon, "Your wisdom and prosperity are far beyond what I was told...Praise the LORD your God, who delights in you" (1 Kings 10:7,9).

7

ONE NATION DIVIDED

THE FIRST 100 YEARS

TIMELINE *(dates are approximate)*

960 BC	The Jerusalem temple is under construction.
930 BC	Solomon dies, and Israel splits in two.
900 BC	Assyria becomes the Middle East superpower.
853 BC	An Assyrian archer kills Ahab in the Battle of Qarqar.
850 BC	King Mesha runs Jews out of Moab (Jordan).
841 BC	Jezebel and her son are killed in a coup.
800 BC	Homer writes of the Trojan War in *Iliad* and its sequel, *Odyssey*.

On the map:

MEDITERRANEAN SEA

SYRIA

PHOENICIA

LEBANON

DAN

ARAM

GOLAN HEIGHTS

ISRAEL'S SACRED CALF AT DAN

SEA OF GALILEE

THE NORTHERNERS
ISRAEL

RAMOTH

CAPITAL OF NORTHERN KINGDOM SHECHEM (NABLUS)

JABBOK RIVER

ISRAEL'S SACRED CALF AT BETHEL

SHILOH

BETHEL

JORDAN RIVER

GEZER

GIBEON

WEST BANK

JERUSALEM

JORDAN

HEBRON

DEAD SEA

THE SOUTHERNERS
JUDAH

0   10   20 MILES
   20   30 KILOMETERS

ARNON RIVER

MOAB

ISRAEL

NEGEV BADLANDS

THE JEWISH PEOPLE'S MOST SACRED OBJECT, THE ARK OF THE COVENANT THAT HELD THE TEN COMMANDMENTS KEPT IN THE JERUSALEM TEMPLE

KADESH-BARNEA

EGYPT

EDOM

Meet God here. After Israel's northerners seceded from the union, their king set up two worship centers in his territory so northerners wouldn't have to worship at the southland temple in Jerusalem. What puzzles Bible experts is why he put golden calves in each shrine as though Moses would have approved. Israel had crafted a golden calf at Sinai, and Moses "took the calf they had made and…ground it into powder, threw it into the water, and forced the people to drink it" (Exodus 32:20). Then he executed 3000 for idolatry. (See "God, the Bull Rider," page 101.)

ISRAEL SPLITS IN TWO
NORTHERNERS HATE SOUTHERN HOSPITALITY

[King Rehoboam:] "If you think life under my father was hard, you haven't seen the half of it."
[Northern Jews:] "Get lost… We've had it with you."

1 KINGS 12:11,16 MSG

King Solomon died dumb, spiritually speaking—out of sync with God.

According to Jewish law, "The king must not take many wives" (Deuteronomy 17:17). But Solomon married enough women to fill 20 buses—1000, the Bible reports.

Many, if not most, were foreigners who worshipped idols. An accommodating husband,

Solomon "built a shrine for each of his foreign wives" (1 Kings 11:8 CEV). In his old age, he let some of his wives convince him to worship their gods.

By the time Solomon died, most Jews in the country were fed up with what they told his son, crown prince Rehoboam, were "harsh labor demands and heavy taxes that your father imposed on us" (1 Kings 12:4).

The rookie ruler consulted his advisers, young and old. His seasoned advisers seemed to say he should cut the people some slack. Or maybe they were simply suggesting he tell the people what they wanted to hear so they would go ahead and crown him king.

His freshman advisers, however, urged him to show the people who's boss, and that's what he did.

Northerners had a poetic response for the crown prince. They knew that their grandparents had embraced David as king by chanting the poem, "We're on your side, O David, we're committed, O son of Jesse" (1 Chronicles 12:18 MSG).

So now they chanted the flip side of that poem: "Get lost, David! We've had it with you, son of Jesse!" (1 Kings 12:16 MSG). The northern tribes went home and crowned their own king—Jeroboam.

Solomon's son, Prince Rehoboam, ended up with only the southern tribe of Judah and the tiny border tribe of Benjamin, which was eventually absorbed into the tribe of Judah.

Israel had split into two countries with two kings. Northerners became known as Israel. Southerners, Judah.

GOD, THE BULL RIDER

Northern Jews had a big problem. By Jewish law, the only place they could worship was in the country from which they had just seceded—Judah. That's where their only temple was, in Jerusalem, hometown of the king they had told to "get lost" (1 Kings 12:16 MSG).

Northerners didn't have anything like the sacred Ark of the Covenant, which rested in the Jerusalem temple's holiest room. Jews considered this gold-plated chest that held the Ten Commandments "God's footstool" (1 Chronicles 28:2).

So their king came up with his own sacred object for each shrine—"two gold calves" (1 Kings 12:28).

Bible experts debate whether those calves were idols. Many scholars speculate they were intended as pedestals for God—a kind of footstool, like the Ark of the Covenant.

Riding high. Storm god Adad, worshipped throughout the ancient Middle East, wields a fistful of lightning bolts while perching himself on a bull pedestal, perhaps to show that the god is stronger than even the most powerful creature known to the region. The art is from Syria, chiseled in the 700s BC. That's a couple of centuries after Jews started worshipping in shrines that featured gold calves, perhaps intended as pedestals for God, some scholars speculate.

AHAB'S FAMILY WAR MACHINE
HOW TO START A DYNASTY

"Turn the horses and get me out of here!" Ahab groaned to the driver of his chariot. "I'm badly wounded!"
1 KINGS 22:34

Split in two, the Jewish nations of Israel and Judah were just a couple of tiny speed bumps directly in the path of two competing empires that wanted to control the Middle East:

- *Egypt in the south,* about the combined size of Texas, Oklahoma, and Kansas.

- *Assyria in the north,* in what is now Iraq, also about the size of Egypt—and growing.

To get a sense of the David-and-Goliath proportion of the Jewish problem, imagine northern New Jersey seceding from the state. Now you've got two tiny New Jerseys, each at the other's throat. That's Israel and Judah.

Jews had to worry not only about each other and their hostile neighboring kingdoms in what are now the Arab countries of Syria, Jordan, and Lebanon. They also had to worry about the ancient version of an annihilation-level nuclear attack from the two Big Boy empires.

King Omri (ruled about 885–874 BC), a former general and the father of northland Israel's most infamous king—Ahab (874–853 BC)—earned himself a reputation as a savvy ruler who knew how to protect his borders and then some.

- *South border:* Judah. He made peace with the south Jewish kingdom.

- *Northwest border:* Phoenicia (Lebanon). He sealed a peace treaty with the king by

Jewish king, chiseled in stone. Nicknamed the Moabite Stone, this ancient slab of black rock from about 840 BC adds support to the Bible claim that Israel's King Omri conquered Moab, in what is now Jordan. Chiseled into the stone: "Omri was king of Israel, and oppressed Moab for many days...His son succeeded him, and he also said, 'I will oppress Moab.'" The notes add that Omri and his son occupied the land 40 years. That's about the length of Omri's four-king family dynasty (roughly 48 years).

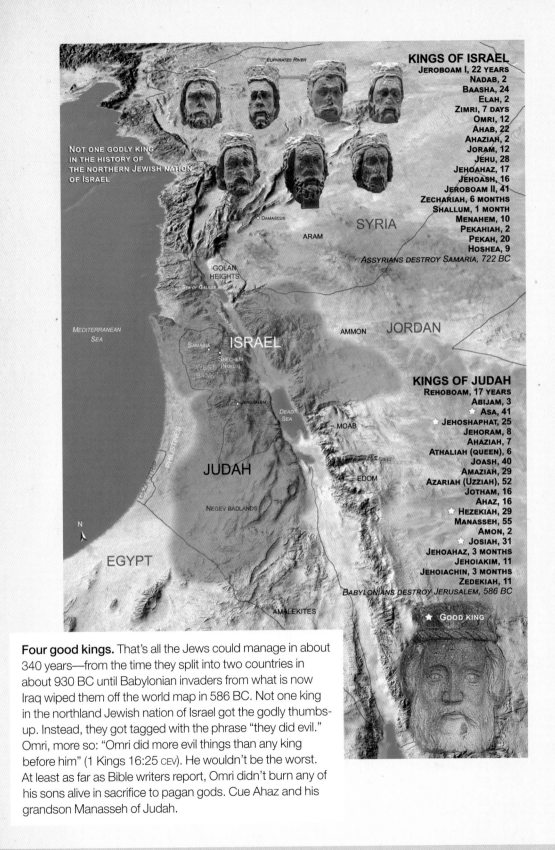

KINGS OF ISRAEL

JEROBOAM I, 22 YEARS
NADAB, 2
BAASHA, 24
ELAH, 2
ZIMRI, 7 DAYS
OMRI, 12
AHAB, 22
AHAZIAH, 2
JORAM, 12
JEHU, 28
JEHOAHAZ, 17
JEHOASH, 16
JEROBOAM II, 41
ZECHARIAH, 6 MONTHS
SHALLUM, 1 MONTH
MENAHEM, 10
PEKAHIAH, 2
PEKAH, 20
HOSHEA, 9
ASSYRIANS DESTROY SAMARIA, 722 BC

NOT ONE GODLY KING
IN THE HISTORY OF
THE NORTHERN JEWISH NATION
OF ISRAEL

KINGS OF JUDAH

REHOBOAM, 17 YEARS
ABIJAM, 3
☆ ASA, 41
☆ JEHOSHAPHAT, 25
JEHORAM, 8
AHAZIAH, 7
ATHALIAH (QUEEN), 6
JOASH, 40
AMAZIAH, 29
AZARIAH (UZZIAH), 52
JOTHAM, 16
AHAZ, 16
☆ HEZEKIAH, 29
MANASSEH, 55
AMON, 2
☆ JOSIAH, 31
JEHOAHAZ, 3 MONTHS
JEHOIAKIM, 11
JEHOIACHIN, 3 MONTHS
ZEDEKIAH, 11
BABYLONIANS DESTROY JERUSALEM, 586 BC

☆ GOOD KING

Four good kings. That's all the Jews could manage in about 340 years—from the time they split into two countries in about 930 BC until Babylonian invaders from what is now Iraq wiped them off the world map in 586 BC. Not one king in the northland Jewish nation of Israel got the godly thumbs-up. Instead, they got tagged with the phrase "they did evil." Omri, more so: "Omri did more evil things than any king before him" (1 Kings 16:25 CEV). He wouldn't be the worst. At least as far as Bible writers report, Omri didn't burn any of his sons alive in sacrifice to pagan gods. Cue Ahaz and his grandson Manasseh of Judah.

marrying one of his sons, Prince Ahab, to Phoenician Princess Jezebel.

- *Southeast border:* Moab (Jordan). Omri attacked and conquered the kingdom.

- *Northeast border:* Aram (Syria). He attacked this Damascus-based kingdom, recapturing some territory King Solomon once controlled east of the Jordan River.

With these local threats neutralized, Omri turned his attention to sprucing up the looks of his kingdom—a makeover.

He had wealth from which to draw. The northern Jewish nation got the best land in what had once been the united tribes of Israel—great farmlands and grazing pastures, including the Valley of Jezreel, which remains Israel's breadbasket today.

EGYPT ON A KILLING SPREE

When David's dynasty cracked and split, Egyptian King Shishak I (reigned about 943–922 BC) decided it would be a wonderful time to go shopping in what is now Israel.

He took his army.

They marched up the coastal trade route known as the Way of the Philistines. They overran

the city of Gezer—once a Philistine city that an earlier Egyptian king had captured and given to his daughter as a wedding present when she married King Solomon.

Hieroglyphics on a temple he built in Karnak say he was prodded into this war by "Asiatic attacks on Egyptian frontier settlements." That might have been a reference to southland cities Solomon fortified, including Kadesh-Barnea in what is now Egypt.

The same hieroglyphics name more than a dozen of the cities the king overran and pillaged, in both Jewish nations.

Archaeologists poking around in the ruins speculate that these attacks were more like raids than complete destruction since the fortresses were quickly rebuilt.

Jews under arrest. Bearded captives from what is now Israel show up in ancient Egyptian art. They're on display at a temple complex in the Egyptian city of Karnak. The relief, chiseled into stone, may have been a way of thanking the Egyptian gods for victory on the battlefield—while getting in a little bragging about the king, shown here in firm control of the situation.

ELIJAH: A BALL OF FIRE

QUEEN JEZEBEL WAS NOT HIS BIGGEST FAN

Jezebel was killing all the LORD's prophets.

1 KINGS 18:4 NCV

Rest stop. Elijah collapses, exhausted, in the Judean badlands. He's on the run from Queen Jezebel, who wants him executed for assassinating her entourage of pagan priests. Elijah asks God to let him die. Instead, God sends an angel of a baker, who delivers hot bread and water. God wasn't finished with Elijah.

Jezebel, queen of the Jews, was anything but a Jew.

Her dad, King Ethbaal of Sidon, in what is now Lebanon, married her off to Israel's King Ahab, the son of King Omri. It was part of a peace deal—which seems a bit ironic, given her tendency to kill people. She had one farmer stoned to death (1 Kings 21:14) and confiscated his property near her summer getaway palace so her hubby could plant veggies there.

Among the baggage she brought with her into Israel was a religion she tried to force on the Jews.

She started killing off all God's prophets. About 100 escaped by hiding "in two caves" (1 Kings 18:4). At God's command, the prophet Elijah announced a multiyear drought and left the country, staying in the seaside village of Zarephath (Sarafand, Lebanon) near Jezebel's hometown. It was about a four-day walk north of Ahab's capital in Samaria, some 80 miles (129 km).

When Elijah finally came back three years later, he was a man on a mission with a message.

His message: God would soon end the drought.

His mission: Put an end to Jezebel's crowd of idol-worshipping religious leaders—"450 prophets of Baal and the 400 prophets of Asherah who are supported by Jezebel" (1 Kings 18:19).

For many non-Jewish natives of the region, Baal was the go-to god for rain. Ancient pictures often show him holding thunderbolts. Asherah, as some ancient writings report, was Baal's lover and the go-to goddess for people wanting babies or lots of lovin'. Asherah knew about that stuff, the ancients reported, since she was the mother of 70 gods.

Elijah challenged Jezebel's religious leaders to a battle of the gods—advantage storm god Baal because the weapon in the duel would be lightning.

On a hilltop in the Mount Carmel range, Elijah and leaders of Jezebel's preferred religion each built an altar and topped it with a dead bull.

Elijah's challenge: "Call on the name of your god, and I will call on the name of the LORD. The god who answers by setting fire to the wood is the true God!" (1 Kings 18:24).

Jezebel's people tried all day. Elijah offered some advice: "Pray louder...Maybe he's daydreaming or using the toilet" (1 Kings 18:27 CEV).

At day's end was Elijah's turn. He drenched the altar three times with water, spoke about a 20-second prayer, and then perhaps stepped back a ways. "Immediately the fire of the LORD flashed down from heaven and burned up the young bull, the wood, the stones, and the dust. It even licked up all the water in the trench!" (1 Kings 18:38).

A crowd of Jews had gathered to watch the showdown. At Elijah's command, they arrested Jezebel's priests, escorted them down the mountain, and executed them. The drought ended.

Jezebel did not convert to Judaism. At her summer getaway palace in nearby Jezreel, she put a hit out on Elijah.

He ran for his life—"forty days and forty nights to Mount Sinai" (1 Kings 19:8). That was about a 15-day walk, traveling 20 miles (32 km) a day—about 300 miles (483 km).

COUP: AHAB'S DYNASTY DIES

JEZEBEL GOES OUT WEARING FRESH MAKEUP

This is what the LORD, the God of Israel, says... You are to destroy the family of Ahab, your master. In this way, I will avenge the murder of my prophets and all the LORD's servants who were killed by Jezebel.

2 KINGS 9:6-7

If looks could kill. Queen Mother Jezebel, hearing she's about to be assassinated, reaches for her makeup. She's sitting pretty when her servants—acting on an invitation from a rebel military commander—shove her out an upstairs window to her death.

There's a delicious twist in the Bible story of Jezebel ordering a hit on the prophet Elijah in retaliation for him executing her pagan priests. Elijah ordered a hit on her—though he may not have realized it.

Elijah indirectly ordered the hit twice when he followed God's instruction: "Anoint Jehu son of Nimshi to be king of Israel, and anoint Elisha...to replace you as my prophet" (1 Kings 19:16).

These two acts would end Jezebel years later, after "Elijah was carried by a whirlwind into heaven" (2 Kings 2:11). By then, Jezebel was the Queen Mother. Ahab had died in battle, and their son Joram had become king.

The Bible doesn't say whether Elijah ever got around to anointing Jehu—and if he did, whether Jehu took him seriously. The commander of a chariot corps, Jehu certainly didn't take it seriously when Elijah's successor, Elisha, showed up at Ramoth-Gilead to anoint him. Ramoth of Gilead, as it's sometimes called, was an Israelite frontier town where Jehu and his men guarded Israel's eastern border after a recent battle there against the armies of Aram, in what is now Syria.

Elisha met with Jehu privately, anointing him with oil and telling him to destroy the family of Ahab. When Jehu's men asked him later what the prophet had said, Jehu answered, "You know how a man like that babbles on" (2 Kings 9:11).

His men pressed him: "You're hiding something."

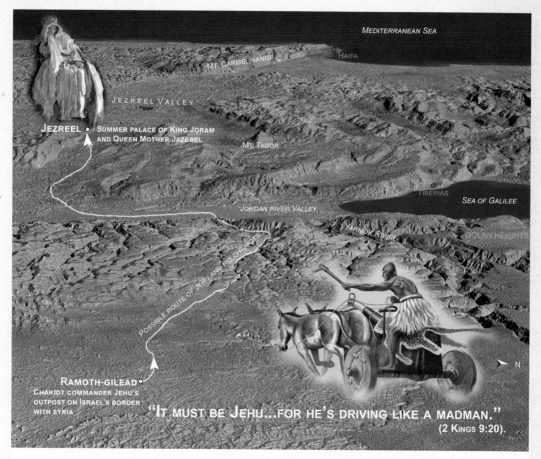

MEDITERRANEAN SEA

MT. CARMEL RANGE

HAIFA

JEZREEL VALLEY

JEZREEL • — SUMMER PALACE OF KING JORAM AND QUEEN MOTHER JEZEBEL

MT. TABOR

TIBERIAS

SEA OF GALILEE

JORDAN RIVER VALLEY

YARMUK RIVER

GOLAN HEIGHTS

POSSIBLE ROUTE OF JEHU AND HIS CHARIOTS

N

RAMOTH-GILEAD • CHARIOT COMMANDER JEHU'S OUTPOST ON ISRAEL'S BORDER WITH SYRIA

"IT MUST BE JEHU...FOR HE'S DRIVING LIKE A MADMAN." (2 KINGS 9:20).

Forty miles (64 km) to a coup. Freshly anointed by the prophet Elisha as Israel's future king, Jehu takes charioteers he commands to Jezreel, where they kill Ahab's son and successor, King Joram, along with Queen Mother Jezebel. King Ahaziah of the southern Jewish nation of Judah had picked a bad time to visit the northern king. Jehu killed him too.

When Jehu told his men what Elisha had said, "they quickly spread out their cloaks on the bare steps and blew the ram's horn, shouting, 'Jehu is king!'" (verse 13).

The coup was on.

King Joram was recovering from wounds he suffered in the recent battle at Ramoth-Gilead. He and Queen Mother Jezebel were at the family's summer getaway in Jezreel, a city on the crest of a ridge overlooking the massive Jezreel Valley.

Lookouts there saw a cloud of dust in the eastern valley blowing toward the palace, so they dispatched two messengers to find out who was coming so quickly. The messengers never returned. They joined forces with Jehu.

One of the lookouts recognized Jehu by his reckless driving. So King Joram decided to rush out and meet his commander. He may have figured Jehu was driving in a hurry to report an invasion.

"Do you come in peace, Jehu?" the king cried out as he approached the oncoming chariot corps.

Jehu said, "How can there be peace as long

as the idolatry and witchcraft of your mother, Jezebel, are all around us?" (2 Kings 9:22).

King Joram turned his horses around to flee, but Jehu shot him in the heart with an arrow.

When Jezebel heard what had happened, "she painted her eyelids and fixed her hair and sat at a window" (verse 30).

On orders from Jehu, Jezebel's servants pushed her out the window. Below, Jehu's chariots and horses trampled her body. Dogs ate what was left.

Jehu sent word back to Samaria, capital of Israel, ordering the heads of all male descendants of Ahab. He didn't want them showing up later to claim the throne.

Rather than risk fighting Jehu's army, "the leaders killed all seventy of the king's sons. They placed their heads in baskets and presented them to Jehu at Jezreel" (2 Kings 10:7).

Coup done.

BAAL'S TOILET TEMPLE

In a fake-out ploy to flush out Baal worshippers, Jehu booked a revival service at the temple of Baal in Israel's capital city, Samaria. He said he wanted to worship with everyone who served the Canaanite god.

At hallelujah time, while Jehu's sacrifice was burning on the pagan altar, he ordered his soldiers who had been hiding nearby to kill everyone else in the temple. The soldiers also wrecked the place. Afterward, locals used it as "a public toilet" (2 Kings 10:27).

Jehu takes a bow in Iraq. King Jehu of Israel is the first person in the Bible to show up in pictures. Less than regal, he's bowing before the most powerful man in the world at the time, Assyrian King Shalmaneser III, the leader of the Middle Eastern superpower based in what is now Iraq. The obelisk describes "the tribute of Jehu," which are taxes Assyrians required from small kingdoms in the region—"silver, gold, a golden bowl, a golden vase with pointed bottom, golden tumblers, golden buckets, tin, a staff for a king, and spears."

8

JEWS EVICTED FROM ISRAEL

TIMELINE *(dates are approximate)*

855 BC	Elijah kills pagan priests of Queen Jezebel.
850 BC	The Moabite Stone records the king bragging of defeating Israel.
722 BC	Assyrians erase Israel from the political map.
701 BC	On the Taylor Prism, Assyrian king brags of surrounding King Hezekiah's Jerusalem.
609 BC	Good King Josiah dies fighting to block Egyptian army.
612 BC	The Babylonian army defeats the Assyrians.
586 BC	Babylonians erase Judah; no Jewish nation remains.

Moabite Stone   Assyrians   Taylor Prism   Egyptians kill King Josiah

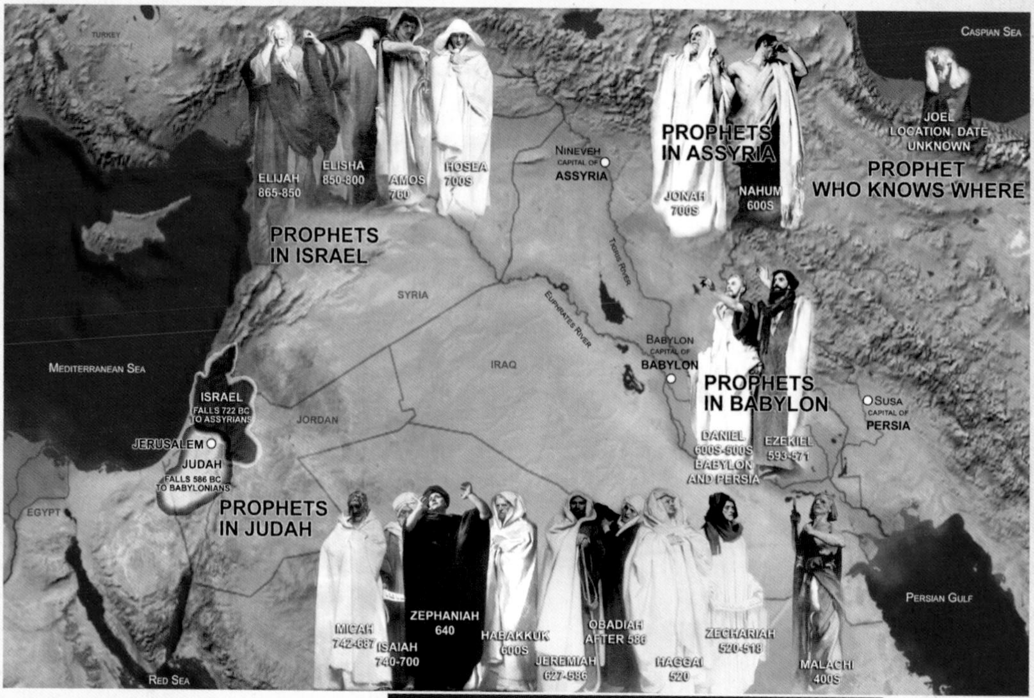
TURKEY
ELIJAH
865-850
ELISHA
850-800
AMOS
760
HOSEA
700S
PROPHETS
IN ISRAEL
NINEVEH
CAPITAL OF
ASSYRIA
PROPHETS
IN ASSYRIA
JONAH
700S
NAHUM
600S
CASPIAN SEA
JOEL
LOCATION, DATE
UNKNOWN
PROPHET
WHO KNOWS WHERE
SYRIA
TIGRIS RIVER
EUPHRATES RIVER
MEDITERRANEAN SEA
IRAQ
BABYLON
CAPITAL OF
BABYLON
PROPHETS
IN BABYLON
SUSA
CAPITAL OF
PERSIA
ISRAEL
FALLS 722 BC
TO ASSYRIANS
JORDAN
JERUSALEM
JUDAH
FALLS 586 BC
TO BABYLONIANS
DANIEL
600S-500S
BABYLON
AND PERSIA
EZEKIEL
593-571
EGYPT
PROPHETS
IN JUDAH
PERSIAN GULF
MICAH
742-687
ISAIAH
740-700
ZEPHANIAH
640
HABAKKUK
600S
OBADIAH
AFTER 586
JEREMIAH
627-586
HAGGAI
520
ZECHARIAH
520-518
MALACHI
400S
RED SEA

PROPHETS AT WORK

PINNING PROPHETS TO A MAP

I, the L*ORD*, *speak to prophets in visions and dreams. But my servant Moses. . . sees me face to face.*

NUMBERS 12:6-8 CEV

Like press secretaries, prophets spoke for someone else. They spoke for God. As spokesfolks, they worked as the yin to the yang of priests.

- Priests took the people's requests to God.
- Prophets took God's requests to the people.

Prophets generally received their celestial requests in "visions and dreams," as we see in the Scripture verse above. Or sometimes in extraordinary encounters, like Moses at the burning bush.

Folks didn't apply to work as prophets. They got a call. From God, one way or another.

It's not a call that some of the headliners wanted. Several famous prophets, handpicked by God, tried to weasel out.

Moses: "I stutter" (Exodus 4:10 MSG).

Isaiah: "I am a foul-mouthed sinner" (Isaiah 6:5 TLB).

Jeremiah: "I'm too young" (Jeremiah 1:6 CEV).

Jonah: "Jonah ran away from the LORD" (Jonah 1:3 NIV). God told him to go east. Jonah

PROPHETS: SOUND BITES AND CLAIM TO FAME

PROPHETS IN ISRAEL

Elijah. "Elijah was carried by a whirlwind into heaven" (2 Kings 2:11).

Elisha. "Please let me inherit a double share of your spirit and become your successor" (2 King 2:9, speaking to Elijah).

Amos. The people of Israel "walk on poor people as if they were dirt, and they refuse to be fair to those who are suffering" (Amos 2:7 NCV).

Hosea. "They sow the wind, and reap the whirlwind" (Hosea 8:7 NKJV).

PROPHETS IN JUDAH

Micah. "They will beat their swords into iron plows and their spears into pruning tools" (Micah 4:3 CEB).

Isaiah. "For a child is born to us,
a son is given to us.
The government will rest on his shoulders.
And he will be called:
Wonderful Counselor, Mighty God,
Everlasting Father, Prince of Peace" (Isaiah 9:6).

Zephaniah. "I, the Lord, now promise
to destroy everything
on this earth—
people and animals,
birds and fish" (Zephaniah 1:2-3 CEV).
(These are words many Bible experts say is an exaggeration for emphasis, to give the Jews a sense of what it's going to feel like when their nation collapses and survivors are exiled.)

Who wants to be a prophet? It was not a coveted job. That explains why Jonah went in the opposite direction God told him to go. Prophets often had to deliver bad news. But on top of that, God told Jonah to deliver it in person to the capital of Israel's most vicious enemy—the Assyrians, an empire that decorated its palace with pictures of impaled Jews. Think of Jonah as a rabbi going to Germany in the 1940s to warn Hitler that his capital, Berlin, was doomed.

Habakkuk. "The righteous live by their faith" (Habakkuk 2:4 NRSV).

Jeremiah. "Can a leopard change his spots?" (Jeremiah 13:23 NCV).

Obadiah. "As you have done...so it will be done to you" (Obadiah 1:15).

Haggai. "You say this isn't the right time to build a temple for me. But is it right for you to live in expensive houses, while my temple is a pile of ruins?" (Haggai 1:2-4 CEV).

Zechariah. "People of Jerusalem, shout!
See, your king comes to you.
He always does what is right.

He has the power to save.
He is gentle and riding on a donkey" (Zechariah 9:9 NIRV).

Malachi. "You ask, 'How have we robbed you?'
"The tithe and the offering—that's how!...Bring your full tithe to the Temple treasury so there will be ample provisions in my Temple. Test me in this and see if I don't open up heaven itself to you and pour out blessings beyond your wildest dreams" (Malachi 3:8-10 MSG).

PROPHETS IN ASSYRIA

Jonah. "The LORD had arranged for a big fish to swallow Jonah. And Jonah was inside the fish for three days and three nights" (Jonah 1:17).

Nahum. "The LORD is slow to get angry, but his power is great, and he never lets the guilty go unpunished" (Nahum 1:3).

PROPHETS IN BABYLON

Daniel. "My God sent his angel to shut the lions' mouths so that they would not hurt me" (Daniel 6:22).

Ezekiel. "Dry bones, hear the word of the LORD" (Ezekiel 37:4 NCV).

PROPHETS WHO KNOWS WHERE

Joel. "Beat your plowshares into swords
And your pruning hooks into spears" (Joel 3:10 NKJV).

booked passage on a ship headed west. Cue the big fish.

There's good reason no one wanted the job. Prophets usually delivered bad news. It often went something like this:

- "Israel has acted like a prostitute by turning against the LORD and worshiping other gods" (Hosea 1:2).
- "I have decided to strike you with disaster" (Jeremiah 18:11 CEV).

Jews had broken their ancient agreement to serve God in return for his protection and blessing. So they had to face the consequences written into the ancient contract: "The LORD will scatter you among all the nations" (Deuteronomy 28:64).

Yet most Bible-writing prophets who preached doom to their sinful generation of Jews ended their books with hope. They offered the promise of a second chance for a new generation—a clean slate and a fresh start: "Do not be afraid, for I am with you...I will say to the north and south, 'Bring my sons and daughters back to Israel from the distant corners of the earth'" (Isaiah 43:5-6).

But first, the two Jewish nations of Israel and Judah had to go.

ASSYRIANS ON THE RISE
TERRORISTS FROM IRAQ

Assyrians will attack you: handsome young captains and lieutenants, all of them important men and all riding horses.

EZEKIEL 23:23 NCV

A ssyrians would bully the Middle East for more than 300 years.

Their reign of terror as a superpower based out of what is now northern Iraq stretched from about 934 to 609 BC. That's almost as long as the northern Jewish nation, Israel, survived after separating from the southern Jewish nation, Judah, in 930 BC.

In fact, Assyrians in 722 BC would erase Israel off the world map. About 20 years later the Assyrians would come within one city of doing the same to Judah. They whacked 46 Judean cities, according to their own surviving records (see page 122, "Comparing Notes"). But when they got to Jerusalem, something whacked them. "The angel of the LORD…killed 185,000 Assyrian soldiers" (2 Kings 19:35). Many scholars say it sounds like a plague. The surviving Assyrians quit that siege and limped home.

"I am important, I am magnificent."
That's what he says—Ashurnasirpal II (883–859 BC), the Assyrian king who started his nation's aggressive expansion to take over the Middle East. What follows his brag-quote, chiseled here in wedge-shaped cuneiform script, includes a report of his first five military campaigns: "With their blood I dyed the mountain red as red wool."

HOW TO GROW AN EMPIRE

Back in Abraham's time, around 2100 BC, Assyrians served a stronger kingdom—Babylonians, based out of what is now Iraq's southland.

Assyrians, mainly herders and farmers, lived at the top of the Fertile Crescent (civilization's birth land) on a patchwork quilt of desert and grazing pasture wedged between two of the biggest rivers in the Middle East, the Tigris and Euphrates. Assyrians claimed a stretch of land about 300 (480 km) miles east to west and 200 miles (320 km) north to south. That's about as much turf as Florida.

As Assyrian population grew, their kings started making land grabs, eventually snatching control of most of the livable parts of the Middle East as far away as Egypt's Nile River Valley.

BIG ASSYRIA 600 BC

LITTLE ASSYRIA 900 BC

TURKEY

CARCHEMISH •

EUPHRATES RIVER

QARQAR •
AHAB AND ALLIES TEMPORARILY STOP
ASSYRIA'S INVASION HERE IN BATTLE.

TADMOR •

SYRIA

• HALAH
WHERE SOME JEWS OF SAMARIA WERE DEPORTED

KING OF ASSYRIA

• NINEVEH
LATER CAPITAL OF ASSYRIA

• ASHUR
EARLY CAPITAL OF ASSYRIA

TIGRIS RIVER

CYPRUS

MEDITERRANEAN SEA

LEBANON

• DAMASCUS

EUROPE
MIDDLE
EAST
AFRICA

SAMARIA
CAPITAL OF ISRAEL •
JERUSALEM •
CAPITAL OF JUDAH

ISRAEL

JORDAN

DEPORTED. Assyrians deported conquered
Jews east, to Iraq and Iran and conquered
Syrians and Babylonians west, to Israel. Assyrians were first on record to deport war
prisoners, perhaps to make it harder for
them to mount a comeback revolt.

HIT •

BAGHDAD •
• CUTHAH (TELL IBRAHIM)
• HOME OF BABYLONIANS DEPORTED TO ISRAEL
BABYLON •
CAPITAL OF BABYLONIAN EMPIRE

IRAN

• SUSA
CAPITAL OF PERSIAN EMPIRE

UR •

IRAQ

MEMPHIS •

NILE RIVER

RED SEA

EGYPT

THEBES •

VISITING THE KING. A delegate from
a defeated or surrendered nation
brings annual gifts to the Assyrian king
as a tax payment.

KUWAIT

PERSIAN
GULF

SAUDI ARABIA

N

0   200 KM
       100 MILES   200 MILES

Starting small. Assyria's empire began as a kingdom of herders and farmers on a stretch of land about the size of Florida, wedged between the Euphrates and Tigris Rivers. In time, Assyrians controlled most of the livable land in the ancient Middle East, collecting taxes from kingdoms and nations from what is now Turkey in the north to Egypt in the south.

All for god: Ashurnasirpal II (883–859 BC). The land grab started big-time with this king, who claimed he was reaching out to other people for religious reasons—to convert them to the enlightened Assyrian religion and its worship of the god Ashur.

When people refused to be enlightened, he lightened them—removing their heads or other important body parts. Surviving Assyrian art, carved in stone and hung on the palace walls, preserves pictures of this for us today.

How to make a Jewish king kneel: Shalmaneser III (858–824 BC). Ashurnasirpal's son picked up where Daddy left off, hoping to push their empire all the way to the Mediterranean Sea. That would give him control of all caravan trade routes and toll fees between northern Middle Eastern kingdoms, such as those in what are now Turkey and Syria, and kingdoms in southland countries, such as Egypt and Saudi Arabia.

It took a few battles.

One of the most famous was the stalemate Battle of Qarqar (853 BC), a city in what is now Syria, about 150 miles (240 km) north of Damascus. The Bible doesn't mention this fight, but Shalmaneser did in a cuneiform record chiseled in stone and discovered in 1861.

The report says his army defeated coalition forces of Israel's King Ahab, who had teamed up with Syrian armies based out of Damascus and the city of Hamath. Shalmaneser's records say he won. But historians say the two sides fought to a draw, with the Jews and Syrians stopping Assyria's advance. Temporarily.

Ahab died later fighting his former allies, the Syrians. "Someone, without aiming, shot an arrow randomly into the crowd and hit the king of Israel in the chink of his armor" (1 Kings 22:34 MSG).

Ahab's family dynasty ended a dozen years later in a coup led by one of the Jewish generals. By then, Assyrians had worn down the Syrians and Jews, forcing them to pay tribute taxes to the empire. Israel's King Jehu, the general who had ended Ahab's dynasty by assassinating Ahab's son King Joram, shows up on an Assyrian stone picture bowing at the feet of King Shalmaneser (see page 109).

Roadblock. Assyrian king Shalmaneser's own cuneiform report of the Battle of Qarqar says Israel's King Ahab fought against him as part of a coalition trying to block the Assyrian push to the Mediterranean Sea. The report, known as the Kurkh Monolith, says Ahab's army included "2,000 chariots and 10,000 soldiers." Shalmaneser's report claims victory. But most history experts say Ahab and company stopped the Assyrians in their tracks.

GOODBYE ISRAEL
NORTHERN JEWISH NATION FALLS

The king of Assyria invaded the entire land, and for three years he besieged the city of Samaria... Samaria fell, and the people of Israel were exiled to Assyria.

2 KINGS 17:5-6

City on a hill. Capital of the northern Jewish nation of Israel, Samaria crowned a hilltop with its walls, along with houses and businesses inside and out. Assyrian invaders from what is now Iraq surrounded the city and starved the people into surrendering three years later.

Jews in the northland Jewish country of Israel got about a generation-long break from Assyrian intrusion. That's because Assyrian kings who followed Shalmaneser III seemed more interested in their own local politics than in collecting taxes from distant kingdoms.

Boy did that change with Assyrian King Tiglath-pileser III (744–727 BC). He wanted not only taxes but also to annex countries and kingdoms into his empire.

Israel's King Pekah (about 740–732 BC) built a coalition army to stop the Assyrians. He joined forces with neighboring kingdoms, including Syrians based out of Damascus and the kingdom of Tyre in what is now Lebanon.

He tried to get King Ahaz of the southern Jewish nation of Judah to join the coalition. But Ahaz wanted nothing to do with that fight. Coalition forces brought the fight to him, trying to replace him with a king who would join the battle.

Ahaz sent a message to Assyria's King Tiglath-pileser, asking for help.

The Assyrian army came with sharp objects.

They crushed the coalition forces, defeating the kingdoms of Syria, Tyre, Ashkelon, and most of Israel—sparing only the area around Samaria, the capital city.

Assyrians deported most of the Jewish survivors to a scattering of other lands the Assyrians had conquered in what are now south Iraq along with Iran. Assyrians repopulated Israel with settlers deported from other conquered kingdoms. It was a population flip-flop of entire cities.

Historians can only guess why the Assyrians did it. One guess is to make it tougher for conquered people to work up a good rebellion—living in new digs among people who speak a different language.

When Tiglath-pileser died, the next Assyrian king, Shalmaneser V (726–722 BC), didn't care much about distant kingdoms and policing his empire. In a fatal mistake, Israel's King Hoshea took that as an invitation to stop sending tax payments to the empire.

Shalmaneser may not have cared much about empire building, but he did care about income. He sent his army to conquer the last of Israel's diminishing kingdom, based out of Samaria. His army surrounded the hilltop city, laying siege to it and cutting off supplies from the outside for three years.

Shalmaneser died while the siege was going on. His replacement, Sargon II (722–705), refused to wait around for the Jews to starve or surrender. He sent reinforcements to storm the city.

Sargon's own report brags that he deported 27,000 Jews from Samaria and the surrounding region. He moved them to "colonies in Halah, along the banks of the Habor River in Gozan, and in the cities of the Medes" (2 Kings 17:6). Halah is now Habur, a city about 60 miles (100 km) north of Assyria's capital in Nineveh (see map on page 116). Medes lived in what is now northwest Iran, along the border with Iraq.

GOOD SAMARITANS

With the northland Jewish nation of Israel dead and gone and many of the Jewish survivors deported, Assyrian pioneers moved in to resettle the vacant land. These Assyrian pioneers were deportees themselves—unwilling settlers who came from what is now south Iraq, a territory conquered by the Assyrian army.

Some settlers married local Jews who had escaped deportation. Descendants of these mixed marriages show up in the New Testament as a new race of people—Samaritans, whom the Jews hated.

Jesus made a "despised Samaritan" (Luke 10:33) the good guy in one of his most famous parables—the story of a Samaritan traveler who helped an injured man after two Jewish religious leaders walked right past the man, leaving him for dead. (See "Parables: The Most Authentic Words of Jesus," page 167.)

Saved. A Samaritan comes to the rescue of a man who has been robbed, beat up, and left for dead. The Samaritan's ancestors were deported to Israel from Iraq. Jews in Jesus's time hated them. But Jesus made one of them the star of perhaps his most famous parable.

JERUSALEM SURROUNDED
ASSYRIANS DESTROY 46 JEWISH CITIES

During Hezekiah's fourteenth year as king, Sennacherib king of Assyria attacked all the strong, walled cities of Judah and captured them.

2 KINGS 18:13 NCV

Ram power. Assyrian soldiers equipped with battering rams and rolling siege towers attack a Judean city near Jerusalem while Jewish defenders on top of the city walls try to fight them off. They die trying.

I have done wrong," King Hezekiah wrote to the invading Assyrian King Sennacherib (704–681 BC). "I will pay whatever tribute money you demand if you will only withdraw" (2 Kings 18:14).

Hezekiah was a little late to the game on that offer. Assyrians had already conquered his entire defensive ring of fortified cities, which were intended to protect the southern Jewish nation of Judah. Forty-six cities fell, according to Assyrian King Sennacherib's own surviving report. He saved the best for last—Jerusalem.

REBEL CRUSHERS

Assyrians invaded Judah in 701 BC because they had excellent intel from what may have been spies in Jerusalem. The spies reported that the Jews and some of their neighboring kingdoms had agreed to join the king of Babylon,

Combat engineers. The Assyrian army's corps of engineers try to bring down the wall of a Jewish city by prying loose the stones and by digging tunnels under the wall. Miners known as "sappers" would dig the tunnel and then pull out the support beams, hoping part of the wall above would crumble into the hole.

a small nation in what is now south Iraq, in a war of independence against Assyria.

What was excellent about the intel was the speed with which it reached King Sennacherib. He got the news even before the Babylonian delegates returned home from their war council meeting in Jerusalem.

Sennacherib mobilized his army. First stop: Babylon, where his soldiers defeated the surprised Babylonian army.

SIDON

TYRE LEBANON

SYRIA

SEA OF GALILEE

JORDAN RIVER

ASSYRIA'S PATH OF DESTRUCTION

MEDITERRANEAN SEA

SAMARIA
Assyrians bypass what used to be the northern Jewish nation of Israel because they defeated it in 722 BC, deported many Jewish survivors and repopulated the land with pioneers from what is now Iraq. People who intermarried with Jews and became known as Samaritans

HEADS, WE WIN
ASSYRIANS FLAUNT THEIR VICIOUS REPUTATION DISPLAYING ART OF SEVERED HEADS AND IMPALED CORPSES ON PALACE WALLS

BENE-BERAK   APHEK

JOPPA

ELTEKEH

AMMON

JORDAN

ASSYRIAN KING LEAVES LIBNAH AND FIGHTS OFF EGYPTIANS AT BATTLE OF ELTEKEH

EKRON (TEL MIQNE)   TIMNAH (TEL BATASH)

JERUSALEM

ASHDOD

AZEKAH (TEL AZEK)   BETHLEHEM

GATH (TEL ZAFIT)

ASHKELON

LIBNAH (TEL BURNA)

JUDAH

BETH-ZUR (KHIRBAT TABAQAH)

DEAD SEA

EGYPTIANS TO THE RESCUE

LACHISH
Commander leaves Lachish with some troops to begin siege of Jerusalem, 30 miles (48 km) north

HEBRON

EGYPTIAN RETREAT

GAZA

ISRAEL

MOAB

N

EGYPTIAN U-TURN
EGYPTIANS RUSH TO RESCUE THEIR ALLIES, THE JEWS BUT ASSYRIANS DEFEAT THEM AT ELTEKEH

EDOM

"The Assyrians came down like the wolf on the fold." That's how Lord Byron described Assyria's invasion in his 1815 poem "The Destruction of Sennacherib." Assyrians made a preemptive strike on a coalition of kingdoms plotting to rebel against them—including King Hezekiah's Judah.

COMPARING NOTES:
THE BIBLE AND AN ASSYRIAN PRISM

King Sennacherib's report of his invasion into Judah tracks nicely with the Bible account.

Scribes wrote his report in about 689 BC using wedge-shaped cuneiform text pressed into a six-sided clay prism. Discovered at the ruins of Nineveh in 1830, it's one of the best preserved documents from ancient Assyria.

Here are a few excerpts from the king's report, alongside the Bible account.

HEADLINE	SENNACHERIB'S REPORT	2 KINGS
Jews revolt	"Hezekiah of Judah did not submit to my authority."	"Hezekiah…revolted against the king of Assyria and refused to pay him tribute" (18:7).
Assyrians take cities	"I attacked and took 46 of his strong, walled cities."	"Sennacherib of Assyria came to attack the fortified towns of Judah and conquered them" (18:13).
Jews pay big fine	"I received one ton of gold, 27 tons of silver, gems, jewels…"	"The king of Assyria then demanded a settlement of more than eleven tons of silver and one ton of gold" (18:14).
Jerusalem survives siege	"Hezekiah I trapped in Jerusalem like a caged bird."	"Sennacherib of Assyria broke camp…He went home" (19:35-36).

Next stop: Judah. Along the way he defeated other kingdoms that had joined the plot to attack him, including Tyre and Sidon, cities on the coast of what is now Lebanon. Three other kingdoms in the area surrendered and pledged allegiance to the Assyrians—Ammon, Moab, and Edom, all in what is now Jordan.

That put Judah in the bull's-eye, surrounded by conquered kingdoms in the north, surrendered kingdoms east and south, the deep blue sea in the west.

Sennacherib wrote a report of the campaign. It has survived almost 2700 years on a clay prism in the ruins of his capital city, Nineveh. He said he captured 46 walled cities, "leveling the walls with battering rams, siege towers, and tunnels under the walls…storming into the city on foot. I captured 200,150 people, great and small, male and female, along with horses, mules, donkeys, camels, cattle, and more sheep than anyone could count. I took them away as war trophies."

Taylor Prism 689 BC

GONE: JEWISH NATION

BABYLONIANS OF IRAQ WIPE JUDAH OFF THE MAP

Nebuchadnezzar of Babylon led his entire army against Jerusalem... He [the king's general] burned down the Temple of the LORD... He destroyed all the important buildings in the city. Then he supervised the entire Babylonian army as they tore down the walls.

2 KINGS 25:1,9-10

Lights out. "We cannot see the fire signals of Azekah." That's the frantic message a soldier scribbled on this broken piece of pottery found in the scorched ruins of Lachish, a city ten miles (16 km) south of the city of Azekah. King Nebuchadnezzar's army conquered both of these walled towns on his march to level Jerusalem.

The worst day in Jewish history, some Jews say, is the day Jerusalem died—July 17, 586 BC.

Babylonian invaders from what is now Iraq slaughtered most of the defenders. Then they ripped Jerusalem apart, stone by stone. Israel's Holy City became Rock City.

The last surviving Jewish nation—with every notable town destroyed—became the invisible nation, erased from the world map. No capital. No king. No people but scattered survivors—many banished as refugees, forced to live in what are now Iraq and Iran.

Some of those Jews must have thought God lied to their ancestor Abraham: "I will give you the whole land of Canaan. You will own it forever. So will your children after you" (Genesis 17:8 NIRV). Others probably knew better. They had read the fine print: "Abraham, you and all future members of your family must promise to obey me" (Genesis 17:9 CEV).

As the prophets tell it, Jews did everything but obey God.

Moses had warned the Jews about the price of disobedience. "You will be torn from the land…the LORD will scatter you among all the nations" (Deuteronomy 28:63-64).

IRAQI INVASION 1

Suddenly a superpower, the Babylonian Empire—led by its most famous king, Nebuchadnezzar—has just knocked the block off the former bully of the Middle East, the Assyrian Empire.

With Babylon's only major threats silenced, Nebuchadnezzar turns his army south. His men plunder their way through what is now Syria and Lebanon before storming into the southland Jewish nation of Judah, the last surviving Jewish nation (604 BC). The northern Jewish nation, Israel, got erased more than a century earlier by the Assyrians (722 BC).

Babylon's invasion may have prompted a fast in Judah, some scholars speculate. The prophet Jeremiah, in Jerusalem, said Jews

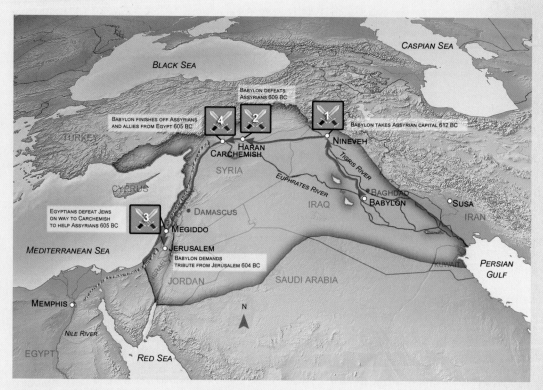

BABYLONIANS MAKE THEIR MOVE

Prepping to manhandle the Assyrian Empire and become the next superpower of the Middle East, Babylonians in what is now south Iraq march north. They…

- decimate Assyria's capital, Nineveh
- search and destroy the regrouping Assyrian army at Haran and finally Carchemish
- defeat Egyptians coming to Assyria's rescue at Carchemish
- march south to Jerusalem and force Jews to start paying taxes

fasted sometime around November or December of that same year, "in late autumn, during the fifth year of the reign of Jehoiakim" (Jeremiah 36:9).

When the Babylonians arrive in Judah, their army…

- overpowers the Jewish city of Ashkelon on the coast
- runs off Egyptians who march up to protect their corner of the Middle Eastern turf
- forces Judah's King Jehoiakim to start paying annual taxes to support Babylon's new empire
- takes Jewish hostages, possibly including the prophet Daniel and his three famously fireproof friends, Shadrach, Meshach, and Abednego

Deported. Jewish headliners—society's elite—get escorted out of the Promised Land and all the way to what is now Iraq. These exiles include Judah's king, his royal entourage, and Judah's best artisans and sharpest thinkers. Among the crowd—a fair bet, scholars say—lion tamer Daniel and his fireproof friends, Shadrach, Meshach, and Abednego.

IRAQI INVASION 2

Jews pay their Babylonian taxes for three years. Then they stop (601 BC).

As far as they're concerned, it's a matter of which bully to bet on—Egypt or Babylon. Judah put her money on Egypt for two reasons.

- *Gratitude to Egypt.* Egypt's King Necho had actually crowned Jehoiakim king of Judah (2 Kings 23:34). Until Babylon arrived, Egypt had been Judah's boss.
- *Confidence in Egypt's army.* Egypt had earlier stopped Babylon at their border. After the Babylonians stormed through Judah, they tried pushing into Egypt but managed to fight only to a draw.

As it turns out, Egypt is the bad bet.

Nebuchadnezzar returned (winter 598 BC). He wanted his Jewish money.

Babylon's army lay siege to Jerusalem. King Jehoiakim died in December, probably during the siege, some scholars say. His son, 18-year-old Jehoiachin, took over and spent three months weighing his options. Likely terrified at the sight of Babylon's newly built siege towers mounted with battering rams, catapults, and archers, he surrendered (March 16, 597 BC).

Babylonians took more than their tax money. Imposing a stiff penalty for late payment, they pillaged Jerusalem. They took "all the gold objects that King Solomon of Israel had placed in the Temple" (2 Kings 24:13)—perhaps stealing the gold-plated Ark of the Covenant, the most sacred Jewish relic. That chest held the Ten Commandments of Moses.

Babylonians took 10,000 hostages too, scraping the cream off the top of society's milk—Judah's best soldiers, the prophet Ezekiel, "and all Jerusalem's elite" (2 Kings 24:15).

Nebuchadnezzar gave the Jews one last chance to learn some respect for Babylonian authority. He appointed a new king—Zedekiah, a 21-year-old uncle of the former king. Too young to know any better, Zedekiah will turn the lights out in Jerusalem—and in all of Judah.

IRAQI INVASION 3

For nine years, Zedekiah plots a path to Jewish independence.

He ignores the prophet Jeremiah's warning that God is using Babylon to punish the Jews: "You must submit to Babylon's king and serve him" (Jeremiah 27:8).

Zedekiah, egged on by his Egyptian ally, repeats the mistake of two Jewish kings before

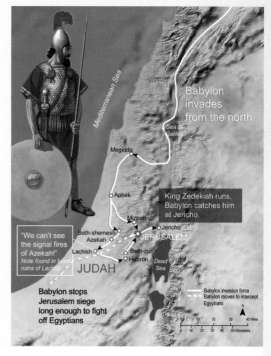

Babylon invades from the north

King Zedekiah runs, Babylon catches him at Jericho.

"We can't see the signal fires of Azekah!" Note found in burnt ruins of Lachish

Babylon stops Jerusalem siege long enough to fight off Egyptians

Babylon invasion force
Babylon moves to intercept Egyptians

Tax collectors with sharp objects. Nine years after Babylon plunders Judah for declaring independence, Jews repeat their mistake. They refuse to send tax money to the current boss of the Middle East. It's the third time a Jewish king has stiffed Babylon's King Nebuchadnezzar. It'll be the last. Within months, Babylon invades from the north. They overrun Judah's major cities. They drive off Egyptians coming to rescue the Jews. Then they level Judah's capital of Jerusalem. Most survivors get executed or deported to what is now Iraq or Iran.

ROCK-SOLID EVIDENCE

"In the seventh year, the month of Kislimu [winter 598–597 BC], the king of Akkad [ancient name for Babylon] mustered his troops. They marched to the Hatti-land [ancient name for Israel's region] and lay siege to the city of Judah [the capital, Jerusalem]. On the second day of the month of Addaru [March 15–16] he captured the city and the king [Jehoiachin]. He appointed another king [Zedekiah] and took massive treasures back to Babylon."

Baked history. This baked clay tablet of Nebuchadnezzar's exploits, found near the Babylon palace, confirms the capture of Jerusalem in 597 BC. The tablet is written in wedged-shaped cuneiform letters pressed into soft clay.

SCENES FROM A SIEGE

It's a horror show inside the walled city of Jerusalem during Babylon's two-and-a-half-year siege. Cut off from all supplies, life is a slow death. The saddest book in the Bible, Lamentations, paints the picture.

- *Kid's meal.* "Loving mothers have boiled and eaten their own children" (4:10 CEV).

- *Cotton mouth.* "Babies are so thirsty that their tongues are stuck to the roof of the mouth" (4:4 CEV).

- *Bone bags.* "Leaders of Jerusalem…their skin clings to their bones" (4:7-8 CEV).

him. He stiffs Nebuchadnezzar. No more Jewish money headed to Iraq (589 BC).

Iraq heads to Jewish money. Babylon's army arrives in the dead of winter on January 15, 588 BC. But they're not coming just to collect taxes. They're coming to kill Jews in the nation that has become a chronic pain in Babylon's neck.

The invaders lay siege to Jerusalem, destroy the outlying cities, and fight off Egyptians coming to Jerusalem's rescue. "Two and a half years later, on July 18 in the eleventh year of Zedekiah's reign, the Babylonians broke through the wall, and the city fell" (Jeremiah 39:2).

In a classic "fight or flight," brave King Zedekiah and his soldiers fly.

Rather than defend Jerusalem's citizens—many of whom are about to get butchered—the king and his army charge downhill, away from the enemy. They run for their lives to the Jordan River Valley some 16 miles (25 km) east. That's where Babylonian soldiers catch up to the king, near Jericho.

The last sight King Zedekiah sees is Babylonian soldiers slaughtering his sons. "Then they gouged out Zedekiah's eyes, bound him

in bronze chains, and led him away to Babylon" (Jeremiah 39:7).

As for Jerusalem, Babylonians tear down the walls and burn the buildings—temple, palace, and all. Archaeologists have found scorch scars on bedrock—imprints of limestone blocks that disintegrated in the heat of the fire.

Most of Jerusalem's survivors were executed or led to Babylon as captives. Some of the poorest are left behind to tend the fields and vineyards for Babylon.

Israel is dead.

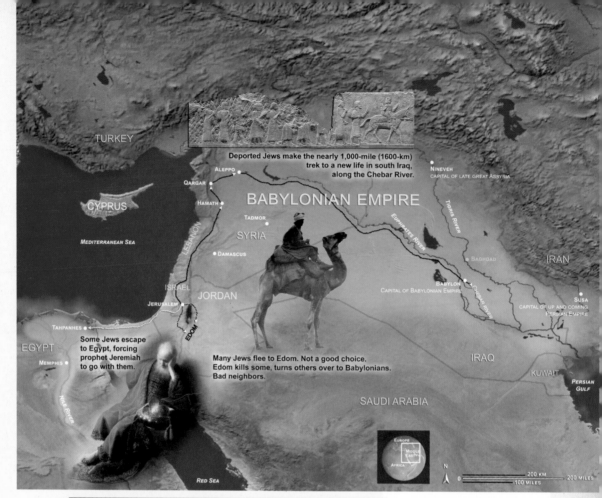

Deported Jews make the nearly 1,000-mile (1600-km) trek to a new life in south Iraq, along the Chebar River.

TURKEY

NINEVEH
CAPITAL OF LATE GREAT ASSYRIA

ALEPPO

QARGAR

CYPRUS

HAMATH

BABYLONIAN EMPIRE

TIGRIS RIVER

TADMOR

SYRIA

EUPHRATES RIVER

MEDITERRANEAN SEA

DAMASCUS

BAGHDAD

IRAN

LEBANON

ISRAEL

JORDAN

BABYLON
CAPITAL OF BABYLONIAN EMPIRE

JERUSALEM

SUSA
CAPITAL OF UP AND COMING
PERSIAN EMPIRE

EDOM

TAHPANHES

Some Jews escape
to Egypt, forcing
prophet Jeremiah
to go with them.

Many Jews flee to Edom. Not a good choice.
Edom kills some, turns others over to Babylonians.
Bad neighbors.

EGYPT

MEMPHIS

IRAQ

KUWAIT

PERSIAN
GULF

SAUDI ARABIA

NILE RIVER

EUROPE
MIDDLE EAST
AFRICA

N

0   100 MILES   200 KM   200 MILES

RED SEA

DEPORTED: JEWS SCATTER
LIFE IN IRAQ AND IRAN

*Beside the rivers of Babylon, we sat and
wept as we thought of Jerusalem.*

Psalm 137:1

When Jerusalem fell in 586 BC, Jews fulfilled an ancient prophecy: "The Lord will scatter you among all the nations from one end of the earth to the other" (Deuteronomy 28:64).

That was one of the consequences written into the fine print of the ancient contract between God and the Jews. If Jews broke the contract by worshipping other gods, the Lord would let neighboring countries invade and scatter the Jews.

Exodus out of the Promised Land. By the time Babylonians deported their fourth wave of Jews, most of the Jews had escaped or been killed or deported. Yet some remained. Archaeological evidence confirms that Mizpah, four miles (6 km) north of Jerusalem, remained a busy town. The Bible says that's where Babylonians set up their base camp to govern "the few people still living in Judah" (2 Kings 25:22 CEV).

About one in five Jews estimated to have lived in Judah were deported to what is now south Iraq. According to numbers reported in the Bible books of 2 Kings and Jeremiah, the Babylonians deported about 14,000 of the estimated 75,000 Jews who lived in Judah. Jeremiah should know—he was there when the city fell.

Deportation was a technique Assyrians had developed, apparently to prevent a conquered people from mounting a rebellion. Babylonians obviously thought the technique worked. They replanted Jews along the Chebar River, south of Baghdad and Babylon, in what is now southern Iraq.

Sad song. Transplanted to what is now Iraq, Jewish refugees get what sounds like a cruel request. With their holy city of Jerusalem destroyed, they are asked to sing a happy song about the city. "Sing us one of those songs of Jerusalem!" (Psalm 137:3). Imagine a country conquering the United States, nuking Washington DC, and then asking American refugees to sing "America the Beautiful."

Babylon prime. Babylon was never bigger, stronger, and richer than when King Nebuchadnezzar ran the empire. Babylon's capital—also called Babylon—covered six square miles (16 sq km) alongside the Euphrates River. Double walls protected downtown Babylon. Dominating the cityscape was a 30-story ziggurat topped with a temple to the patron god, Marduk.

9

REBUILDING FROM A ROCK PILE

TIMELINE *(dates are approximate)*

539 BC	Persians defeat Babylonians.
536 BC	A clay cylinder confirms Cyrus freed Jews.
515 BC	Jews dedicate rebuilt temple.
445 BC	Nehemiah rebuilds Jerusalem walls.
333 BC	Alexander the Great defeats Darius III of Persia.
160 BC	Jews win independence from Greeks.
63 BC	Romans invade, ending Jewish independence.

Alexander the Great
(reigned 559–530 BC)

Cyrus cylinder

Roman soldier

RUSSIA

CYRUS II (THE GREAT)
FOUNDER OF A 200-YEAR PERSIAN DYNASTY

EUROPE

BLACK SEA   GEORGIA   CASPIAN SEA   TURKMENISTAN
ARMENIA

TURKEY

GREECE

PERSIAN EMPIRE OF CYRUS, 530 BC
2500 MILES (4000 KM)   ECBATANA
CYRUS CYLINDER FOUND HERE,
IN OLDEST-KNOWN PERSIAN CITY   AFGHANISTAN

SYRIA

IRAN

IRAQ   BABYLON   SUSA
CAPITAL OF BABYLON   CAPITAL OF PERSIA   INDIA

MEDITERRANEAN SEA   PASARGADAE
CAPITAL OF CYRUS'S PERSIA   PAKISTAN

ISRAEL   LEBANON   JORDAN   KUWAIT   LITTLE PERSIA
600 BC

SAUDI ARABIA   PERSIAN GULF

EGYPT   ARABIAN SEA

NILE RIVER

RED SEA

SUPERPOWER NEXT
PERSIANS OF IRAN

Your kingdom has been divided and given to the Medes and Persians.

Daniel 5:28

World's biggest empire. In a generation, Persia's footprint grew from about the size of Florida to a stretch of land about the distance from New York City on the East Coast to Los Angeles on the West Coast. Persians swallowed up more territory than either the Assyrians or the Babylonians before them.

One really odd thing about the world's next superpower (Persia, based out of what is now Iran): The Jewish Bible predicted its king. By name. More than a century before the king was born. "Cyrus...is my shepherd...he will command, 'Rebuild Jerusalem'; he will say, 'Restore the Temple'" (Isaiah 44:28).

Many Bible experts say this part of Isaiah was written after the time of Cyrus as history, not prophecy. Many, if not most, scholars say the book of Isaiah was written by two or more writers at different times in history. The Bible says the prediction came from Isaiah, prophesying sometime in the 700s BC.

If the Jews actually had this prophecy when Cyrus showed up, how handy. The Jews could have taken the prophecy to the Persian king to show him what God said he would do—free the Jews.

As the Bible tells it, Cyrus the Great (reigned 559–530 BC) seems to have bought into that prophecy. Another Bible writer said Cyrus issued the following statement:

The LORD, the God of heaven, has given me all the kingdoms of the earth. He has appointed me to build him a Temple at Jerusalem, which is in Judah. Any of you who are his people may go to Jerusalem in Judah to rebuild this Temple of the LORD, the God of Israel, who lives in Jerusalem. And may your God be with you! (Ezra 1:2-3).

Then Cyrus ordered his officials to return to the Jews all of the sacred temple objects looted by King Nebuchadnezzar a generation earlier: "5,400 articles of gold and silver" (Ezra 1:11).

Not all Jews went home. After spending half a century in exile, most of the surviving Jews had grown up in what is now Iraq. Babylon was their home. Yet many Jews did return to their homeland in one caravan wave after another.

First wave: "A total of 42,360 people returned to Judah" (Ezra 2:64).

Handwriting on the wall. Babylon's king, Belshazzar, sees a disembodied hand scrawl a cryptic message on the palace wall. Not good news. Babylon is about to fall. "That same night, the king was killed. Then Darius the Mede…took over his kingdom" (Daniel 5:30-31 CEV).

JEREMIAH'S QUESTIONABLE MATH: DID HE GET THE NUMBERS WRONG?

Gifts for the king. Foreign ambassadors bring tribute to the king of Persia—a sampling of the expensive gifts representing the empire's required tax payments. This stone carving is from a wall in a Persian palace.

"You will be in Babylon for seventy years. But then I [God]…will bring you home" (Jeremiah 29:10).

That's the prophet Jeremiah predicting Jews would live in exile for 70 years. As it turns out, it was more like 50.

In 586 BC, Jerusalem fell to Babylonian invaders. Jeremiah saw it happen. He was inside Jerusalem at the time, one of the lucky survivors.

Forty-eight years later, in 538 BC, Persians defeated Babylon and freed the Jews.

Some Jews, however, may have been exiled for almost 70 years—66, which would round up to 70. Bible experts say that King Nebuchadnezzar of Babylon probably took hostages back with him during his first tour of the region in 604 BC. That was right after he finished off the Assyrian army and then called the summit of regional kings, ordering them to submit to the Babylonian Empire—an order the Jews obeyed.

FREE TO BE JEWISH
THE LONG ROAD HOME

Jewish exiles...returned to Jerusalem and the other towns in Judah where they originally lived.

EZRA 2:1

Loaded for the long haul. A camel caravan trudges along a Judean trail near Jerusalem in a photo taken in the early 1900s. Jews who returned from exile in what is now Iraq probably traveled in caravans like this.

Persians were nice, compared to your average invader. Consider the Assyrians or Babylonians, who...

- impaled your grandpa on a fence post
- skinned your mother alive
- burned your city to the ground
- deported you a thousand miles (1600 km) away

Persians, led by their conquering king, Cyrus II, abandoned terror tactics. They kept their conquered people on a leash, but it was a long leash.

Cyrus organized his Middle Eastern empire into what amounts to states ruled by governors. But in the Persian lingo of Aramaic, they were called *provinces* ruled by *satraps*.

What's surprising is that Cyrus not only freed the political prisoners to go back to their homeland, he often appointed a member of the royal family from that region to rule as governor.

Perhaps even more surprising, he gave back all the sacred objects that Babylonians had looted from worship centers throughout the Middle East. He allowed the exiles to take these back to their homeland, and he encouraged the people to rebuild their worship centers. He even helped pay for the rebuilding.

His decree shows up in surviving documents from his own day, along with this statement, preserved in the Bible:

I am King Cyrus of Persia.

The LORD God of heaven, who is also the God of Israel, has made me the ruler of all nations on earth. And he has chosen me to build a temple for him in Jerusalem, which is in Judah. The LORD God will watch over and encourage any of his people who want to go back to Jerusalem and help build the temple.

Everyone else must provide what is needed. They must give money, supplies, and animals, as well as gifts for rebuilding God's temple (Ezra 1:2-4 CEV).

Cyrus set up Judah as a province of the Persian Empire.

He appointed as governor a man who seems to have come from the family of King David—"Sheshbazzar the prince of Judah" (Ezra 1:8 MSG). This prince may have been the deported son of one of Judah's last kings, Jehoiachin. A similar-sounding name shows up on a list of deported family members: "taken prisoner by the Babylonians...Shenazzar" (1 Chronicles 3:17-18). Or perhaps Sheshbazzar was the king's grandson.

"I am Cyrus, king of the universe." So says the writer of this 2600-year-old clay cylinder, reporting on the Iran–Iraq war of 539 BC. This cylinder, nine inches long (23 cm), backs up the Bible report that says Cyrus freed the Jewish political prisoners in Babylon to go home and rebuild their temple. The cylinder is more general, though. It talks about all political prisoners with their gods and their sacred objects. Cyrus says, "I freed them...I sent them home...across the Tigris River to where their temples lay in ruins." Cyrus ends by asking all those people and their gods to pray for him every day "for a long life."

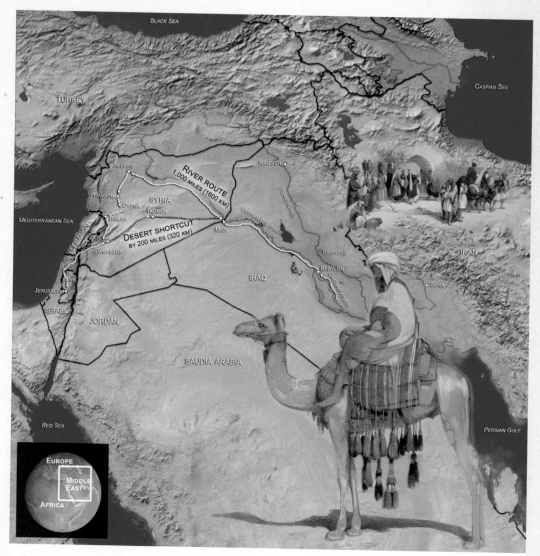

Some go, some stay. Freed by King Cyrus of Persia, some Jews leave their riverside communities south of Babylon to make the 1000-mile (1600 km) trek home to the ruins of what is now Israel. Many Jews, including some of the sharpest minds, opt to stay where they have lived for the past half century. In Iraq, they compile some of the most sacred Jewish writings, including the Babylonian Talmud, a collection of Jewish traditions and Bible commentary by rabbis gathered from throughout the centuries.

The Bible isn't clear on how many Jews rode the first wave home. A priest named Ezra, writing a century later, said "42,360 people returned to Judah, in addition to 7,337 servants and 200 singers" (Ezra 2:64-65). But that may have been a later group of people, since Sheshbazzar was not listed as the leader—the top leader was Zerubbabel (Ezra 2:2), which some Bible experts speculate was simply another name for Sheshbazzar.

It's not even clear which route they took home. They may have taken the 800-mile-long (1290 km) shortcut through the Syrian desert. But as a group of nonprofessional caravan travelers, they may have been inclined to follow the more popular, nicely watered trade route, a marathon of about 1000 miles (1600 km) alongside the Euphrates River.

Many Jews, if not most, stayed where they had been replanted in Iraq for the past generation. They maintained a strong and respected Jewish presence there for about 1000 years—until Islamic leaders began persecuting people of other religions. One caliph, Umar II (ruled AD 717–720), outlawed construction of new synagogues and churches.

SYRIA

SEA OF
GALILEE

SAMARIA

MEDITERRANEAN SEA

JORDAN

JORDAN RIVER

ONO

JOPPA

AMMON

BETHEL

GEZER   MIZPAH

GIBEAH

EKRON
(TEL MIQNE)   JUDAH   JERUSALEM

ASHDOD

AZEKAH   BETHLEHEM

GATH
(TEL ZAFIT)

ASHKELON

ISRAEL   HEBRON

DEAD SEA

GAZA   EN-GEDI

IDUMEA   MOAB

EDOM

N

JEWS COME HOME TO A LAND IN RUINS. MORE BAD NEWS: LOCALS DON'T WANT THEM TO REBUILD.

STARTING OVER
TINY PROVINCE OF JUDAH

Things are not going well for those who returned to the province of Judah. They are in great trouble and disgrace. The wall of Jerusalem has been torn down.

NEHEMIAH 1:3

No longer a country or a kingdom, the Jewish homeland gets downgraded to a province on the Persian frontier, way out west.

Jews freed to go home are led by descendants of King David—Sheshbazzar first and Zerubbabel next—but those royal princes never get to rule as kings. Demoted, they run the Jewish province as governors.

Downsizing. The Jewish homeland, now in ruins, shrinks to roughly one-fiftieth the size of King Solomon's Israel. Judah is now just a Persian province some 40 miles wide and 25 miles north to south (64 by 40 km). That's about Phoenix and Nashville combined, for snowbirds who like banjos. Surrounding the Jews are not-so-friendly neighbors who work the Persian system to block the Jews from rebuilding. These neighbors bribe officials and even write letters of protest to Persian kings, who eventually order the building halted.

Jerusalem under construction. Returning home from exile in what is now Iraq, Jews find Jerusalem in ruins. It will take more than a century to rebuild.

Within a century, David's descendants won't even rule as that. King David's sputtering dynasty finally dies on what appears to be an order of Persian King Artaxerxes (reigned 465–425 BC). The king puts a priest in charge.

> Ezra, use the wisdom God has given you and choose officials and leaders to govern the people of Western Province. These leaders should know God's laws and have them taught to anyone who doesn't know them (Ezra 7:25 CEV).

THE FIRST CENTURY OF REBUILDING

Survival was probably tough for the first caravans of Jews returning to what is now Israel. Bible experts say the first groups were likely small with huge obstacles. Two of the biggest:

- Major cities, such as Jerusalem, lie in ruins, a massive pile of charred rocks.

- Neighbors don't want the Jews to re-establish themselves as a nation. They know the history of Jews driving out non-Jews.

In what appears to have been the first order of business, Jews clear the temple area in Jerusalem and lay a foundation for a new temple. But it's shaping up to be a poor excuse of a worship center compared to the one King Solomon had built 400 years earlier.

One clue: the building fund. Jews took up an offering and raised half a ton of gold and three tons of silver to rebuild the temple.

Sounds like a lot. But it's spit in a barrel compared to what King David had stockpiled for construction of Solomon's temple: 4000 tons of gold and 40,000 tons of silver.

If we convert that to cash, when gold sells for $1000 an ounce and silver for $20 an ounce, we get these round numbers:

Solomon's temple building fund: $130 billion.

Replacement temple building fund: $16 million.

In other words, Solomon's Temple got more than $8000 for every penny the new temple got.

When some of the old-timers who remembered Solomon's temple saw the foundation layout of the new temple, "they sobbed" (Ezra 3:12 NIRV). The Bible writer doesn't say if they were crying for happy or crying for sad. Maybe both.

While the Jews had been away in exile for the past 50 years, settlers had moved in. The last thing those settlers wanted was a resurrection of Israel, a nation of people who might confiscate their land and drive them away. Been done before.

These locals managed to roadblock the rebuilding process. Over a stretch of about 15 years, "they kept bribing government officials to slow down the work" (Ezra 4:5 CEV). They wrote letters to succeeding kings of Persia, eventually managing to get all work stopped on the rebuilding of Jerusalem and the temple.

Walls. A painting from the early 1800s showcases the walled city of Jerusalem. A close-up photo of the wall taken in the early 1900s on Jerusalem's sunrise east side shows evidence of patchwork repair—perhaps like the work Nehemiah did. A coalition of non-Jewish leaders from Samarian, Ammonite, and Arabian tribes plotted to stop this repair by assassinating Nehemiah—an attempt that failed. Judah's neighbors didn't want the Jewish nation to come back from the dead apparently because they felt threatened by it.

They pulled this off by reminding the king about Israel's long history of rebellion.

Two prophets—Haggai and Zechariah—relit a fire under the Jews to get them back to building the temple. The Jews had suffered a terrible harvest, and Haggai said it was God's punishment for living in the land almost 20 years without bothering to rebuild the temple. Quoting God, Haggai said, "Why are you living in luxurious houses while my house lies in ruins?" (Haggai 1:4).

Jews resume work on the temple within weeks, by September 520 BC. Without Persian permission. Locals appeal to Darius, the new king of Persia. They accuse the Jews of disobeying the previous king's orders. But when Darius checks court documents, he sees that the original order from Persia's first king, Cyrus, was for the Jews to rebuild their temple.

Darius gives the Jews the green light. They finish the temple five years later, on March 12, 515 BC.

That's 70 years and a few months after Babylonian invaders from what is now Iraq destroyed the temple. The timing must have prompted Jews to remember Jeremiah's prophecy that the exile would last 70 years (Jeremiah 29:10). The physical exile stretched only about 50 years. But the spiritual exile—separation from their only worship center—stretched a full 70.

REBUILDING THE WALLS

Ezra (a Jewish priest) and Nehemiah (a Jewish wine-taster for the Persian king) show up in Jerusalem about 100 years after the first wave of Jews started returning home.

Ezra arrives first, as the Bible reports it, in about 458 BC. A priest with a reputation as an expert in Jewish law, Ezra received permission from King Artaxerxes to "go to Jerusalem and Judah to find out if the laws of your God are being obeyed" (Ezra 7:14 CEV).

Ezra assembles a caravan of Jewish people that includes priests and their associate workers, the Levites. Once he reaches Jerusalem, he lays down the law, but good. He's perhaps most famous for condemning mixed marriages. He even goes so far as to order Jewish men who are married to non-Jewish women to divorce their wives and send them away with their children.

The problem, as Ezra sees it, isn't only that mixed marriages are forbidden in the laws of Moses. Many Jews said that they ended up in exile partly because their ancestors broke this very law. They married non-Jews and then allowed themselves to get lured into worshipping the idols that their spouses brought to the marriage.

Ezra didn't want to see a rerun.

Nehemiah comes to Jerusalem about 13 years later in 445 BC. A wine steward who made sure poisoned wine never reached the lips of the Persian king, Nehemiah seems an unlikely construction foreman. But when his brother comes back from a visit to Jerusalem and tells him the city walls are torn down, Nehemiah slips into a funk. For months.

One day, he puts on a sad face in front of the king. Given what follows, the story reads as though Nehemiah anticipated the king would ask what he could do to help. Nehemiah is ready for that question.

- *Leave of absence.* "Send me back to Judah, so that I can rebuild the city where my ancestors are buried."

- *Safe passage.* "Give me letters to the governors of the provinces west of the Euphrates River, so that I can travel safely to Judah."

- *Free timber.* "I will need timber to rebuild the gates of the fortress near the temple and more timber to construct the city wall and to build a place for me to live" (Nehemiah 2:5,7-8 CEV).

The king gives him all this and more, including an armed escort.

Excited Jerusalem-area Jews mobilize a work force to help Nehemiah raise the walls. Non-Jewish neighbors go berserk. No way do they want the Jews to rebuild defensive walls around Jerusalem. Samaritans in the north along with Ammonites and Arabs in the east go so far as to try luring Nehemiah into a meeting, where they intend to assassinate him.

Nehemiah says he doesn't have time for a meeting—he's working on the wall.

The speed with which the wall is completed terrifies the non-Jewish neighbors. The Bible records Nehemiah saying, "They realized this work had been done with the help of our God" (Nehemiah 6:16).

JEWISH ORPHAN-QUEEN OF IRAN

A Jewish orphan girl raised by one of her cousins, Esther becomes queen of the Persian Empire after she wins a beauty contest.

The former queen, Vashti, had refused a request from King Xerxes (reigned 486–465 BC) to come to a drinking party he was throwing for the top men in his kingdom. Xerxes wanted all the guys to see how pretty his woman was. But Vashti didn't want to show off her face or anything else, so the king decided to put his trophy wife on the shelf and keep her there. In a royal guy moment, Xerxes demoted Vashti to just another squeeze in the harem.

Esther is best known for stopping what would have been an empire-wide holocaust of the Jews led by the king's top official. Earlier, that official, Haman, had decided to kill all the Jews in retaliation against one Jew who disrespected him by refusing to bow when he walked by.

Overkill.

Lousy on intel, Haman didn't get the memo about the queen being a Jew. When Esther revealed that to her king husband, the king ordered Haman executed. Jews today still celebrate that holocaust missed with a springtime Mardi Gras–style festival called Purim.

PERSIAN CALVARY

323 BC
OUTER LIMITS OF ALEXANDER'S EMPIRE
BEFORE SHRINKING
AND BREAKING INTO KINGDOMS

RUSSIA

CASPIAN SEA

AFGHANISTAN

CHINA

BLACK SEA

MACEDONIA

OTHER GREEK KINGDOMS

ROME

HELLESPONT
SHIPS FERRY GREEK ARMY
INTO TURKEY

TURKEY

NINEVEH

HECATOMPYLOS
RETREATING PERSIANS KILL
THEIR KING, DARIUS III

INDIA

GREECE

AEGEAN SEA

ISSUS
GREEK'S DEFEAT
PERSIA IN BATTLE 2 OF 3

SELEUCID KINGDOM

IRAN

PAKISTAN

CYPRUS

CRETE

SYRIA

BABYLON

SUSA

CONTESTED BY
SELEUCUS AND PTOLEMY

DAMASCUS

IRAQ

PERSEPOLIS
DESTROYS PERSIAN CAPITAL

MEDITERRANEAN SEA

JERUSALEM

JORDAN

PTOLEMY KINGDOM

PERSIAN GULF

EGYPT

SAUDI ARABIA

LIBYA

NILE RIVER

RED SEA

ALEXANDER THE GREAT

ALEXANDER'S GREAT ADVENTURE
THE MIDDLE EAST GOES GREEK

The Greek Empire will break into four kingdoms, but none as great as the first.

DANIEL 8:22

Why a 22-year-old kid barely old enough to shave decided to take his army of 40,000 soldiers and conquer the civilized world is anyone's guess.

One popular theory: His mother, Olympias, was the ancient version of a soccer mom. She had big dreams for her boy, Alexander (356–323 BC).

Another guess: Alexander believed the legend that he was the son of the Greek top god, Zeus. Greek historian Plutarch (AD 45–120) reported that legend as fact.

Who knows? Maybe Olympias planted that idea in her boy's head after her husband, King Philip of Macedonia, got himself assassinated in 336 BC.

Alexander's fleet of ships in 334 BC ferried his army and cavalry across the mile-wide (1.6 km) strait known as Hellespont. This narrow finger of the Aegean Sea separated what is now Europe

Alexander's bigger empire. Defeating the Persians and then pushing out the boundaries of the Middle Eastern empire farther than ever before, Alexander managed to capture most of the livable land between Greece and India, a stretch of about 3200 miles (5150 km). That's Seattle to Miami for some sunshine, and then back to Atlanta for peaches and cream. When Alexander died at age 32, his generals divided the conquered Middle East among themselves. The two biggest kingdoms went to generals Seleucus and Ptolemy. Those two kingdoms butted heads at their border, fighting over who got what is now Israel.

from Turkey in the Middle East. The story goes that as Alexander's ship approached Turkey, he threw his spear into the ground and said the land they were about to invade could be taken by spear.

As it turned out, the kid was right.

His Macedonian army from what is now northern Greece fought three major battles with a Persian army double their size and led by their King Darius III (reigned six years, 336–330 BC). Darius was a descendant of Xerxes I (reigned twenty-one years, 486–465 BC), the king famous for burning Athens after defeating King Leonidas of Sparta in the Battle of Thermopylae, immortalized in the blockbuster movie *300*.

Alexander and his Greeks had a score to settle with this particular family of kings.

They settled it. They defeated the Persians in all three battles, crushing them most decisively in the second match—the Battle of Issus in 333 BC. Persians retreated deep into their territory. But Alexander caught up with them again two years later a little east of Nineveh, near what is now Mosul, Iraq.

After that defeat, King Darius's own men assassinated him.

As Alexander marched throughout the Middle East, many cities and kingdoms surrendered. They had no intention of trying to stop an army that was strong enough to walk over a seemingly overwhelming force of Persian soldiers. Jews in the tiny Persian province of Judah were among those who surrendered.

By force or surrender, Alexander captured what is now Israel, Egypt, Lebanon, and the livable parts of Syria and Jordan. From there he pushed east into what had been the heart of the Persian Empire. He took all of Persia and its top cities, including Babylon, Susa, and the capital at the time—Persepolis, which he destroyed.

Ten years after his decisive victory at the Battle of Issus, Alexander lay dead from a fever.

General Ptolemy claimed Egypt and what is now Israel. General Seleucus took most of the rest of the Middle East. About a century later, his descendant Antiochus III snatched Israel from Ptolemy V.

JEWISH REVOLUTION

Eight rulers deep into the Seleucid dynasty, Antiochus IV Epiphanes (ruled 175–163 BC) made a big mistake that would lose him the Jewish homeland.

On his way back from a failed attempt to conquer Egypt, Antiochus apparently decided to pump up his deflated ego by thumping Jerusalem a good one. He marched his army there, expecting a fight.

But Jerusalem's citizens welcomed him warmly, especially those who appreciated Greek culture.

King Antiochus decided to assimilate the rest of the Jews into the Greek world. He outlawed Jewish worship of God. He ordered everyone to offer sacrifices to Greek gods. To enforce this, he sent representatives to each of the villages, forcing the people to publicly make a sacrifice to one of the gods.

One priest in a small village about 20 miles (32 km) west of Jerusalem killed the Seleucid representative. Then he fled to the Judean hills along with his three sons, Judas, Jonathan, and Simon.

The Jewish revolution was on in 166 BC.

This time the Jews were fighting not only for their land but also for their identity as the people of God—for the right to worship the only God they said existed.

They took back Jerusalem two years later in December 164 BC. They purified and rededicated the defiled temple with cleansing rituals in an event the Jews still celebrate—the festival of Hanukkah.

Jews and Seleucids reached an agreement in 152 BC. Jews agreed to become an independent province of the Seleucid kingdom. Ten years later the Seleucid king recognized Judea as an independent kingdom, no longer affiliated with the Seleucid kingdom.

The Jews were free. But it didn't last.

Scribe at work. Jewish scribe Sholomo Washadi, in 1935, creates a fresh, handwritten copy of the Torah—the first five books in the Jewish Bible. Two thousand years ago, an isolated community of Jews some 15 miles (24 km) east of Jerusalem made it their business to preserve sacred Jewish writings. Their library included 800 books, unearthed in the 1940s and '50s and known today as the Dead Sea Scrolls. The library includes at least fragments of every book in the Jewish Bible except Esther—a book that doesn't mention God. Scholars today use these ancient copies to help translate the Bible into modern languages.

JEWISH MONKS: MAKERS OF THE DEAD SEA SCROLLS

Some Jews got ticked when Jonathan Maccabeus, a leader of the Jewish war for independence, snatched for himself the titles of king and high priest.

Problem was, he wasn't kosher, so he didn't qualify as a high priest.

All high priests for the past 800 years had been descendants of King Solomon's high priest, Zadok. Jonathan wasn't. He was a priest descended from another family.

In protest, one group of Jews bailed on worship at the Jerusalem temple. They withdrew to monk-like isolated communities, breaking contact with Jewish leaders in Jerusalem. Jewish historians writing in the first century (Josephus and Pliny the Elder) called them Essenes.

One of these groups managed to preserve a library of 800 sacred Jewish writings, now famous as the Dead Sea Scrolls. A shepherd boy discovered the first of them in a cave during the winter of 1946–47. And the search was on for more.

This ancient library included copies of the Jewish Bible 1000 years older than the copies scholars used to translate the revered King James Version of the Bible.

Remarkably, there was very little difference between the ancient Dead Sea copies of the Bible and the more recent copies. Clearly, scholars agree, scribes throughout the centuries took extreme care when they copied sacred material from one fading scroll to a new scroll for the next generation of readers.

ROMANS TO THE RESCUE

Facing the Romans. Roman general Pompey the Great stares front and center in this museum display of busts from Roman times. Jews invited Pompey to settle a power struggle between two Jews who wanted to be king. Pompey's solution, enforced by his army: No king but Caesar. Romans came, they saw, they conquered. Italian guests who refused to leave. More than a century later, they would destroy the Jewish temple, exile Jews from the city, and rename the Judean homeland Palestine.

Jews were free. But they weren't happy.

The freedom they wanted was the freedom to be Jewish, to return to Jewish tradition and worship. But the Maccabean leaders of the revolution made a power grab. They took not only the palace but also the temple. Maccabean rulers declared themselves both kings and high priests.

They became known as the Hasmonean Dynasty, named after the great-grandfather of Mattathias, the priest who started the Jewish war of independence.

By Jewish tradition, the high priest was supposed to come not only from the family of Aaron, Israel's first high priest, but more specifically from the family of Zadok, a later high priest in the time of Solomon, the king who built the first Jewish temple.

Maccabean boys were not that.

Maccabeans ran the country for about a century until two brothers couldn't agree on who should be the combo king–high priest.

Civil war followed.

Jews on both sides went shopping for allies in 63 BC.

Italy seemed like a good idea at the time, since there was a Roman army an easy one-week march north of Jerusalem, about 140 miles (225 km) away in Damascus. The general on duty was Pompey (106-48 BC), one of Rome's finest. Rome's Senate had commissioned him to spread the Italian way of life into the Middle East. Pompey had already fought his way across Turkey and into Syria, and he hadn't stopped.

Three Jewish delegations propositioned him with invitations to what is now Israel.

General Pompey appointed Hyrcanus, the oldest royal Maccabean brother, high priest and *ethnarch*, a title that means "prince." Not a king. There would be no king. The Jewish homeland of Judea would now be a province of Rome.

Italy owned it.

Jews would try to take it back. Three times. Three wars of independence. Three failures.

After the third failure in the AD 130s, Romans got fed up with the Jewish obsession over their homeland. Romans erased the Jewish name off the world map and renamed the area Palestine, a name that comes from Philistine, a warrior race of people who, for centuries, had fought Jews for the right to live there. As Palestinians to do today.

HOW SYNAGOGUES GOT STARTED

God told the Jews they couldn't worship him by offering sacrifices at just any ol' place. "You may do so only at the place the LORD will choose within one of your tribal territories" (Deuteronomy 12:14).

God chose the temple King Solomon built in Jerusalem.

After Solomon built the temple and prayed a prayer of dedication, God appeared to him one night and said, "I have heard your prayer and have chosen this Temple as the place for making sacrifices" (2 Chronicles 7:12).

Big problem: Babylonians from what is now Iraq tore the temple to the ground in 586 BC and scattered Jewish survivors throughout the Middle East.

Suddenly, Jews seemed to have no way to worship God. Their one and only worship center was gone.

Somewhere along the way, Jews developed the idea of getting together in the community buildings where they lived. These meeting places became known as synagogues, from a Greek word that means "house of assembly." In other words, "a place to meet."

Many Bible experts say Jews came up with the idea in the 500s BC. But so far, the oldest reference to a synagogue goes back only to an Egyptian note written in the 200s BC, after Alexander had spread his Greek culture throughout the Middle East.

Jews met in these synagogues to study their laws, read their sacred writings, and offer the only sacrifices they were able to offer without a temple: "When I lift up my hands in prayer, may it be like the evening sacrifice" (Psalm 141:2 NIRV).

Bible study. Ultraorthodox Jews in their local synagogue keep up on Jewish law by reading the Torah, the first five books in the Bible. Synagogues developed into worship centers for Sabbath Day services on Friday evening and Saturday. They also multitasked as religious schools for adults as well as children— places to study Jewish laws and tradition and to discover what it means to be Jewish.

WORLD'S FIRST BIBLE TRANSLATION: IT WAS GREEK TO THE JEWS

Singing in Greek. A fragment of Psalm 90, copied during the AD 400s in Greek, the language of the first Bible translation. A scribe wrote this on a sheet of papyrus—paper pressed from the spongy tubes inside stalks of reeds that grew beside lakes and rivers.

Thanks to Alexander, most Jews throughout the Middle East spoke Greek instead of their native language, Hebrew.

That was a problem. Imagine folks today having to make do with Bibles written in the obsolete language of the Roman Empire, Latin. That was Hebrew to most Jews.

The solution came from an Egyptian librarian at the ancient world's most famous library, in Alexandria, Egypt. The librarian sent a proposal to the king, Ptolemy II Philadelphus (285–246 BC): "The laws of the Jews are worth translating, and they deserve a place in your library."

Ptolemy, proud of his world-renown library, agreed.

He struck a deal with the high priest in Jerusalem, according to ancient reports. He would free his Jewish political prisoners if the high priest would loan him a team of 72 scholars—six from each of Israel's 12 tribes. These scholars would translate the Hebrew Bible into Greek, the international language of the day.

Deal.

The world's first-known Bible translation got tagged with the name Septuagint, from the Latin word *septuaginta*, which means "70."

Many historians say they doubt this story. They say the Septuagint has a lot of Alexandrian words and phrases, suggesting that Jewish scribes living in Egypt did most of the work.

The translators started with the most revered books in the Jewish Bible—the first five books: Genesis, Exodus, Leviticus, Numbers, and Deuteronomy. These books contain the heart of Jewish law and tradition.

Translation work continued off and on for centuries until the entire Jewish Bible was translated into Greek.

Scholars even added the Apocrypha, a collection of books that report Jewish history between the time of the Old and New Testament. These books also preserve wise sayings, prayers, and poetry.

The Apocrypha did not, however, make the cut when Jews put together a formal collection of their Bible. They didn't make the cut for Protestant Christians either. But these additional books do show up in Bibles of other Christian groups, including the Roman Catholic Church and the Eastern Orthodox Church.

10

JESUS ON A MISSION

TIMELINE *(dates are approximate)*

73 BC	Herod the Great is born.
63 BC	Romans occupy Jewish homeland.
40 BC	Roman senate declares Herod the Great king of Jews.
6 BC	Jesus is born.
4 BC	Herod dies.
AD 26	Pilate starts ten-year rule as Judea's governor.
AD 29 or 30	Jesus begins ministry.
AD 30 or as late as 33	Romans crucify Jesus.

Pilate (ruled AD 26–36)

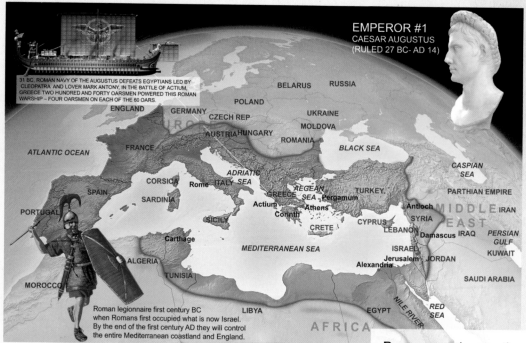

31 BC. ROMAN NAVY OF THE AUGUSTUS DEFEATS EGYPTIANS LED BY CLEOPATRA AND LOVER MARK ANTONY, IN THE BATTLE OF ACTIUM, GREECE. TWO HUNDRED AND FORTY OARSMEN POWERED THIS ROMAN WARSHIP – FOUR OARSMEN ON EACH OF THE 60 OARS.

Roman legionnaire first century BC when Romans first occupied what is now Israel. By the end of the first century AD they will control the entire Mediterranean coastland and England.

HEROD THE NOT-SO-GREAT
ARAB KING OF THE JEWS

Herod was furious when he realized that the wise men had outwitted him. He sent soldiers to kill all the boys in and around Bethlehem who were two years old and under.

MATTHEW 2:16

Romans snuck up on the Middle East. No one saw them coming, it seems. Roman legend says Rome was born in the mid-700s BC—founded by twin brothers Romulus and Remus. Early on, it was just a seven speed-bump burg. It existed as seven tiny settlements on seven neighboring hills. By the time of Jesus, Rome controlled most of the land framing the Mediterranean Sea.

I would rather be Herod's pig than his son."

That's a quote attributed to Caesar Augustus, though some historians seem to doubt he would have said that about a man he approved as king of the Jews.

Whoever said it, the line was a hoot. What made it funny is that it was true. Herod, a convert to the Jewish faith who observed Jewish traditions (at least outwardly), wouldn't kill a pig. Pigs weren't kosher. But he killed at least three of his sons, whom he suspected of plotting to take his job.

SUCKING UP TO ROMANS

Herod and his father rose to power in what is now Israel because they both got on the good side of the Romans, beginning as early as 63 BC, when General Pompey first invaded the Jewish homeland. The Roman senate declared him king of the Jews and loaned him an army to take control of the region. (Continued on page 153.)

Jerusalem temple. Herod's renovated and expanded Jewish temple dominated Jerusalem's cityscape, as seen in this large-scale model. The tourist in the foreground gets a view similar to the one people in Jesus's time would have seen while standing on the Mount of Olives, just across the narrow Kidron Valley. The temple's large courtyard, framed in pillared walkways, was open to Jews and non-Jews. But only Jews were allowed inside the central walled areas near the sanctuary building. Only priests were allowed inside the sanctuary building.

Roman road. A stretch of the Appian Way leading to Rome, this is a road the apostle Paul likely walked. Romans built a road system, mainly to make sure their army could quickly get from one place to another. In time, the road network covered about a quarter of a million miles (400,000 km) with about 50,000 miles (80,000 km) of it paved in stone. By comparison, the United States has about 47,000 miles (76,000 km) of interstate highway. When the Romans paved the roads with stone, they elevated the center of the road a tad so water drained to gutters at the sides.

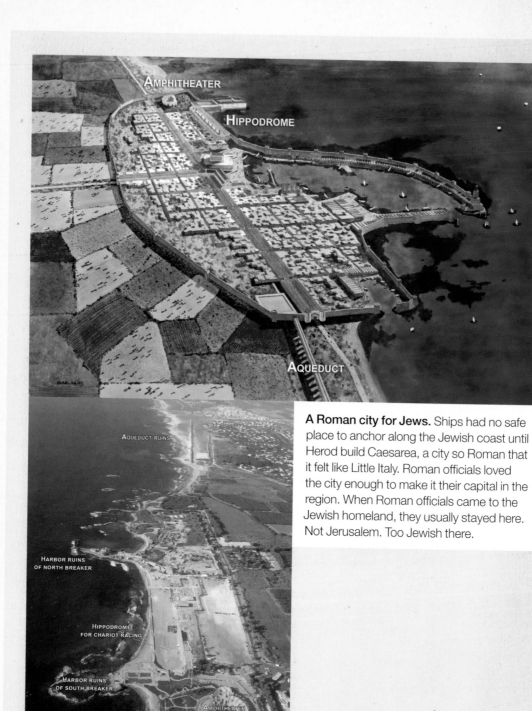

AMPHITHEATER

HIPPODROME

AQUEDUCT

AQUEDUCT RUINS

HARBOR RUINS
OF NORTH BREAKER

HIPPODROME
FOR CHARIOT RACING

HARBOR RUINS
OF SOUTH BREAKER

AMPHITHEATER

N

A Roman city for Jews. Ships had no safe place to anchor along the Jewish coast until Herod build Caesarea, a city so Roman that it felt like Little Italy. Roman officials loved the city enough to make it their capital in the region. When Roman officials came to the Jewish homeland, they usually stayed here. Not Jerusalem. Too Jewish there.

By race, Herod's family was Idumean. That's Greek for the Hebrew word Edomite. Herod's ancestors came from the kingdom of Edom in what is now Jordan. Invaders drove them west, into the Jewish homeland, as refugees.

HEROD, A BUILDER ON STEROIDS

Herod seemed compelled to build a nation fit for a king—him.

Roman-style cities, aqueducts to carry water into the cities, hilltop fortresses, luxurious palaces, sprawling temples...he built them all.

His most state-of-the-art project was the port city of Caesarea, which he smartly named after Caesar Augustus. (If the emperor's not happy, nobody's happy.) Herod did such a fantastic job of shaping it into a Roman city that the Romans would use it as their capital of the region for more than 600 years.

Herod built the city and harbor for the money he thought they would bring once ships started showing up. He was right about that. Before Herod, the Jewish homeland didn't have a harbor where boats could drop anchor and find protection against surging waves.

Herod built the Caesarea harbor with massive stones, each one about the size of a tractor-semitrailer rig. First-century historian Josephus said each stone measured about 50 feet long, 18 feet high, and 9 feet wide (15 by 5 by 3 m).

Archaeologists say that Herod's engineers—possibly the best in the Roman Empire—also used hydraulic concrete, history's first-known use of this technique. They built wooden frames where the protective walls would go. Then they filled those frames with the concrete mixture, similar to Portland cement—paste-like mortar, rocks, sand, and a binder, such as lime or gypsum.

The harbor, perhaps the most impressive of its time, wowed the Romans. So did the city of Caesarea, built on a Roman-style grid pattern. This town, destined to become the largest in the Judean province, had it all.

- aqueduct, channeling spring water from Mount Carmel ten miles north (16 km)
- sewage system, flushing out the bad water
- theater for shows
- forum for meetings
- hippodrome for chariot races
- Roman public baths, a bit like the pool and gym at the YMCA
- temples for Romans
- synagogues for Jews

As impressive as Caesarea and its harbor were, Herod's show-stopping feat was his makeover of the Jewish temple in Jerusalem. A project 80 years in the making, he started it in 20 BC. Work continued long after his death—wrapping up in AD 62.

Of all the Jewish temples that ever existed, Herod's was the biggest and most breathtaking. Sadly, it was also the shortest-lived. Eight years and dead. Romans leveled it when they crushed a Jewish revolt in AD 70.

Before Herod, the temple had been a modest one. Former Jewish refugees built it about 500 years earlier, after they got back from exile in what is now Iraq. They didn't have much money then.

Herod wanted to turn this temple into one of the biggest in the world. He did just that. Archaeologists rank it number two behind the temple complex in Karnak, Egypt.

Jerusalem's hilltop wasn't big enough to

accommodate Herod's vision for the temple. No problem. He made the hilltop bigger. He brought in fill dirt to extend the flat platform on top. He shored up the sides of that extension with retaining walls built of huge stones.

One of those retaining walls has survived. It's the most sacred spot on earth for Jews. They call it the Western Wall. Some folks call it the Wailing Wall, a nickname most Jews don't like.

This wall is a place of prayer for the Jewish people. It's as close to their temple as they can get because what rests on the hilltop now is a 1300-year-old Muslim shrine—Jerusalem's most famous landmark, the Dome of the Rock.

Divorce by execution. King Herod imposes the death sentence on his wife, Miriamne, the mother of his four children. He seems to suspect that Miriamne, a Hasmonean princess, is trying to resurrect her Jewish family dynasty. Herod later regrets his decision so much that he names his next wife Miriamne II. Which must have been great for her self-esteem.

ALEXANDRIA

EGYPT   CAIRO   GOSHEN
   RAMESES

SINAI PENINSULA

MEDITERRANEAN SEA

BETHLEHEM-ALEXANDRIA
375 M (600 KM)

JOSEPH: BUILDER
HOMETOWN: NAZARETH

GAZA

JESUS: BORN IN BETHLEHEM

HEBRON

BETHLEHEM   JERUSALEM   ISRAEL
   BETHANY   BETHEL

DEAD SEA

JUDEAN HILL ROUTE
NAZARETH-BETHLEHEM
80 M (130 KM)

JERICHO
   SHECHEM   SAMARIA
   (NABLUS)

MEGIDDO

JEZREEL VALLEY

NAZARETH

JORDAN RIVER

JORDAN RIVER ROUTE
NAZARETH-BETHLEHEM 90 M (145 KM)

900 MILES (1450 KM) ROUND-TRIP

N

JORDAN

BABY JESUS
FROM BETHLEHEM TO EGYPT

Jesus was born in Bethlehem in Judea,
during the reign of King Herod.

MATTHEW 2:1

Bethlehem bound. Nazareth locals Joseph and very pregnant Mary walk south to Bethlehem to register for a Roman-ordered census. They may have traveled the most direct route, along the crest of the Judean hills. Or they may have taken the longer route through the Jordan River Valley. When King Herod ordered baby boys in Bethlehem killed, Joseph took Mary and young Jesus somewhere in Egypt—possibly to Alexandria, home to a large community of Jews. The family moved back to Nazareth after Herod died.

Jesus's birth story could have been worse for him. God could have named him Sue.

Life as a boy named Sue might seem to have fit nicely into the mix of other hardships the Bible writers say Jesus faced from the get-go.

- tagged as what folks today might call illegitimate because when his mother got pregnant, she was only "engaged to be married" (Luke 1:27)

- born in a barn, or what passed as one, and forced to sleep in a poor excuse of a crib—a "feeding box" (Luke 2:12 NCV)

- introduced to the world by society's bottom-dwellers—shepherds, who were about as classy as a birth announcement on a Waffle House napkin

- targeted for execution by paranoid King Herod, who was trying to protect his family dynasty from threat of a coup by someone Jews might think fulfilled prophecies about the coming Messiah, king of the Jews

Reading Jesus's story, newcomers to the Bible are left wondering why God didn't make more fitting arrangements for the birth of his own Son. Yet as the story unfolds, most Christians say they see God all over the details in glorious fashion—protecting Jesus and making the point that he cares about everyone, rich and poor. Especially the poor.

THE ANNOUNCEMENT: IT'S A BOY

Gospels Matthew and Luke both report that an angel told Mary—a Nazareth virgin engaged to a carpenter named Joseph—that she was going to give birth to "the Son of God" (Luke 1:35).

That was news to her fiancé.

When Joseph found out Mary was pregnant, "He decided to break the engagement quietly" (Matthew 1:19). An angel convinced him otherwise, appearing to him in a dream and explaining that Mary's child "was conceived by the Holy Spirit…For he will save his people from their sins" (Matthew 1:20-21).

Matthew said this fulfilled a 700-year-old prophecy from Isaiah:

> Look! The virgin will conceive a child!
> She will give birth to a son,
> and they will call him Immanuel,
> which means "God is with us" (Matthew 1:23).

That link to Isaiah is a bit of a stretch, many Bible experts agree. They say Isaiah was talking

THE GOOD NEWS GOSPELS

Almost everything we know about Jesus comes from four books in the Bible: Matthew, Mark, Luke, and John.

Gospels. That's what Bible aficionados call these books. The word comes from the Old English term *god-spell*. It means "good news."

These books are not biographies of Jesus. If they were, we would know more about him. A good biography would tell us what he looked like, what kind of house he lived in, what kind of education he got, and what he did for a living during the one or two decades of his adult years, before he started his ministry.

We get none of that in these books. Only Matthew and Luke even bother to briefly mention the astonishing circumstances around his birth. Mark and John skip those, as though they are no big deal compared to what they have to say about him.

What we get are stories about his short ministry of two or three years—stories that make the case that Jesus was not only the Messiah but also the Son of God.

Born in a barn. This Nativity scene, chiseled in stone during the AD 500s, is one of the oldest pictures of Baby Jesus. He's resting in a feeding trough. One physician from Jesus's time, Soranus, said a feeding trough made an excellent crib because it was tilted, which allowed the baby to rest with its head slightly elevated for easier breathing.

about a child born in his time to a "young woman" (Isaiah 7:14 NRSV). Only the Greek edition of the Hebrew Bible translated "young woman" as "virgin." Isaiah was not necessarily talking about a virgin. The Hebrew word he used could go either way—young woman or virgin. But the Greek word that Matthew used meant "virgin."

Some Bible experts say Matthew went a bit overboard in trying to show that Jesus fulfilled Old Testament prophecies about the Messiah-king who would save Israel. Matthew links Jesus to about 60 of those—twice as many as the runner-up Gospel, Mark, which has about 30.

Yet many scholars say Isaiah's prophecy seems tailored for a double shift whether Isaiah knew it or not. They say his prediction works on both timelines—in Isaiah's day in the 700s BC and in the time of Christ.

BETHLEHEM OR BUST

Nine months pregnant doesn't seem like the ideal time for an 80-mile (130 km) hike from one end of the Judean hills to the other. Or 90 miles (145 km) through the gentler Jordan River Valley.

Either way, it's normally a walk of four or five days. But anyone who has ever traveled long-distance with a pregnant woman knows that normal is not normal.

As Luke tells the story, Joseph had no choice about making the trip. He had to report to his ancestral hometown for a census ordered by the Roman emperor, presumably to help Romans get an idea about how much tax money they could expect from the Jews.

Some Bible experts say Luke probably got that part of the history wrong. They suggest several reasons.

- There's no record of the Romans ordering this census.

- Luke said the census was taken "when Quirinius was governor of Syria" (Luke 2:2). Roman records say Quirinius was not governor of Syria until a decade later, AD 6–7.

- Romans counted people where they lived. They didn't order them to go back to where their ancestors used to live.

Some Bible experts defending Luke's account say Quirinius may have served two terms as governor. And they speculate that tradition-minded Jewish leaders may have made the recommendation to Romans that it would be best for Jews to go back to their ancestral home to be counted.

Joseph and Mary got to Bethlehem just in time to increase the census by one.

"There was no lodging available for them" (Luke 2:7), possibly because of the swarm of people who came for the census. An ancient tradition said Jesus was born in one of the many caves in the area that people used as homes or barns. Bethlehem's Church of the Nativity—Christianity's oldest surviving church, built in the AD 300s immediately after Romans legalized Christianity—is built over what remains of that cave. Pilgrims visit the cave by going down steps that seem to be leading into a basement. But it's a cave.

Baby Jesus's first visitors were not regal dignitaries worthy of an audience with a newborn prince. They were shepherds from a nearby field, alerted to the birth by an angel "joined by a vast host of others—the armies of heaven—praising God" (Luke 2:13).

Shepherds were the opposite of regal dignitaries. When it came to social status, shepherds were a challenged lot. Maybe a bit like garbage

collectors today—important to society, but not a job to brag about over shrimp cocktails.

Yet God put them at the front of the line. That's how most Bible experts interpret the story. They say the entire saga of Jesus's birth is scripted to throw a spotlight on God's concern for people who are poor and struggling to survive. The honor of basking in "the radiance of the Lord's glory" (Luke 2:9) goes to…

- a humble carpenter ordered by Roman occupiers to take his pregnant wife on a long march
- a peasant woman giving birth in a barn
- shepherds working the night shift

Jupiter, Saturn, Pisces Constellation

STAR OF BETHLEHEM?

This was Jerusalem's night sky in 7 BC, looking south toward Bethlehem, according to some stargazers. Many Bible experts say the star of Bethlehem may have been a lining up of Jupiter and Saturn alongside the Pisces constellation.

- Jupiter represents kings because Jupiter is the Roman name for the king of gods (Zeus to the Greeks).

- Saturn represents Jews because they worship on Saturday, the day devoted to the god Saturn.

- Pisces refers to the Jewish homeland because Pisces is the Greek word for "fish." It represented the land around the Mediterranean Sea, including the Jewish homeland.

As the theory goes, "wise men from eastern lands" (Matthew 2:1) would have put the pieces of this puzzle together and figured the Jews were about to get a new king. That might explain why the wise men did not go directly to Bethlehem, but went instead to the capital of the Jewish nation, Jerusalem.

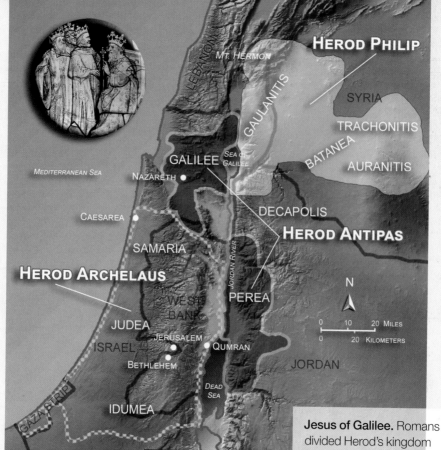

HEROD PHILIP

MT. HERMON

LEBANON

GAULANITIS

SYRIA

TRACHONITIS

BATANEA

AURANITIS

GALILEE
SEA OF GALILEE

MEDITERRANEAN SEA

NAZARETH

DECAPOLIS

CAESAREA

HEROD ANTIPAS

SAMARIA

JORDAN RIVER

HEROD ARCHELAUS

PEREA

N

WEST BANK

JUDEA

0   10   20 MILES
0   20 KILOMETERS

JERUSALEM

QUMRAN

ISRAEL

BETHLEHEM

JORDAN

DEAD SEA

GAZA STRIP

IDUMEA

HOLY LAND

ISRAEL DURING JESUS'S MINISTRY

Tiberius Caesar had been ruling for 15 years.
Pontius Pilate was governor of Judea. Herod
was the ruler of Galilee. His brother Philip
was the ruler of Iturea and Traconitis.

LUKE 3:1 NIRV

Jesus of Galilee. Romans divided Herod's kingdom among his three sons. But they fired Herod Archelaus after ten years because he kept riling up the locals. Romans appointed governors, called prefects, like Pontius Pilate to rule the south-land territory. Prefects reported to the regional governor, who lived in what is now Syria. Jesus spent most of his two or three years of ministry in Galilee, a land ruled by Herod Antipas, the man who executed John the Baptist at a birthday party.

When Herod the Great died, Romans split his kingdom between his three sons—and regretted it.

Herod Archelaus: 18-year-old wannabe king (reigned 4 BC–AD 6). Archelaus inherited the throne to rule over the main part of the Jewish homeland—Judea, Samaria, and Idumea. But when he presented himself for approval to Caesar Augustus, the emperor demoted him to *ethnarch,* "ruler of the people." Not quite a king.

Herod Antipas: John the Baptist killer (reigned 4 BC–AD 39). Antipas inherited Galilee, where Jesus lived in Israel's northland. He also got a narrow string of land called Perea along the east bank of the Jordan River in what is now the Arab country of Jordan. His title was tetrarch, or "governor of a fourth." Romans had divided the Jewish homeland four ways among Herod's three sons: half to the oldest son, a fourth to Antipas, and a fourth to Philip.

Antipas married his brother Philip's ex-wife, a lady who apparently considered Antipas a husband upgrade. Antipas probably considered the marriage a political upgrade. Herodias was a Hasmonean princess, granddaughter of Herod the Great's wife, Miriamne. That marriage linked Antipas to Jewish rulers during Israel's age of independence, before Romans arrived.

When the prophet John the Baptist called the marriage an incestuous violation of Jewish law, the little lady took issue. Then she took his head.

Herod Philip I: wife left him for his younger brother (reigned 4 BC–AD 34). Philip, also known as Herod II, got what is now the Golan Heights area, northeast of the Sea of Galilee. First-century Jewish historian Josephus described him as mild-mannered and approachable.

"Boring," his wife Herodias may have said. She left him for his richer brother, Antipas, who ruled a more lucrative region. Philip's people were mostly nomads. But Antipas's Galilee had lots of cities and farms.

JOHN THE BAPTIST: PROPHET WITHOUT A HEAD

Rich kid grows up and renounces the rich life. That might describe John the Baptist, son of Jerusalem priest Zechariah.

John might have been a priest too, living the cushy life of a man drawing a regular salary from his share of temple offerings. Instead, "he lived in the wilderness until he began his public ministry to Israel" (Luke 1:80).

John inaugurated Jesus's ministry by baptizing him, at Jesus's request.

Bible writers report that the ruler of Galilee, Herod Antipas, beheaded John. First-century historian Josephus confirmed the story in his history of the Jews. He added this:

Some Jews thought the destruction of Herod's army [in a battle with Herod's ex-father-in-law, who was livid about Herod divorcing his daughter to marry Herodias] was God's punishment for what he did to John, called the Baptist. Herod killed him. John was a good man who encouraged the Jews to respect each other, to honor God, and to get baptized.

Getting a head. Salome waits with a platter for the head of John the Baptist. It's her prize for dancing so well at a birthday party for her stepfather, Herod Antipas. Herod told her to make a wish. She consulted her mother, Herodias, who hated John for condemning her marriage as incest. She wanted his head. Herod didn't want to kill John. But more than that, he didn't want to "lose face with his guests" (Matthew 14:9 MSG). So John lost his head.

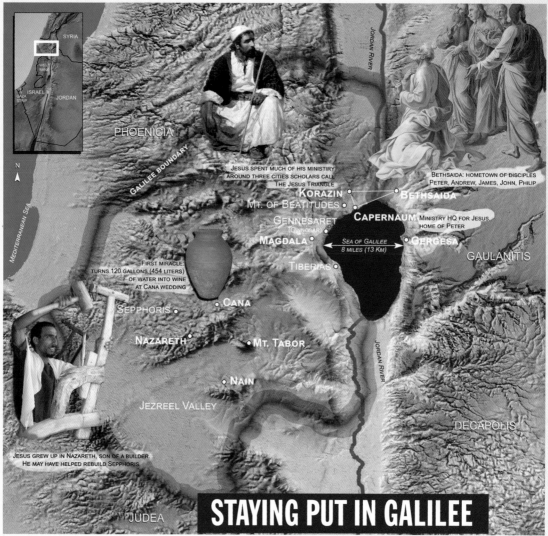

PHOENICIA

MEDITERRANEAN SEA

N

GALILEE BOUNDARY

JORDAN RIVER

JESUS SPENT MUCH OF HIS MINISTRY
AROUND THREE CITIES SCHOLARS CALL
THE JESUS TRIANGLE

KORAZIN

MT. OF BEATITUDES

GENNESARET
(GINNOSAR)

MAGDALA

BETHSAIDA

BETHSAIDA: HOMETOWN OF DISCIPLES
PETER, ANDREW, JAMES, JOHN, PHILIP

CAPERNAUM MINISTRY HQ FOR JESUS,
HOME OF PETER

SEA OF GALILEE
8 MILES (13 KM)

GERGESA

GAULANITIS

TIBERIAS

FIRST MIRACLE:
TURNS 120 GALLONS (454 LITERS)
OF WATER INTO WINE
AT CANA WEDDING

SEPPHORIS

CANA

NAZARETH

MT. TABOR

NAIN

JORDAN RIVER

JEZREEL VALLEY

DECAPOLIS

JESUS GREW UP IN NAZARETH, SON OF A BUILDER.
HE MAY HAVE HELPED REBUILD SEPPHORIS

JUDEA

STAYING PUT IN GALILEE
JESUS'S SEASIDE MISSION

*Jesus traveled throughout the region of Galilee, teaching in
the synagogues and announcing the Good News about the
Kingdom. And he healed every kind of disease and illness.*

MATTHEW 4:23

Not a big traveler, Jesus made a name for himself by staying close to home. Very close.

As Bible writers tell it, he seems to have done most of his teaching and healing within
about a one-hour walk of his ministry headquarters in the fishing village of Capernaum, on
the north shore of a lake known as the Sea of Galilee. The leader of his disciples, Peter, owned a
house there.

Some Bible experts describe Jesus's main mission field as a tiny plug of ground—a triangle anchored by three neighboring cities: Capernaum, Korazin, about two miles (4 km) north, and Bethsaida, about four miles (6 km) east.

Why Jesus spent most of his ministry in his hometown region of Galilee is anyone's guess. But the location tracks nicely with a line from a poem by Isaiah, a man from 700 years before Jesus who had so many prophecies seemingly fulfilled by Jesus that some scholars call the book of Isaiah "the fifth Gospel."

> There will be a time in the future when Galilee…will be filled with glory. The people who walk in darkness will see a great light (Isaiah 9:1-2).

THIRTY-SOMETHING JESUS LAUNCHES HIS MISSION

Bible writers say almost nothing about what Jesus did during his first 30-something years. Son of a builder, Jesus likely helped his dad with the family business—perhaps working on construction projects in neighboring Sepphoris, a city an hour's walk away that was being rebuilt during Jesus's growing-up years. Romans had burned it in 4 BC, crushing a Jewish revolt. Herod Antipas, Galilee's ruler, ordered it rebuilt into one of the most beautiful cities in Galilee—a project that took a couple of decades.

Here's to the bride and groom. At a wedding in Cana, the wine runs out. Jesus's mother convinces him to produce some. He tells servants to fill six jugs with water—a total of at least 120 gallons (454 liters). He turns it all into fine wine—enough for more than 1000 people to get drunk by today's measure of drunkenness. Weddings, however, typically lasted for about a week. Wine needed to last that long too.

Jesus launched his ministry perhaps a year or more after John the Baptist started his in "the fifteenth year of the reign of Tiberius" (Luke 3:1)—about AD 28 or 29.

"Jesus was about thirty years old when he began his public ministry" (Luke 3:23). He was at least 33 because he was born before Herod the Great died in 4 BC. Possibly as old as 37.

"Thirty," many Bible experts say, was the traditional Jewish way of saying a man was mature—thinking with a brain nicely aged with insight. Age 30 is when King David started his reign (2 Samuel 5:4) and when

Joseph started working for the king of Egypt (Genesis 41:46).

Jesus began his ministry after...

- baptism in the Jordan River by John the Baptist

- a 40-day stretch of prayer and fasting in the nearby Judean badlands, just west of Jordan's river valley

"Forty days" (Luke 4:2) is a round number that many Bible experts say means a long time. In this case, the writer may have intended

GALILEE

Good to grow. As in the time of Jesus, farms still texture Galilee's landscape, pictured here in the fertile Jezreel Valley at the foot of knobby Mount Tabor in the distance, center.

SPECS FROM A FIRST-CENTURY ROMAN BOOK

- *Villages:* 204
- *Souls:* 15,000
- *Footprint:* 1000 square miles (1600 sq km), double the size of Greater Nashville or Los Angeles
- *Character:* "Surrounded by so many foreign nations, Galileans have been hardened by war since childhood. They are never short of courage and always put up a strong resistance in wartime."
- *Work:* "The soil is so rich that even the laziest person could make a living at farming. The land is full of farms and fruit tree orchards. Farmers work all of the land. They don't leave any part of it idle."

JOSEPHUS (AD 37–100),
ANTIQUITIES OF THE JEWS

Crowds still come. Tourists visit the Chapel of the Beatitudes on the crest of a hill above the Sea of Galilee. An old tradition says Jesus preached his most famous sermon on this hilltop, which is less than a mile from his Capernaum mission headquarters.

to link Jesus to Moses, who spent 40 years in the badlands. Some scholars say they see Bible writers portraying Jesus as the new Moses who came to replace the old Jewish laws Moses delivered. Serving his disciples wine at their last meal, Jesus said, "This cup is the new covenant between God and his people—an agreement confirmed with my blood, which is poured out as a sacrifice for you" (Luke 22:20).

Bible experts disagree on exactly when Jesus started his ministry and how long it lasted. One popular guess is that Jesus started in AD 29. Crucifixion: sometime between AD 30 and 33.

DISCIPLES: THE B-TEAM

It's odd that Jesus picked any disciples at all, many scholars say. Normally it worked the other way around. Jewish disciples picked their rabbis in much the same way doctoral students today choose professors under whom they want to study.

What's even odder is the 12-man team Jesus put together. Not quite the A-team by any measure of men other than whatever measuring tape Jesus used.

Jesus apparently didn't require biblical savvy. The dicey dozen didn't seem to have much of that—even after spending somewhere between one and three years with Jesus. After Jesus's crucifixion and resurrection, Peter and John, the most articulate disciples, appeared before the top Jewish council. The scholars were amazed at the bravery of the two, but "they could see that they were ordinary men with no special training in the Scriptures" (Acts 4:13).

No wonder. At least four disciples—brothers Peter and Andrew, along with brothers James and John—were fishermen, better with worms than words.

Matthew was a tax collector—a professional traitor, as far as many Jews were concerned. Taxmen collaborated with the Roman occupiers by bidding for tax jobs. Highest bidder got to collect taxes from their fellow Jews.

Simon was a Zealot, possibly referring to the political group of militant Jews trying to force out the Romans by assassinating them and their Jewish collaborators. If that guess about Simon is right, he and Matthew probably didn't start out as besties.

JESUS'S SURPRISE TEACHINGS

So it's fair to say Jesus didn't act like your normal rabbi. He didn't sound like one either. He didn't go around reciting Jewish laws and quoting what long-dead Jewish rabbis had to say about those laws. "The crowds were amazed at his teaching, for he taught with real authority—quite unlike their teachers of religious law" (Matthew 7:28-29).

Jesus didn't seem to waste much time retelling familiar stories or talking about abstract philosophy and vague religious principles. If he did, the Gospel writers didn't seem to remember much of it.

What the writers did remember are the stories Jesus told. Parables, Bible experts call them. They were down-to-earth stories with spiritual messages, a bit like many Hallmark movies. But shorter, and often with a surprise ending—not always a happy one.

More than anyone else in the Bible, Jesus seemed to love telling these stories. What he talked about most: the kingdom of God.

JESUS IN ROMAN HISTORY BOOKS

Jesus wasn't a make-believe person who shows up only in the Bible. He shows up in Roman history too.

A GOOD MAN

There was a wise man called Jesus, a good person who could work wonders…He attracted many followers—Jews and non-Jews. Pilate, at the request of our [Jewish] leaders, sentenced him to death by crucifixion…Jesus's disciples remained loyal to him. They told people that Jesus appeared to them three days after his crucifixion, and that he was alive…The brother of Jesus, called the Christ, was James.

JOSEPHUS (AD 37–100),
ANTIQUITIES OF THE JEWS

CRUCIFIED

Nero blamed the fire that destroyed much of Rome on a group of people he found so disgusting

that he ordered them tortured in horrifying ways. They were Christians. They got their name from Christus [Christ], a man who suffered the ultimate penalty at the hands of a procurator, Pontius Pilate, when Tiberius was emperor of Rome.

TACITUS (ABOUT AD 55–120),
ANNALS OF IMPERIAL ROME

TROUBLEMAKER

Emperor Claudius expelled Jews from Rome because Chrestus [Christ] got them so upset that they were constantly causing public disturbances.*

SUETONIUS (AD 70–130),
LIVES OF THE TWELVE CAESARS

* Possible link to the Bible: "Aquila had come from Italy with his wife Priscilla, because Emperor Claudius had ordered the Jewish people to leave Rome" (Acts 18:2 CEV).

PARABLES

THE MOST AUTHENTIC WORDS OF JESUS

At Sunday lunch, if someone asked us what the preacher said in the sermon that morning, we might not remember anything except the illustrations. Stories are easiest to remember because they aren't abstract. They paint pictures in our heads. Jesus told powerfully engaging stories to illustrate how people should live as citizens of God's kingdom.

Even the most skeptical Bible scholars—those who say Bible writers probably misquoted Jesus a lot—agree that the parables Jesus told contain some of the most authentic quotes in the Bible.

In perhaps his most famous parable of all, Jesus said a Jewish man got mugged while walking on a trail in the middle of nowhere, between Jericho and Jerusalem. In this fictional tale, two Jewish worship leaders walked right past the injured man as if he were invisible. The person who finally stopped to help him was a Samaritan—a local race of people whose intense animosity with the Jews rivaled that of today's Palestinians with Israelis.

Jericho road. Riding donkeys, two travelers wind their way up toward Jerusalem from Jericho. This is the barren setting for Jesus's famous parable about a Good Samaritan helping a lone traveler who got mugged and robbed on the 14-mile (23 km) stretch through the badlands between Jericho and Jerusalem.

Jesus told this parable as a way of answering a Jewish scholar's question about the law that says Jews should help their neighbors. The scholar wanted to know who qualifies as a neighbor. Some Jews taught that this law refers only to helping fellow Jews.

After Jesus told the story of the Samaritan saving the Jewish man, he asked the scholar, "Which of these three would you say was a neighbor to the man who was attacked by bandits?"

"The one who showed him mercy," the man replied.

Jesus said, "Yes, now go and do the same" (Luke 10:36-37).

Last-second zingers like that were a common feature of the parables Jesus told. One more reason they were easy to remember.

- "Jesus said, 'How can I describe the Kingdom of God? What story should I use to illustrate it?'" (Mark 4:30).

- "One day the Pharisees asked Jesus, 'When will the Kingdom of God come?' Jesus replied, 'The Kingdom of God can't be detected by visible signs. You won't be able to say, "Here it is!" or "It's over there!" For the Kingdom of God is already among you'" (Luke 17:20-21).

- "Seek the Kingdom of God above all else, and live righteously, and he will give you everything you need" (Matthew 6:33).

Even with everything Jesus said about the kingdom of God, Bible experts debate what he meant by it. Some say he was talking about life in Israel after the Romans left. Some say he was talking about life after death.

But at the moment most seem to say he was talking about neither of those. Not a place on a map. Not a place in a celestial dimension.

Instead, Jesus was saying that God's kingdom is wherever God's people are—people who pledge their allegiance to him and try to live their lives in a way that would please him. People in this life. People in the next.

As Jesus taught it—probably to the great surprise of most Jewish scholars of his day—God's kingdom is here and now. And God's kingdom will be then and there. It's not waiting on a Messiah to rally the Jews, drive out the Romans, and restore the glory of King David's Israel.

Jesus's most famous sermon, the Sermon on the Mount, sums up the heart of his message about what it means to be a citizen in God's kingdom. It's a message that clearly portrays him as anything but a warrior-Messiah: "Love your enemies! Pray for those who persecute you!" (Matthew 5:44).

HEALING: THE MAIN ATTRACTION

Jesus knew that his miracles were the main attraction. And at times, that seemed to frustrate him.

- When a man asked him to come and heal his son, Jesus replied, "Will you never believe in me unless you see miraculous signs and wonders?" (John 4:48).

- After feeding a crowd of 5000, Jesus said, "You want to be with me because I fed you, not because you understood the miraculous signs" (John 6:26).

But as long as he healed people and performed creation-style miracles, such as turning water into wine, the people kept coming. And when they came, he kept teaching them.

His teachings were so extraordinary and seemingly impossible at times—"be perfect" (Matthew 5:48)—that people may not have swarmed him the way they did had he not performed miracles of healing people.

Crowds seemed to follow him wherever he went. Once, when he sat down on a hillside by the Sea of Galilee, "a vast crowd brought to him people who were lame, blind, crippled, those who couldn't speak, and many others. They laid them before Jesus, and he healed them all" (Matthew 15:30).

DR. JESUS

PHYSICIAN WITH A ROMAN TOUCH

Roman science writer Pliny (AD 23–79), who died in the eruption of Mount Vesuvius, recorded a long list of medical treatments used in the time of Christ. Some of these treatments, preserved in Pliny's 37-volume *Natural History*, add evidence to back up stories about Jesus healing people.

MENSTRUAL BLEEDING

A woman in the crowd had suffered for twelve years with constant bleeding. She had suffered a great deal from many doctors, and over the years she had spent everything she had to pay them, but she had gotten no better. In fact, she had gotten worse.

MARK 5:25-26

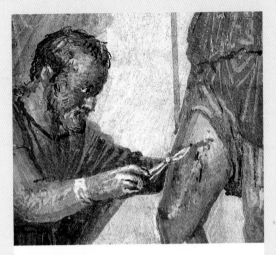

You'll feel a little sting. A wall painting recovered from Pompeii, a Roman city destroyed in the AD 79 eruption of Mount Vesuvius, shows a physician using forceps to remove an arrowhead buried in a soldier's thigh.

Docs today say they suspect the woman Jesus healed had suffered from menorrhagia, which produces prolonged, heavy menstrual bleeding. *Natural History* lists dozens of treatments for that very problem—more than enough to bleed a woman of her life's savings. Here's a sampling.

- *Crush a jellyfish, apply topically.* Ouch—physically and financially. Where's an inland farmer to get a jellyfish?

- *Mix ashes of a horse's head with vinegar, apply topically.* Yuck. And a horse's head doesn't sound cheap.

MUD IN THE EYE

He [Jesus] spit on the ground, made mud with the saliva, and spread the mud over the blind man's eyes.

JOHN 9:6

Like Jesus, Romans used spit and mud to treat eye problems. Excerpts from *Natural History*:

- "To cure inflammation of the eyes, wash the eyes each morning with spit from your overnight fast."

- "To protect your eyes from developing eye diseases…Each time you wash dust off your feet, touch your eyes three times with the muddy water."

JESUS ON THE ROAD
OUTSIDE GALILEE'S COMFORT ZONE

Jesus left Galilee and went north to the region of Tyre. He didn't want anyone to know which house he was staying in, but he couldn't keep it a secret.

MARK 7:24

Welcome to Bethany. In Bethany, a village on the outskirts of Jerusalem, Jesus visits the home of Mary, Martha, and their brother Lazarus, whom Jesus had recently raised from the dead. Deeply grateful, Mary breaks open a 12-ounce (327 g) jar of expensive perfume. "She anointed Jesus' feet with it, wiping his feet with her hair" (John 12:3).

Jesus took his miracles and teachings on the road from time to time, sometimes with unsettling results. Case in point: "Jesus left Galilee and went north to the region of Tyre" (Mark 7:24). That was about a two-day walk, some 35 miles (55 km) to the Mediterranean coast in what is now Lebanon.

The unsettling part for many readers is the quote from Jesus to a woman asking for his help. The woman had apparently heard of his ability to heal people. She came to him, dropped at his feet, and begged him to exorcise a demon that had possessed her daughter.

In what seems a bigoted and heartless reply, Jesus tells her, "First I should feed the children—my own family, the Jews. It isn't right to take food from the children and throw it to the dogs."

A sharp wit, the woman replied "That's true, Lord, but even the dogs under the table are allowed to eat the scraps from the children's plates."

"Good answer!" Jesus said. "Now go home, for the demon has left your daughter" (Mark 7:27-29).

Jesus was no bigot, most Bible experts agree. Had he been unwilling to help non-Jews, they explain, he would not have taken his ministry on the road to Gentile territories. One theory is that he knew what the woman would say, so he was giving her a voice and essentially turning this scene into a living parable with a message: God cares as much about Gentiles as he does about Jews. He heals them both.

When the woman returned home, she found her daughter lying quietly. "The demon was gone" (Mark 7:30).

From there, Jesus traveled another day's walk north to the area near the coastal city of Sidon before doubling back to the east side of the Sea of Galilee, what is now the Golan Heights. But in his day it was a Roman province called Ten Cities (Greek: Decapolis) on Rome's eastern border, mainly in what is now the Arab countries of Jordan and Syria.

There, he healed a deaf man with a speech impediment. "Jesus…put his fingers into the man's ears. Then, spitting on his own fingers, he touched the man's tongue. Looking up to heaven, he sighed and said…'Be opened!'" (Mark 7:33-34).

One of his most famous miracles in the Ten Cities area outside Jewish territory was the exorcism of a man possessed by so many demons that they called themselves Legion (Mark 5:9). That word is Latin, Rome's preferred language. It referred to a military unit with 3000 to 6000 infantry reinforced with cavalry.

Jesus didn't just exorcise the demons, casting them out to who knows where. At their request, he sent them into a herd of about 2000 pigs (Mark 5:13). Pigs gone wild, they charged down a steep hillside, fell into the lake, and drowned. The fall must have killed them—pigs can swim.

The pig herder, suddenly herdless, ran to a nearby town, where he herded up a crowd of humans. The people followed the herder to Jesus. When they saw him and the healed man, they were more terrified than impressed. They asked Jesus to leave, which he did, returning to his ministry base at Capernaum.

JESUS HEADS TO THE BIG CITY

It's tough to figure out how many times Jesus went to Jerusalem during his stretch of ministry. Bible experts can't even agree on how long that stretch of ministry was—one year or more. But at some point, Jesus seemed to get fed up with people in the Jesus Triangle between the villages of Korazin, Bethsaida, and Capernaum.

> What sorrow awaits you, Korazin and Bethsaida! For if the miracles I did in you had been done in wicked Tyre and Sidon, their people would have repented of their sins long ago…And you people of Capernaum, will you be honored in heaven? No, you will go down to the place of the dead (Luke 10:13-15).

The people heard his teachings and saw his miracles, but they didn't change the way they lived. It was time for Jesus to move on. Jerusalem ahead.

Along the way, Jesus continued to teach and heal the people who crowded around him.

Jewish leaders at the top of the theological food chain had been scouting him like a rival they needed to take down. They didn't like what they saw in him any more than he liked what he saw in them.

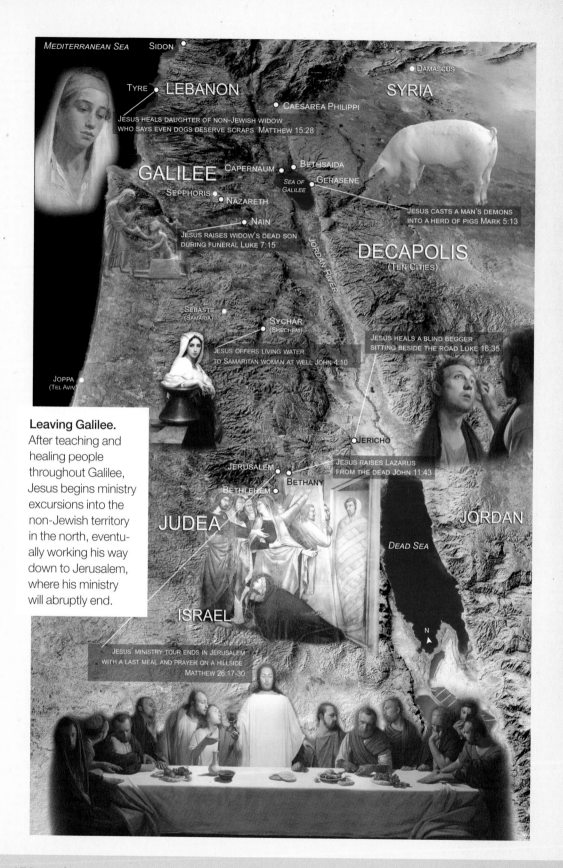

MEDITERRANEAN SEA   SIDON •

DAMASCUS •

TYRE • LEBANON

SYRIA

CAESAREA PHILIPPI •

JESUS HEALS DAUGHTER OF NON-JEWISH WIDOW
WHO SAYS EVEN DOGS DESERVE SCRAPS MATTHEW 15:28

GALILEE   CAPERNAUM •   • BETHSAIDA

SEPPHORIS •   • NAZARETH

SEA OF
GALILEE   • GERASENE

JESUS CASTS A MAN'S DEMONS
INTO A HERD OF PIGS MARK 5:13

• NAIN

JESUS RAISES WIDOW'S DEAD SON
DURING FUNERAL LUKE 7:15

JORDAN RIVER

DECAPOLIS
(TEN CITIES)

SEBASTE
(SAMARIA) •

• SYCHAR
(SHECHEM)

JESUS OFFERS LIVING WATER
TO SAMARITAN WOMAN AT WELL JOHN 4:10

JESUS HEALS A BLIND BEGGER
SITTING BESIDE THE ROAD LUKE 18:35

JOPPA •
(TEL AVIV)

• JERICHO

Leaving Galilee.
After teaching and
healing people
throughout Galilee,
Jesus begins ministry
excursions into the
non-Jewish territory
in the north, eventu-
ally working his way
down to Jerusalem,
where his ministry
will abruptly end.

JERUSALEM •

JESUS RAISES LAZARUS
FROM THE DEAD JOHN 11:43

• BETHANY

BETHLEHEM •

JUDEA

JORDAN

DEAD SEA

N

ISRAEL

JESUS' MINISTRY TOUR ENDS IN JERUSALEM
WITH A LAST MEAL AND PRAYER ON A HILLSIDE
MATTHEW 26:17-30

- *Pharisees:* "He can cast out demons because he is empowered by the prince of demons" (Matthew 9:34).

- *Jesus:* "You're hopeless, you religion scholars and Pharisees! Frauds! You're like manicured grave plots, grass clipped and the flowers bright, but six feet down it's all rotting bones and worm-eaten flesh. People look at you and think you're saints, but beneath the skin you're total frauds" (Matthew 23:27-28 MSG).

Jesus had probably visited Jerusalem many times throughout his life, since Jews typically celebrated religious holidays like Passover in Jerusalem. But this trip was different. Somehow he knew it would be his last. "Jesus began to tell his disciples plainly that it was necessary for him to go to Jerusalem…He would be killed, but on the third day he would be raised from the dead" (Matthew 16:21).

Jesus and his entourage continued south, heading toward Jerusalem to console the family of Lazarus, who had died. The disciples knew if they followed their controversial rabbi into the city, they would be in danger too. "Thomas, nicknamed the Twin, said to his fellow disciples, 'Let's go, too—and die with Jesus'" (John 11:16).

Gauntlet to Calvary. Jesus carries his cross from the place of his beating to the site of his execution. Most artists show him carrying the full cross. But historians speculate that Romans kept the vertical posts in place at Calvary (Rome's Latin language for "Place of the Skull"). If so, Jesus carried only the crossbeam, perhaps 30 to 40 pounds (13–18 kg). That's the weight of about four or five standard two-by-four boards, each eight feet long (5 by 10 cm, 2.5 m long).

JESUS'S LAST WEEK
PALM SUNDAY TO EASTER

A large crowd was in Jerusalem for Passover. When they heard that Jesus was coming for the festival, they took palm branches and went out to greet him. They shouted… "God bless the King of Israel!"

JOHN 12:12-13 CEV

J ewish leaders decided to kill Jesus for two reasons, according to Bible writers.

He raised Lazarus from the dead. "If we allow him to go on like this, soon everyone will believe in him," Jewish leaders said. "Then the Roman army will come and destroy both our Temple and our nation" (John 11:48).

They were talking about Jesus conning folks into believing he was the Messiah and then leading them into a doomed war of independence, which the Romans would crush—exactly the way they crushed the Jewish revolt 40 years later, in AD 70.

"From that time on, the Jewish leaders began to plot Jesus' death" (verse 53).

Jesus bought himself more time by leaving town, returning later to celebrate Passover in Jerusalem.

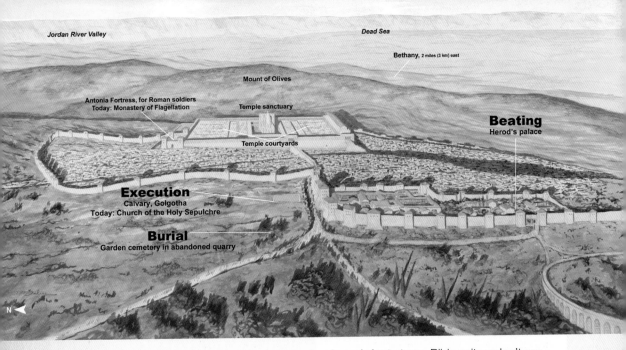

Jordan River Valley

Dead Sea

Bethany, 2 miles (3 km) east

Mount of Olives

Antonia Fortress, for Roman soldiers
Today: Monastery of Flagellation

Temple sanctuary

Beating
Herod's palace

Temple courtyards

Execution
Calvary, Golgotha
Today: Church of the Holy Sepulchre

Burial
Garden cemetery in abandoned quarry

N

He chased merchants out of the temple courtyards. These merchants—who may have paid temple priests a rental fee for their booth space in the courtyard—provided a service to worshippers. Merchants sold priest-approved sacrificial animals so Jews didn't have to bring their own animals long-distance, only to risk having priests declare the animals unfit. Merchants also exchanged Roman coins for temple-approved coins. Roman coins had pictures of the emperor. Jewish law prohibited any "graven image" (Exodus 20:4 KJV) because it could be worshipped as an idol.

"The leading priests, the teachers of religious law, and the other leaders of the people began planning how to kill him" (Luke 19:47).

Jesus justified running off the merchants: "The Scriptures declare, 'My Temple will be called a house of prayer,' but you have turned it into a den of thieves!" (Matthew 21:13, quoting Jeremiah 7:11).

What Jesus meant by that is unclear. Some scholars say he may have been protecting the courtyard because it was the only place in the temple area where non-Jews were allowed to

Jesus's last steps. Bible writers don't say how far Jesus carried his cross. One guess scholars offer—a third of a mile (500 m). That assumes soldiers beat Jesus either near Herod's palace, where Pilate likely stayed, or at their barracks in Antonia Fortress, where they kept an eye on Jews at the temple. It's also based on an ancient tradition that his execution and burial sites are both marked by the Church of the Holy Sepulchre, one of the oldest churches. Christians built it in the early AD 300s, right after the Roman Empire legalized Christianity.

worship. Or perhaps, others say, this cleansing may have been a symbolic gesture to announce that God was doing away with the temple system of worship. It died 40 years later when Romans crushed a Jewish revolt and leveled the temple, which has never been rebuilt. A 1300-year-old Muslim shrine sits on the site—the Dome of the Rock, Jerusalem's most famous landmark.

JESUS'S BIG ENTRANCE

Miracle-working Jesus was perhaps the best-known Jew on earth by the time he rode a donkey into Jerusalem on what has become known as Palm Sunday. The Jewish crowd that saw him coming seemed to think they were witnessing a historic event—the arrival of the Messiah, who would save Israel from the Romans. They had three clues.

Jesus rode a donkey. Many Jews would have been familiar with a prophecy from 500 years earlier, which many linked to the coming Messiah: "Everyone in Jerusalem, celebrate and shout! Your king has won a victory, and he is coming to you. He is humble and rides on a donkey" (Zechariah 9:9 CEV).

Royal welcome. "A large crowd of Passover visitors took palm branches and went down the road to meet him" (John 12:12-13). "As he rode along, the crowds spread out their garments on the road ahead of him" (Luke 19:36). That's how Jews welcomed home soldiers who won a previous war of independence. In the victory procession, Jews entered Jerusalem "with praise and palm branches" (1 Maccabees 13:51).

Three cheers for the king. The crowd cheered Jesus with quotes from the last line of a popular Passover song that pleads for God to save his people: "Blessings on the King who comes in the name of the Lord!" (Luke 19:38, quoting Psalm 118:26).

ONE LAST MEAL

On his last day as a free man, Jesus told two of his disciples to go into Jerusalem and meet a man who would take them to an upstairs room, where they would prepare the Passover meal for Jesus and his disciples.

This room was above a synagogue, according to a Christian tradition that dates back to at least the AD 300s, when the Roman Empire finally legalized Christianity. Pilgrims today visit what may be the site, which is called the Room of the Last Supper. Excavations there have uncovered precisely cut stones from what may have been a first-century worship center.

It was Thursday night, according to the writers of Matthew, Mark, and Luke, "on the first day of the Festival of Unleavened Bread, when the Passover lamb is sacrificed" (Mark 14:12).

By morning, the Lamb of God would be sacrificed.

This was a pivotal moment in Jewish history, as New Testament Jewish writers report it. Jesus told his disciples that his sacrifice would mark the end of the covenant agreement—the contract God made with his people through Moses.

One prophet had predicted this 600 years before Jesus. "'The day is coming,' says the Lord, 'when I will make a new covenant with the people of Israel…I will put my instructions deep within them, and I will write them on their hearts'" (Jeremiah 31:31,33).

The day had come. Holding a cup of wine, Jesus said, "This is my blood which is the new agreement that God makes with his people" (Mark 14:24 NCV).

Moments earlier, Jesus took a piece of flatbread and then "broke it in pieces and gave it to the disciples, saying, 'This is my body, which is given for you. Do this to remember me'" (Luke 22:19).

Ever since that night, Christians have been doing this to remember Jesus. The ritual goes by various names: Lord's Supper, Communion, Eucharist, Mass.

After the meal, Jesus and most of his disciples took a short walk—less than a mile (1.5 km)—to a place of prayer in what may have been an olive grove on the Mount of Olives hillside. It was a quiet place because it was springtime, and olives don't ripen until late summer.

One disciple, Judas, slipped away to tell

Jewish priests that this would be a good time to arrest Jesus. Historians can only guess why Judas betrayed Jesus: for the reward, to provoke Jesus to react with miracle-working power to drive out the Romans, or demon possession—"Satan entered into Judas Iscariot" (Luke 22:3).

Judas led the temple police and the arresting entourage to Jesus and then identified Jesus by greeting him with a kiss on the cheek—the ancient Middle Eastern version of a handshake.

SPEEDY TRIAL

Jesus was bounced through a pinball of a trial overnight and Friday morning, running up against one judge after another—five appearances in all.

Annas. For questioning "they took him to Annas, the father-in-law of Caiaphas, the high priest at that time" (John 18:13). Annas was the high priest emeritus—retired. Annas asked Jesus about what he had been teaching his disciples. Jesus, apparently with a bit of an attitude, said his teachings were obvious because he had taught them openly in synagogues and the temple. A guard slapped him for dissing the elderly priest.

Caiaphas. For arraignment, "Annas bound Jesus and sent him to Caiaphas, the high priest" (John 18:24). Overnight, Jesus endured questioning and accusations. "Many false witnesses spoke against him, but they contradicted each other" (Mark 14:56). By daylight, Caiaphas and apparently the rest of the 71-member Jewish high council known as the Sanhedrin had charged Jesus with blasphemy for claiming to be God's Son and the Messiah.

Pontius Pilate. Caiaphas and the other Jewish leaders wanted Jesus executed, but they needed Roman approval. So at the break of day they took Jesus to Pontius Pilate, the Roman administrator in charge of keeping the peace in Judea. They told Pilate that Jesus was trying to launch a revolt against Rome "by claiming he is the Messiah, the king" (Luke 23:2). Formerly a judge, Pilate knew how to process a defendant. When he found out Jesus was from Galilee, he referred him to Herod Antipas, Galilee's ruler, who was in town for the Passover festival.

Herod Antipas. A son of Herod the Great, Herod Antipas was the ruler who had executed John the Baptist, a relative of Jesus. "Herod was delighted at the opportunity to see Jesus, because he had heard about him and had been hoping for a long time to see him perform a miracle" (Luke 23:8). When Jesus refused to cooperate, Herod mockingly dressed him in a royal robe and sent him back to Pilate as a joke. "Herod and Pilate, who had been enemies before, became friends that day" (Luke 23:12).

Pontius Pilate. Pilate wanted to release Jesus because he considered the case a religious matter, not a political one. But he was on shaky ground with his Roman bosses for two reasons.

- A few years earlier, in about AD 28, he crushed a Jewish protest by ordering his soldiers to slaughter "a great number," according to Josephus, a first-century historian. Rome noticed.

- The official who had recommended Pilate for the job in Judea, Sejanus, was executed during an attempted coup in AD 31. The emperor executed many of Sejanus's associates too but spared Pilate. If Jesus's trial took place after that, Pilate was on incredibly shaky ground with his bosses.

Perhaps for these reasons, Pilate caved, ordering Jesus crucified.

WHAT ROMANS SAID ABOUT CRUCIFIXION

- "Each criminal who goes to execution must carry his own cross on his back."

    PLUTARCH (ABOUT AD 46–120)

- "Some hang their victims upside down. Some impale them through the private parts. Others stretch out their arms onto forked poles."

    SENECA (ABOUT 4 BC–AD 65)

- "Would any human being willingly choose to be fastened to that accursed tree, especially after the beating that left him deathly weak, deformed, swelling with vicious welts on shoulders and chest, and struggling to draw every last, agonizing breath? Anyone facing such a death would plead to die rather than mount the cross."

    SENECA

Slow death. It could take a healthy man two days to die on a cross, which is why Romans typically beat the victims to weaken them. Cause of death was often a combination of shock, exhaustion, and asphyxiation. Victims had to push themselves up to breathe because of the pressure on their lungs from the stretched arms and the angle of their crucified body. In time, they ran out of strength to push. Sometimes that didn't happen soon enough to suit the Romans, so, "soldiers came and broke the legs of the two men crucified with Jesus" (John 19:32).

Thomas, the hard sell. None of the disciples believed the women when they came back from the tomb on Easter morning and said they had seen Jesus vertical. So it may not be fair to tag Thomas as Doubting Thomas simply because he didn't believe the disciples when they told him the same thing after Jesus appeared to them on Easter Sunday evening. Thomas, like the other disciples, had to see Jesus for himself. Once that happened, Jesus told him, "You believe because you have seen me. Blessed are those who believe without seeing me" (John 20:29).

JESUS'S CRUCIFIXION

Roman reports indicate a healthy man could survive two days on a cross. Romans often expedited the process by beating their victims with whips embedded with chunks of bone and metal. Blood loss weakened the victim, sometimes producing shock and sometimes killing them.

By about nine Friday morning, according to Mark's report, Jesus was nailed to the cross. He was dead about six hours later.

One Jewish member of the high council that had convicted Jesus—Joseph of Arimathea—got permission to bury him. Joseph and others rushed to get Jesus's body into Joseph's tomb before sundown, when the Sabbath began and Jews had to abandon all work for 24 hours.

THE RESURRECTION

Jews had convinced Pilate to post a guard by the tomb because Jesus had predicted he would rise on the third day, and they were afraid Jesus's disciples would steal his body and say that's what happened.

When Jesus rose Sunday morning before dawn, the Roman soldiers guarding his tomb did pretty much the opposite—they fainted. "The guards shook from fear and fell down, as though they were dead" (Matthew 28:4 CEV).

Mary Magdalene and several other women went to the tomb at daybreak to prepare Jesus's body for burial because they hadn't had time to do that on Friday afternoon. The tomb was empty.

"He isn't here!" an angel told the women. "God has raised him to life…Tell his disciples" (Matthew 28:6-7 CEV). As the women ran from the tomb, Jesus greeted them and sent them on their way to the disciples.

HOLY WEEK, DAY BY DAY

Piecing together details from all four Gospels, Bible experts say Jesus's last week may have unfolded something like this.

Sunday. Jesus rides a donkey into Jerusalem while crowds cheer him. This day becomes known as Palm Sunday.

Monday. Jesus chases merchants out of the temple courtyard, upsetting the priests, who apparently had approved the merchants being there.

Tuesday. Jesus teaches in the temple.

Wednesday. Judas makes a deal with Jewish leaders to take them to Jesus when he was not around a crowd to defend him from arresting officers.

Thursday. Jesus eats his Last Supper with the disciples and then is arrested in the Garden of Gethsemane while praying.

Friday. Jewish leaders conduct a secret, overnight trial of Jesus and then pressure Pilate into crucifying him by about nine that morning. Jesus is dead by about three that afternoon and is in the tomb by sunset.

Saturday. Roman soldiers guard Jesus's tomb.

Sunday. God raises Jesus from the dead. It's the first Easter.

11

THE CHURCH IS BORN

TIMELINE *(dates are approximate)*

AD 5	Paul (Saul) is born.
AD 29–33?	Jesus ministers publicly.
AD 35	Paul becomes a Christian after seeing a vision of Jesus.
AD 36	Pilate is fired as governor of Judea.
AD 37	Josephus, a Jewish historian, is born.
AD 64	Paul and Peter are executed in Rome.
AD 66	Jews revolt and drive out the Roman army.
AD 70	Romans crush the Jewish revolt and level Jerusalem.
AD 95	John writes the last book in the Bible—Revelation.

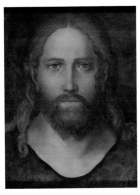

PETER IN CHARGE
THE FIRST SERMON AFTER JESUS

Peter stepped forward with the eleven other apostles and shouted to the crowd, "Listen carefully, all of you, fellow Jews and residents of Jerusalem!"

ACTS 2:14

It didn't take two months for Jesus's disciples to morph from chickenhearted to lionhearted.

They hid during Jesus's crucifixion—apparently figuring that if the top Jewish council wanted their teacher dead, they might want his students dead too. By 50 days later, however, these disciples had picked up where Jesus left off, preaching his message in the streets of Jerusalem, the city that had crucified him—and right in front of the eyeballs of the high priest and other Jewish council leaders who had orchestrated the execution.

A spiritual experience had changed these men, as one Bible writer reports—a physician named Luke, if early Christian tradition is right. Luke accompanied Paul on some of his missionary travels and is credited with writing the Gospel of Luke along with Acts of the Apostles, which is the story of how the church got started.

Luke said that before Jesus ascended into the heavens, he instructed his followers to go to Jerusalem and wait to "receive power when the Holy Spirit comes upon you" (Acts 1:8). They didn't have to wait long. About ten days. On the Jewish holiday of Pentecost, a celestial presence filled the room where 120 followers of Jesus had gathered. Cue the effects.

Peter, top apostle. Catholic Christians call Peter the first pope, explaining that Jesus left him in charge. "I will give you the keys to the kingdom of heaven. What you lock on earth will be locked in heaven. What you unlock on earth will be unlocked in heaven" (Matthew 16:19 NIRV). Pope or not, Peter preached the first known sermon after Jesus left the planet. In response, some 3000 Jews joined the emerging movement called the Way—a name believers may have pulled from something Jesus said: "I am the way, the truth, and the life. No one can come to the Father except through me" (John 14:6). In time, others tagged them as Christians, linking them to their belief that Jesus was the Messiah (or Christ in Greek, the international language of the day).

- *Sound.* "Suddenly, there was a sound from heaven like the roaring of a mighty windstorm."

Come, Holy Spirit. Among the 120 followers of Jesus on hand when the Holy Spirit arrived were 11 of Jesus's original disciples "along with Mary the mother of Jesus, several other women, and the brothers of Jesus" (Acts 1:14).

- *Fire.* "What looked like flames or tongues of fire appeared and settled on each of them."

- *Foreign languages.* "Everyone present was filled with the Holy Spirit and began speaking in other languages" (Acts 2:2-4).

Jews from all over the Middle East had crowded into Jerusalem for the holiday, and many heard the sound. They rushed to see what was going on.

They couldn't believe their ears. "These people [120 followers of Jesus] are all from Galilee, and yet we hear them speaking in our own native languages!" (Acts 2:7-8). There were a lot of languages represented in this crowd of pilgrims from scattered nations in what are now Iran, Iraq, Turkey, Egypt, Libya, and Italy.

Peter figured this was a perfect time to tell the Jews they didn't have to wait any longer for the Messiah. He said that the prophet Joel, centuries earlier, had predicted what the crowd had just witnessed, "God says, 'I will pour out my Spirit upon all people…Everyone who calls on the name of the Lord will be saved'" (Acts 2:17,21).

Peter then made a case for Jesus. He reminded the people of the miracles Jesus had performed, and he announced that Jesus had risen from the dead and ascended into heaven. Peter backed up those bold words by healing people in the crowd.

He convinced about 3000 Jews who joined the Jesus Is Messiah movement. "They worshiped together at the Temple each day, met in homes for the Lord's Supper, and shared their meals with great joy and generosity" (Acts 2:46).

Map legend:
○ CITY WHERE CHRISTIANS LIVED
▮ EXTENT OF CHRISTIANITY BY AD 100

THE SCATTERING
PERSECUTED CHRISTIANS RUN FOR THEIR LIVES

Saul agreed that the killing of Stephen was good. On that day the church of Jerusalem began to be persecuted, and all the believers, except the apostles, were scattered throughout Judea and Samaria.

ACTS 8:1 NCV

Gen-one church. By the time everyone who had ever met Jesus died, the Christian movement had spread throughout the most populated areas along the Mediterranean coast from what is now Israel to Italy. By the time Romans legalized Christianity in the 300s, Christians lived in nearly all the populated areas around the Mediterranean Sea, all the way to France and Spain.

It sounds like communism trumping capitalism. The first wave of Christians "met together in one place and shared everything they had. They sold their property and possessions and shared the money with those in need" (Acts 2:44-45).

That doesn't mean they sold everything and moved into a Jesus commune. But they did seem to wipe out poverty within their group, at least for a while. Well-to-do landowners among the growing community of believers sometimes did what Barnabas did: "He sold a field he owned and brought the money to the apostles" (Acts 4:37).

Peter and the other apostles used donations like this to set up an early version of a Jerusalem soup kitchen to feed the hungry. But managing the soup kitchen took too much of their time, they said. "We apostles should spend our time teaching the word of God, not running a food program" (Acts 6:2). They appointed a team of seven men to direct the food distribution ministry—including Stephen, the man who would become the first Christian martyr.

The stoning of Stephen unleashes a shock wave of persecution in the city where the church is born. Jewish Christians scatter, taking their new faith with them.

Crowds believed the apostles. That's because the miracles the apostles did seemed to confirm that God approved their message.

Some on the high council were furious with the apostles for refusing to observe the council's ban on talking about Jesus. They wanted to kill the disciples. What shut up Jesus, they reasoned, would shut up his students.

One council member convinced his colleagues to chill for the time being. "Let them go! If their plans and actions are only human, they will fail. But if their plans come from God, you won't be able to stop these men" (Acts 5:38-39 NIRV).

FIRST BLOOD

Stephen, who was supposed to help manage the soup kitchen, talked himself to death. Like most believers at the time, he was a Jew who worshipped in a synagogue. He got into a debate one day with some fellow Jews and managed to out-reason them.

They had him arrested for being too free with his speech. They charged him with bad-mouthing God and Moses and with predicting that Jesus would destroy the temple and change the Jewish laws.

When the high council arraigned Stephen and asked him if the charges were true, he bad-mouthed them too. With the truth. First, he gave these scholars a lesson in Jewish history—which would have been insulting enough. Like a student lecturing a history prof on history. Then he gave them what for.

> You stubborn people! You are heathen at heart and deaf to the truth. Must you

From the moment the disciples started teaching about Jesus in Jerusalem, the city that had crucified Jesus a few weeks earlier, the disciples and their followers faced stiff-arm pushback from top Jewish leaders—the 71-man council called the Sanhedrin, which had orchestrated Jesus's execution. The council arrested Peter and John, jailed them overnight, and the next day ordered them to stop teaching that Jesus rose from the dead.

The two refused. "Should we obey you or God? We cannot keep quiet. We must speak about what we have seen and heard" (Acts 4:19-20 NCV).

The council decided it had no choice but to release the two—for the same reason they tried Jesus in secret: "They didn't know how to punish them without starting a riot" (Acts 4:21).

forever resist the Holy Spirit? That's what your ancestors did, and so do you! Name one prophet your ancestors didn't persecute! They even killed the ones who predicted the coming of the Righteous One—the Messiah whom you betrayed and murdered (Acts 7:51-52).

That was a bit like standing in front of Congress and the supreme court and calling them all a bunch of felons raised by felons—and being right about it.

A riot broke out in the court. Angry Jews dragged him outside and stoned him to death.

Guarding the coats of the throwers was Saul, who would later convert to Christianity and become famous as the apostle Paul, the man who would write almost half the books in the New Testament.

Stephen's case enraged orthodox Jews. They let the dogs out. "A great wave of persecution began that day, sweeping over the church in Jerusalem" (Acts 8:1).

Christians scattered, taking their faith with them. Fired-up Jews like Saul hunted them down: "I even had some of them killed. I had others arrested and put in jail. I didn't care if they were men or women" (Acts 22:4 CEV).

Oddly enough, Jesus's disciples stayed in Jerusalem even as other believers ran for their lives.

Staying in Jerusalem proved fatal for one of Jesus's best friends. James is the only apostle whose execution is reported in the Bible. King Herod Agrippa, grandson of the notorious Herod the Great, "began to persecute some believers in the church. He had the apostle James (John's brother) killed with a sword" (Acts 12:1-2).

When he saw how happy this made the Jews, he arrested Peter, who managed to pull

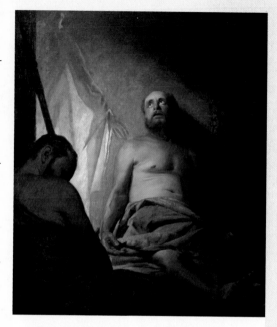

Jailbreak. Chained and locked in a Jerusalem jail, Peter seems destined for execution by sword the next morning. King Herod Agrippa has just executed the apostle James. When Herod saw how happy that made the Jews, he prepared an encore. But an angel leads Peter to freedom, apparently while everyone else at the jail gets their beauty rest. The jailers got a permanent rest the next day—execution.

off a jailbreak with the help of an angel. "The chains fell off his wrists" (Acts 12:7).

The Bible writer implies that this all happened more than a decade after Jesus's death and resurrection—in AD 44. Roman history books say that's the year Herod died. The Bible writer says that after Peter's escape, Herod left Jerusalem for Caesarea, where he suddenly took sick and died of what sounds like a lingering infection that attracted maggots. "He was eaten by worms and died" (Acts 12:23 NCV). That's how his infamous grandfather reportedly died too—of maggot-infested gangrene.

HOW TO CONVERT A HARD-CORE JEW
PAUL SEES THE LIGHT

When Saul [later known as Paul] had almost reached Damascus, a bright light from heaven suddenly flashed around him. He fell to the ground and heard a voice that said, "Saul! Saul! Why are you so cruel to me?"

ACTS 9:3-4 CEV

Jesus arrests Paul. Paul, on his way to find and arrest Jewish Christians in Damascus, gets knocked to the ground by a light brighter than the desert sun—bright enough to blind him for three days. From the light comes a voice: "I am Jesus, the one you are persecuting!" (Acts 9:5).

In the beginning, Paul was a little like FBI agent Melvin Purvis (1903–1960) during Prohibition—the era of no liquor sales.

Instead of going after outlaws who sold hooch, like Purvis did, Paul eagerly hunted down Christians selling what he considered a heresy that insulted God by teaching that God and a Nazareth girl had a Son.

"I went after anyone connected with this 'Way,'" Paul said. "I rounded up men and women right and left and had them thrown in prison" (Acts 22:4 MSG).

Paul described himself as a Pharisee. That was a branch of the Jewish faith—a bit like Christians have denominations: Catholics, Baptists, and Methodists. Pharisees were scholars obsessed with obeying the laws in their Bible. But they also taught that people should obey laws that rabbis and other Jewish scholars added over the years in an attempt to help people know how to apply God's laws to everyday life.

For example, Jewish law ordered people not to work on the Sabbath—sundown on Friday to sundown on Saturday. Pharisees defined work by creating a list of hundreds of Sabbath prohibitions: Don't cook, don't practice medicine, and don't even pick a head of wheat to snack on the kernels.

That's why Pharisees snapped at Jesus for healing people on the Sabbath and for letting his disciples nibble their way through a grain field. "Why are they breaking the law by harvesting?" (Mark 2:24), they asked.

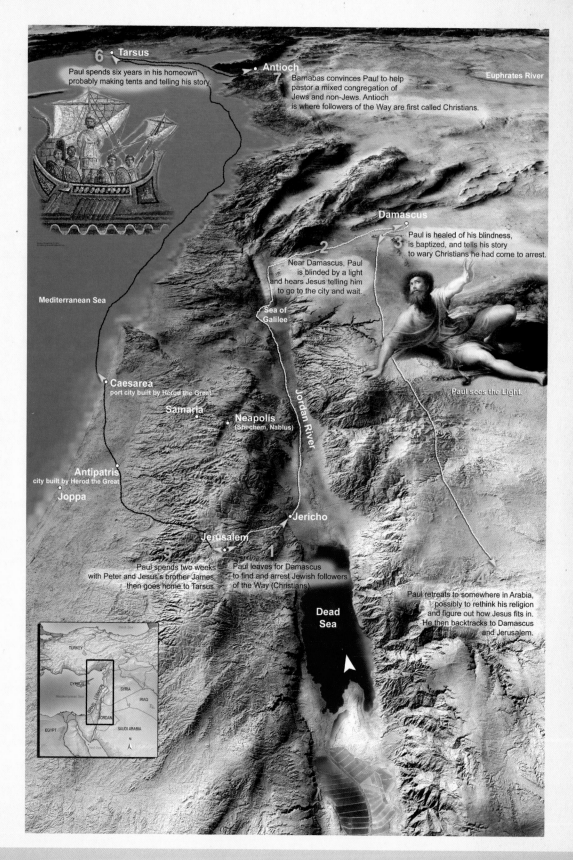

6 Tarsus
Paul spends six years in his hometown, probably making tents and telling his story.

7 Antioch
Barnabas convinces Paul to help pastor a mixed congregation of Jews and non-Jews. Antioch is where followers of the Way are first called Christians.

Euphrates River

Damascus

3 Paul is healed of his blindness, is baptized, and tells his story to wary Christians he had come to arrest.

2 Near Damascus, Paul is blinded by a light and hears Jesus telling him to go to the city and wait.

Sea of Galilee

Mediterranean Sea

Paul sees the Light.

Caesarea
port city built by Herod the Great

Samaria

Neapolis
(Shechem, Nablus)

Jordan River

Antipatris
city built by Herod the Great

Joppa

Jericho

Jerusalem

5 Paul spends two weeks with Peter and Jesus's brother James, then goes home to Tarsus.

1 Paul leaves for Damascus to find and arrest Jewish followers of the Way (Christians)

4 Paul retreats to somewhere in Arabia, possibly to rethink his religion and figure out how Jesus fits in. He then backtracks to Damascus and Jerusalem.

Dead Sea

TURKEY
CYPRUS
SYRIA
IRAQ
LEBANON ISRAEL
JORDAN
EGYPT
SAUDI ARABIA
N

Since Pharisees got upset about stuff that minor, it's easy to see why Paul and other Pharisees went ballistic on Messiah-loving Jews who said Jesus retired the laws of Moses because now "God's law is written in their hearts" (Romans 2:15).

A traveling man by nature, it would seem, Paul managed to get from the Jewish high priest a letter authorizing him to arrest followers of the Way in Damascus, a week's walk north some 150 miles (240 km).

"When Saul had almost reached Damascus, a bright light from heaven suddenly flashed around him. He fell to the ground and heard a voice that said, 'Saul! Saul! Why are you so cruel to me?'"

"Who are you?" Saul asked.

"I am Jesus" (Acts 9:3-5 CEV).

Jesus told Paul to go on into Damascus. That was a little tough because the light had blinded Paul. Men traveling with him had to lead him along the way. Those men "saw the light but didn't understand the voice" (Acts 22:9).

In town, Paul waits. "He remained there blind for three days and did not eat or drink" (Acts 9:9).

Finally, a man named Ananias came to Paul and laid hands on him in a ritual of healing. "Suddenly something like fish scales fell from Saul's eyes, and he could see. He got up and was baptized" (Acts 9:18 CEV).

Paul told his story to the believers he had come to arrest. Then he "went away into Arabia" (Galatians 1:17). Going back to Jerusalem would have been awkward.

Where he went in Arabia is anyone's guess. Some scholars suggest Mount Sinai. This is the mountain where Moses got the Ten Commandments and where the prophet Elijah retreated and heard God in "a gentle whisper" (1 Kings 19:12). Paul wanted to hear from God too.

It's probably a fair guess that Paul spent the three years of that retreat rethinking his religion in light of the Light.

Afterward, he went back to Damascus and then moved on to Jerusalem, where he spent 15 days staying with Barnabas, his future partner in the first mission trip. While Paul was there, he met Peter along with James the brother of Jesus, who by that time seems to have become pastor of the first Christian church, in Jerusalem.

From there, Paul headed home to the city

Rulekeeper. This rabbi, painted at the turn of the 1900s, wears a prayer shawl—standard issue among Pharisees like young Paul. Pharisees were famous for trying to live the holy life by keeping all the rules—including man-made rules a bit like some we might find in church manuals today. The rules aren't in the Bible, but they're written with the good intention of helping people know how to apply Bible principles to life today. The principle of resting on the Sabbath, for example, generated 39 categories of prohibited work, such as cooking, tying, and putting out a fire. Each category is like an umbrella with a crowd of laws beneath it.

PAUL, ON THE CLOCK   *(dates are approximate)*

PAUL'S AGE	YEAR AD	EVENT
	5	Paul is born.
15–25	20–30	He studies the Jewish Bible in Jerusalem under famous rabbi Gamaliel.
28–30	33–35	He persecutes Christians.
30	35	After converting to Christianity, he retreats to Arabia for three years to rethink his religion.
33	38	He spends two weeks in Jerusalem meeting with Peter and James (the brother of Jesus) and then goes home to Tarsus for about six years.
39	44	Barnabas convinces him to help pastor the church in Antioch, where believers are first called Christians.
41	46	Barnabas and Paul make the first known missionary journey (two years—Cyprus and south Turkey).
44	49	Paul helps convince Jerusalem church leaders not to require non-Jews to follow Jewish traditions, such as circumcision and eating only kosher food. He makes his second mission trip (three years—Turkey and Greece) and writes 1 and 2 Thessalonians, considered the oldest books in New Testament.
48	52	After a short visit in Jerusalem, he takes his third mission trip (four years—Turkey and Greece). He stays in Ephesus three years and writes Galatians (AD 53), 1 and 2 Corinthians (AD 55), and Romans (AD 57).
52	57	Falsely accused, Paul is arrested in Jerusalem and moved to prison in Caesarea and held for two years.
54	59	He sails to Rome for trial in the emperor's supreme court.
55	60	Under house arrest in Rome for two years, Paul writes letters to Philippians, Ephesians, Colossians, and Philemon.
58	63	Paul was possibly released and may have traveled to Spain. He writes 1 Timothy and Titus.
59	64	Arrested in Rome during Emperor Nero's persecution of Christians, Paul writes 2 Timothy and is eventually executed.

of Tarsus, some 400 miles (640 km) north, along the southern coast of what is now Turkey. During the next six years, he may have worked at his trade, making tents. But scholars say it's hard to imagine him not telling his story to fellow Jews and anyone else who would listen.

Perhaps his success there at convincing non-Jews to believe in Jesus is what got him his job preaching. Or maybe it was simply that Barnabas knew his story. For whatever reason, Barnabas tracked him down and convinced Paul to help him pastor a mixed congregation of Jews and non-Jews in Antioch—about 100 miles (160 km) away by ship, in what is now Antakya, Turkey. This congregation would become the launching pad for Paul's...

- three missionary trips throughout what are now Turkey and Greece
- thirteen letters—almost half of the books in the New Testament

SAUL IS PAUL

It's anyone's guess why the writer of Acts—presumably physician Luke, who traveled with Paul—decided to call him by his Hebrew name, Saul, and then to call him Paul after the conversion story.

It wasn't until Paul and Barnabas were traveling abroad on their first mission trip that the writer revealed that Saul had a second name: "Saul, also known as Paul" (Acts 13:9).

"Paul" was the name the apostle chose to use while traveling and writing letters to cities throughout the Roman Empire, where people spoke...

- Latin, the official language of the Roman Empire (his name: Paulus)
- Greek, the international language of the day (his name: Paulos)

People sometimes do the same thing today when traveling abroad. In Mexico, Stephen becomes Esteban. In Greece, he's Stephanos.

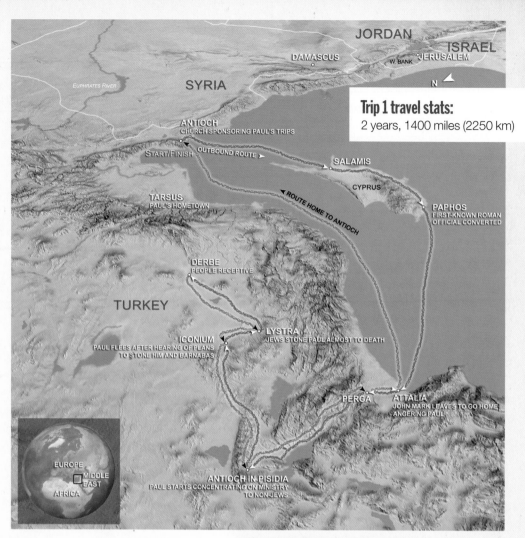

JORDAN

ISRAEL

DAMASCUS

W. BANK   JERUSALEM

Euphrates River

SYRIA

N

Trip 1 travel stats:
2 years, 1400 miles (2250 km)

ANTIOCH
CHURCH SPONSORING PAUL'S TRIPS

START/FINISH   OUTBOUND ROUTE ►

SALAMIS

CYPRUS

TARSUS
PAUL'S HOMETOWN

◄ ROUTE HOME TO ANTIOCH

PAPHOS
FIRST-KNOWN ROMAN
OFFICIAL CONVERTED

DERBE
PEOPLE RECEPTIVE

TURKEY

ICONIUM
PAUL FLEES AFTER HEARING OF PLANS
TO STONE HIM AND BARNABAS

LYSTRA
JEWS STONE PAUL ALMOST TO DEATH

PERGA

ATTALIA
JOHN MARK LEAVES TO GO HOME
ANGERING PAUL

EUROPE

MIDDLE
EAST

AFRICA

ANTIOCH IN PISIDIA
PAUL STARTS CONCENTRATING ON MINISTRY
TO NON-JEWS

FIRST MISSIONARY
PAUL'S THREE TRIPS ABROAD

*One day as these men [church leaders in Antioch] were worshiping the
Lord and fasting, the Holy Spirit said, "Dedicate Barnabas and Saul for
the special work to which I have called them." So after more fasting and
prayer, the men laid their hands on them and sent them on their way.*

ACTS 13:2-3

Paul hits the road, taking his story and his Christian beliefs with him. He plants house churches
throughout what are now Turkey and Greece. Then he writes letters of encouragement to
some congregations and some to his colleagues. Many letters, such as some to Corinth, Ephesus,
and Philippi, survived long enough to get included in the New Testament.

While Paul and Barnabas were leading the mixed congregation of Jews and non-Jews in Antioch near the Mediterranean coast, the Holy Spirit somehow got a message through during a prayer meeting of the church leaders: "Dedicate Barnabas and Saul for the special work to which I have called them" (Acts 13:2).

After prayer and fasting, the congregation sent the two off on a mission trip. The job was a mixed bag.

- Part circuit-riding preacher, going from place to place but without any churches to preach to.
- Part missionary, telling the story of Jesus to people abroad.
- Part diplomat, negotiating with hostile crowds.

Most tradition-minded Jews didn't take kindly to Paul's story about God having a Son. Or that the Son's death and resurrection set up a new covenant that retired the old laws of Moses and replaced them with laws God writes on people's hearts. "Even Gentiles, who do not have God's written law, show that they know his law when they instinctively obey it, even without having heard it. They demonstrate that God's law is written in their hearts" (Romans 2:14-15).

Just about anywhere Paul and Barnabas went, they got pushback. Once, on this first mission trip, Paul got stoned nearly to death.

The two caught a ship to the island of Cyprus, homeland of Barnabas. They took an assistant, John Mark, cousin of Barnabas. They landed at Salamis on the east coast and traveled by land to the west coast city of Paphos, preaching about Jesus along the way. Trip highlights:

- *Paphos.* When a sorcerer tried to

sermon-block him, Paul put a curse on him that temporarily blinded him. Roman governor Sergius Paulus was so impressed that he became the first Roman official on record to convert to Christianity.

- *Perga.* John Mark abandoned the mission and went home to Jerusalem. Perhaps the swampy coastland didn't seem inviting. The Bible doesn't say why John left—only that Paul didn't like it one little bit (Acts 15:38).
- *Antioch of Pisidia.* Many Jews bought into the story when the two preached it at a Sabbath service. But by the next Sabbath, a group of angry Jews did nothing but argue with Paul and trash talk him. Paul said fine, he'd take his good news to the non-Jews. A mob ran the two out of town.
- *Iconium.* Antioch déjà vu. Add stones: "A mob of Gentiles and Jews…decided to attack and stone them" (Acts 14:5). The two fled before rocks flew.
- *Lystra.* Paul healed a man crippled since birth. Crowds praised Paul and Barnabas as gods—Barnabas the boss-god Zeus, and Paul the talker-god Hermes. Paul said they weren't gods. Hotheaded Jews from Antioch and Iconium arrived late and started a riot. The mob stoned Paul and left him for dead. He came to and left town the next day.
- *Derbe.* Nothing bad reported for a change. Paul and Barnabas backtracked through the Turkish towns they visited, checking on the new believers and then returning to their home church in Antioch.

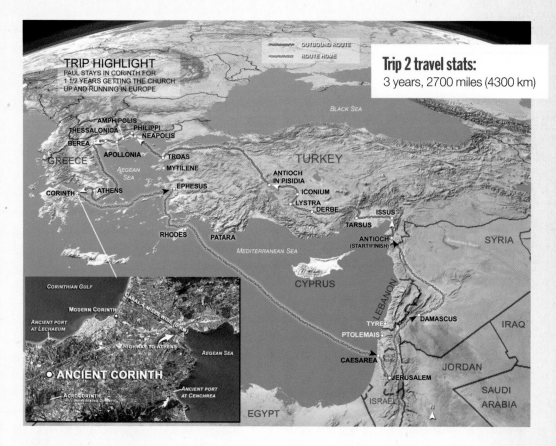

TRIP HIGHLIGHT
PAUL STAYS IN CORINTH FOR
1 1/2 YEARS GETTING THE CHURCH
UP AND RUNNING IN EUROPE

OUTBOUND ROUTE
ROUTE HOME

Trip 2 travel stats:
3 years, 2700 miles (4300 km)

BLACK SEA

AMPHIPOLIS
THESSALONICA   PHILIPPI
NEAPOLIS
BEREA
GREECE   APOLLONIA   TROAS
AEGEAN   MYTILENE
SEA
CORINTH   ATHENS   EPHESUS

TURKEY

ANTIOCH
IN PISIDIA
ICONIUM
LYSTRA
DERBE
ISSUS
TARSUS
RHODES   PATARA   ANTIOCH   SYRIA
(START/FINISH)
MEDITERRANEAN SEA

CYPRUS

DAMASCUS   IRAQ
TYRE
PTOLEMAIS
JORDAN
CAESAREA

Corinthian Gulf
MODERN CORINTH
CANAL 4 MILES WIDE (6 KM)
ANCIENT PORT
AT LECHAEUM
HIGHWAY TO ATHENS   AEGEAN SEA
ANCIENT CORINTH
ANCIENT PORT
ACROCORINTH   AT CENCHREA
HILL OVERLOOKING CORINTH

JERUSALEM
ISRAEL   SAUDI
ARABIA
EGYPT   LEBANON

HELLO EUROPE: MISSION TRIP TWO

Paul and Barnabas decided to go back to the cities they visited on their first mission trip to see how the church plants were doing. But they got into an argument. Barnabas wanted to take John Mark again. Paul said nope because John Mark had bailed on them during the first trip. Paul and Barnabas agree to disagree. They part company and split the mission—Barnabas and John Mark take Cyprus while Paul and a new associate, Silas, take the cities in Turkey.

Paul and Silas started in Derbe, working their way west. They visited the churches Paul had started earlier and also took their sermons all the way to the west coast city of Troas. There, Paul had a vision. He saw a man in Greece pleading, "Come over...help us!" (Acts 16:9). Highlights:

Philippi. A rich businesswoman opened her home for Paul to start the first home-church in Europe. (Christians didn't start building worship centers until Romans legalized the religion in the early AD 300s.) Paul cured a demon-possessed slave who had been making money for her masters by fortune-telling. When she couldn't tell the future anymore, her masters got Paul and Silas thrown into jail and beaten. City officials later apologized for the beating and the lockup once they realized the two were Roman citizens—no beatings allowed without a trial. The two were free to go, and they did.

Thessalonica. Paul preached in the synagogue for three Sabbaths. Riots followed.

Athens. Paul and Silas moved along the Greek coast to Berea and then to Athens—the scholarly Oxford of its day. Philosophers invited Paul to tell them about the new religion. Then they laughed him out of town. They could handle ideas about the soul living forever—that's nicely Greek. But resurrection of someone's dead body is the stuff of a Greek comedy.

Corinth. This busy city with nearby ports in two oceans got the pleasure of Paul's company for a year and a half. Perhaps he figured that with so many people coming and going, this was the perfect place to pass out Gospel seeds that folks could take with them in all directions. After Paul finally left for home, trouble erupted in the Corinthian church. As a result, we have in our New Testament two of the letters he wrote to the folks of Corinth.

I'M BACK: MISSION TRIP THREE

Paul retraced his trail from mission trip two, once again checking in on the churches and then working his way to a city new to him—Ephesus. This city was a wonderful place to tell the story of Jesus because it was one of the five largest cities in the Roman Empire and a major gateway to and from the Middle East. Paul stayed three years—long enough to cause trouble for certain job creators.

TROUBLETOWN
A YEAR AND A HALF IN CORINTH

For an itchy-foot evangelist like Paul, who seldom stayed in any one place more than a few weeks, it's odd that he suddenly decided to plant himself in Corinth for a year and a half. What was the attraction? Bible experts offer a few guesses.

Great shortcut. Corinth perched itself on a four-mile-wide (6 km) strip of land between two different oceans. It had ports on both sides, so ships off-loaded their cargo onto wagons in one port for overland transport to ships in the other port. That cut 200 miles (320 km) off the shipping and avoided the sometimes treacherous sea around the southern tip of Greece.

Busy, dicey town. Corinth was one big deal of a business center—an international crossroads crowded with perhaps 100,000 or more city folk along with visiting sailors and traveling salesmen. Lots of souls to save. The city had a dicey reputation. Its name spawned a verb: *corinthianize*, which today would translate into a blunt word for *fornicate*.

Income available. Paul didn't usually accept offerings for himself but rather paid his own way. In Corinth he worked as a bivocational minister—part-time preacher and part-time tentmaker, helping fellow Christian tentmakers Aquila and Priscilla (Acts 18:1-3).

Letters Paul wrote to this congregation after he left reveal a big bunch of problems in the church. For one, they were fighting a turf battle over whose teachings they should follow. Contenders: Paul, Apollos, Peter, Christ (1 Corinthians 3:21-23).

For another, one of the church members was *corinthianizing* with his stepmother (1 Corinthians 5:1). Paul's recommendation: Show the gent the door.

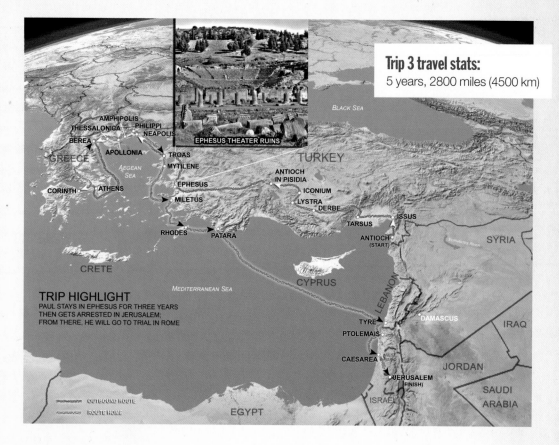

Trip 3 travel stats:
5 years, 2800 miles (4500 km)

EPHESUS THEATER RUINS

BLACK SEA

AMPHIPOLIS
THESSALONICA
PHILIPPI
BEREA
NEAPOLIS

GREECE
APOLLONIA
TROAS
MYTILENE

AEGEAN
SEA

TURKEY

ANTIOCH
IN PISIDIA

CORINTH
ATHENS
EPHESUS

ICONIUM
LYSTRA
DERBE

MILETUS

TARSUS
ISSUS

RHODES
PATARA
ANTIOCH
(START)
SYRIA

CRETE

CYPRUS

MEDITERRANEAN SEA

LEBANON

DAMASCUS

IRAQ

TRIP HIGHLIGHT
PAUL STAYS IN EPHESUS FOR THREE YEARS
THEN GETS ARRESTED IN JERUSALEM;
FROM THERE, HE WILL GO TO TRIAL IN ROME

TYRE
PTOLEMAIS

CAESAREA

JORDAN

JERUSALEM
(FINISH)

SAUDI
ARABIA

ISRAEL

OUTBOUND ROUTE
ROUTE HOME

EGYPT

- *Scribes.* Sorcerers who converted to Christianity burned their scrolls of incantations. "The value of the books was several million dollars" (Acts 19:19).

- *Idol makers and merchants.* They feared, "Everyone will start saying terrible things about our business" (Acts 19:27 CEV).

One of the city's top job creators was Demetrius, a rich guy who owned the Artemis idol industry. Certainly worried about cash flow, he opted to play the religious angle in public. "Artemis—this magnificent goddess worshiped throughout the province of Asia and all around the world—will be robbed of her great prestige!" (Acts 19:27).

A riot followed, and Paul left town. He moved on to what is now Greece, where he stayed for three months—until he heard about Jews planning to end him. He sailed back to Jerusalem, stopping to preach at coastal cities along the way.

As far as the Bible reports it, these were Paul's last months as a free man. In Jerusalem, a Jewish riot would get him arrested and kept in lockup for perhaps half a dozen years—possibly for the rest of his life.

ARTEMIS BUSTERS
THREE YEARS IN EPHESUS

Not counting jail, Ephesus is the one place Paul stayed longest. Like Corinth, Ephesus was a happening city with wonderful opportunities to tell the story of Jesus to open-minded people.

- *Big town.* Ephesus was home to perhaps a quarter of a million citizens, making it one of the five largest cities in the Roman Empire.
- *Major port.* Ephesus was one of the main gateways in and out of the Middle East.
- *Money center.* It served as the main treasury for Middle Eastern taxes collected for Rome.
- *Comm HQ.* Ephesus was the base of military communications for Roman legions in the region.
- *A receptive crowd.* The citizens themselves were the biggest attraction for Paul. They were teachable. Paul convinced so many of them to trade their Greek gods for Jesus that Ephesus job creators in the idol-making business noticed their moneybags getting lighter.

Cue the riot started by "Demetrius, a silversmith who had a large business manufacturing silver shrines of the Greek goddess Artemis" (Acts 19:24). The riot drove Paul out of town but not before he had established a strong community of faith. He would later appoint his best friend and colleague, Timothy, to pastor the church.

Archaeologists have found Demetrius's name on a list of men honored in Ephesus for protecting the Temple of Artemis. This may or may not have been the same Demetrius who shows up in the Bible.

Goddess of Ephesus.
Go-to goddess for women in childbirth, Artemis looks top-heavy with what some guess are breasts for feeding the world. This four-foot-high (130 cm) statue of Artemis, crafted in the AD 100s, was found in the ruins of Ephesus. Until Paul came along, artisans there made a good living by selling figurines and statues of the city's patron goddess.

CHAINED SAINT
PAUL UNDER ARREST

*Jews from the province of Asia [today's Turkey]
saw Paul in the Temple and roused a mob against
him…the [Roman] commander arrested him
and ordered him bound with two chains.*

Acts 21:27,33

Turkish Jews wanted Paul dead. They made that clear enough during his first missionary trip.

- *Mob at Antioch of Pisidia.* "Jews…incited a mob against Paul and Barnabas and ran them out of town" (Acts 13:50).

- *Murder plot at Iconium.* "Jews…poisoned the minds of the Gentiles against Paul and Barnabas…A mob of Gentiles and Jews…decided to attack and stone them. When the apostles learned of it, they fled" (Acts 14:2,5-6).

- *Stoning at Lystra.* "Jews arrived from Antioch and Iconium and won the crowds to their side. They stoned Paul and dragged him out of town, thinking he was dead" (Acts 14:19).

Jews from these towns in the Roman province called Asia in what is now western Turkey may have been the same Asian Jews the Bible writer says went berserk when they spotted Gentile-loving

Paul in their sacred Jewish space, the Jerusalem temple. These Paul-hating Jews did what Asian Jews had done to him before—whipped up the crowd with loud talk and lies.

- *"[He] tells everybody to disobey Jewish laws"* (Acts 21:28). Not true. What he taught was that non-Jews didn't have to observe Jewish customs, such as laws requiring circumcision and kosher food.

- *"He...defiles this holy place by bringing in Gentiles"* (Acts 21:28). Wrong again. They saw him earlier in the day with non-Jews, and they wrongly presumed he brought them into the Jews-only part of the temple—a death-penalty offense. Signs posted on the temple courtyard warned non-Jews they would be killed if they crossed into the courtyards reserved for Jews.

Jews grabbed Paul, dragged him out of the temple, and started beating him, perhaps hoping to shut him up for good. Roman soldiers stationed in a fortress along the north wall rushed through the mob and snatched Paul, arresting him.

The beating was Paul's last free moment in life as far as Acts tells the story.

TWO YEARS IN JAIL

Rome's commander in Jerusalem called in the Jewish priests and the high council, known as the Sanhedrin. He wanted to find out what was going on.

Paul, wonderfully savvy of Jewish politics, managed to turn these Jews against each other—especially the party of the Pharisees against the party of the Sadducees. Paul said, "I am a Pharisee...on trial because my hope is in the resurrection of the dead!" (Acts 23:6). By

Sword ahead: Paul's destiny. At about age 52, Paul gets arrested in Jerusalem, moved to Rome's regional HQ in Caesarea, and held without trial for two years. He is portrayed in many paintings, including this one, with a sword. It's foreshadowing. Christian tradition says Romans beheaded him in Rome after a trial in Nero's supreme court.

putting it the way he did, he turned the Pharisees, who believed in life after death, against the Sadducees, who didn't. Chaos followed.

Soldiers took Paul back to jail.

The next morning a group of Jews vowed not to eat or drink until they killed Paul—no matter how many Romans they had to kill to get to him. We can only assume they lost weight. And that's because Jerusalem's commander got word of the plot. The info came from an informer—the son of Paul's sister. So that same night, the commander ordered a battalion of 470 soldiers to escort Paul to a more secure jail some 50 miles (80 km) northwest in Caesarea, Rome's capital in the region.

JAILBIRD WITH A QUILL

During his 20 years in the ministry—an estimate—Paul spent about five or six years in jail. Two in Caesarea (Acts 24:27). Another two in Rome (Acts 28:30). There were other times as well. Philippi for one (Acts 16:23-24).

Who knows—he may have gotten thrown in jail every time he was beaten. "Five times the Jews gave me thirty-nine lashes with a whip. Three times the Romans beat me with a big stick" (2 Corinthians 11:24-25 cev).

The good news is, Paul wrote some of his most helpful and encouraging letters from prison—Ephesians, Philippians, Colossians, Philemon, and 2 Timothy.

Five days later the high priest and some other Jewish leaders arrived to press charges against Paul. A Roman governor named Felix presided over the hearing, listening to the charges and to Paul's defense.

Felix postponed the hearing indefinitely and kept Paul in jail for two years, allowing Paul's friends to visit him. The writer reporting the story said Felix kept Paul in jail for two reasons.

- "He…hoped that Paul would bribe him, so he sent for him quite often and talked with him" (Acts 24:26).
- "Felix wanted to gain favor with the Jewish people" (Acts 24:27).

Felix was one of many corrupt Roman governors during the reign of bad-boy-emperor Nero (reigned AD 54–68). So reported first-century Jewish historian Josephus, who added that Felix hired the assassins who murdered the high priest. The assassins went to worship carrying daggers.

Two years into Paul's imprisonment, Jews got a new governor, Festus (AD 60–62), the Bible and Josephus agree. Festus, wanting to please the Jews he was just assigned to govern, seemed ready to send Paul back to Jerusalem for trial by the Jews.

That's when Paul played his "Roman citizen" card. "No one has a right to turn me over to these men to kill me. I appeal to Caesar!" (Acts 25:11). Had he been an American, this would have been his appeal to the supreme court. Roman citizens at risk of being executed had the right to be heard in the emperor's court.

"Very well!" Festus said. "You have appealed to Caesar, and to Caesar you will go!"

Up next, a sea voyage to Rome to the emperor, who in AD 64 would launch an empire-wide persecution of Christians. As the story goes, Nero blamed Christians for the July fire that charred much of the city, including parts of Nero's palace. It was a case of terrible timing for Paul.

As Festus confided to one of his distinguished guests, Jewish King Agrippa, "He could have been set free if he hadn't appealed to Caesar" (Acts 26:32). With his Jewish accusers lying in wait, getting set free was the last thing Paul needed.

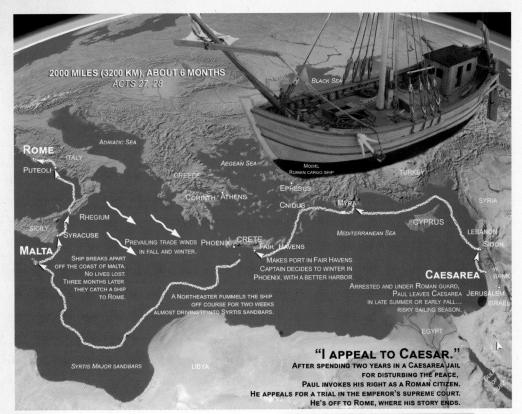

2000 MILES (3200 KM), ABOUT 6 MONTHS
ACTS 27, 28

BLACK SEA

ROME
ITALY
PUTEOLI
ADRIATIC SEA

AEGEAN SEA
MODEL
ROMAN CARGO SHIP

GREECE
TURKEY

CORINTH ATHENS
EPHESUS
CNIDUS
MYRA
SYRIA

RHEGIUM
CYPRUS
LEBANON
SIDON

SICILY
SYRACUSE
MEDITERRANEAN SEA

MALTA
PREVAILING TRADE WINDS PHOENIX CRETE
IN FALL AND WINTER. FAIR HAVENS

SHIP BREAKS APART
OFF THE COAST OF MALTA.
NO LIVES LOST.
THREE MONTHS LATER
THEY CATCH A SHIP
TO ROME.
MAKES PORT IN FAIR HAVENS.
CAPTAIN DECIDES TO WINTER IN
PHOENIX, WITH A BETTER HARBOR.
CAESAREA
W.
BANK
ARRESTED AND UNDER ROMAN GUARD,
PAUL LEAVES CAESAREA JERUSALEM
IN LATE SUMMER OR EARLY FALL... ISRAEL
RISKY SAILING SEASON.

A NORTHEASTER PUMMELS THE SHIP
OFF COURSE FOR TWO WEEKS
ALMOST DRIVING IT INTO SYRTIS SANDBARS.

EGYPT

"I APPEAL TO CAESAR."
AFTER SPENDING TWO YEARS IN A CAESAREA JAIL
FOR DISTURBING THE PEACE,
PAUL INVOKES HIS RIGHT AS A ROMAN CITIZEN.
HE APPEALS FOR A TRIAL IN THE EMPEROR'S SUPREME COURT.
HE'S OFF TO ROME, WHERE HIS STORY ENDS.

SYRTIS MAJOR SANDBARS
LIBYA

PAUL: THE END
VOYAGE TO HIS TRIAL IN ROME

*Paul warned them, "Men, I can see there will be a lot of trouble on
this trip. The ship, the cargo, and even our lives may be lost."*

ACTS 27:9-10 NCV

Paul knew a shipwreck when he saw it coming. "Three times I was shipwrecked. Once I spent a whole night and a day adrift at sea" (2 Corinthians 11:25).

He was headed into shipwreck number four. He figured that much out all by himself. It didn't take a prophet to see it coming. All it took was an experienced traveler—and he had covered roughly 10,000 miles (16,000 km) by land and sea.

On orders of Roman governor Festus, Paul—arrested and escorted by a Roman officer named Julius—sailed for Rome, where he would be tried in the emperor's supreme court.

It wasn't primo sailing season. They set sail from Caesarea in late summer or early fall on a 2000-mile (3200 km) voyage they couldn't possibly finish before winter—when the sea churns nasty and smart sailors get temporarily reacquainted with solid ground. From mid-November to early March, sailing in the Mediterranean was reserved for emergencies.

After a stop in Sidon, they reached Myra on the southern coast of what is now Turkey.

Christians on fire. After Roman emperor Nero accused Christians of setting the AD July 64 fire that burned much of Rome and parts of his palace, he set fire to them. He used them as torches at dusk to light the attraction of other Christians getting turned into cat food.

It was already late September or early October: "the Great Day of Forgiveness [Yom Kippur, or the Day of Atonement] was past" (Acts 27:9 CEV). They were only about a fourth of the way to Rome.

"We encountered strong headwinds that made it difficult to keep the ship on course" (Acts 27:4). They had to zigzag, tacking into the wind.

Leaving Myra, they tried sailing west toward Greece and got close to Cnidus, modern-day Knidos, Turkey. But seasonal trade winds blowing from the northwest pushed them south to Crete. Paul advised the captain to winter in the first harbor they approached—Fair Havens, Crete.

Nope. The captain preferred the better-protected harbor at Phoenix. It would have been a fine place for snowbirds, but they never made it.

What sounds like a typhoon snatched the ship and pummeled it southwest for two weeks, threatening to run the ship aground in the shallow "sandbars of Syrtis off the African coast" (Acts 27:17).

Instead, the wind threw a switch on the direction. The ship ran aground along the coast of Malta, a small island south of Italy and Sicily. All souls were saved. Some could swim. Others floated on "planks or debris from the broken ship" (Acts 27:44).

Three months later, Paul and Julius caught another ship sailing north, with stops at Syracuse, Rhegium, and Puteoli. Christians from Rome who heard Paul was coming met him at Puteoli and walked with him the final week's trek—about 125 miles (200 km) north to Rome.

Here's the odd end of the story. "For the

next two years, Paul lived in Rome at his own expense. He welcomed all who visited him, boldly proclaiming the Kingdom of God and teaching about the Lord Jesus Christ. And no one tried to stop him" (Acts 28:30-31).

Why no report about the trial? Perhaps, some Bible scholars speculate, the writer knew that all of his Christian readers were painfully aware of what happened. Early Christian writers, such as Eusebius of Caesarea (AD 265–340), reported that "Paul was beheaded in Rome."

The question is when. Some say at the end of this trial. Others say the court found him not guilty. As the theory goes, Paul was released, only to get arrested a couple years later, tried again, and executed.

One piece of supporting evidence is from church leader Clement of Rome. Writing in Paul's century, he said Paul traveled to "the extreme west," presumably Spain, on the Roman Empire's western frontier.

Paul never wrote about it in any letter that has survived. But he did tell the Christians in Rome, "I am planning to go to Spain, and when I do, I will stop off in Rome" (Romans 15:24). If that's what happened, he was executed sometime after AD 64, during Nero's purge of Christians, whom he blamed for setting fire to Rome that summer.

Jesus: "Take a letter." Jesus dictates seven letters to a man named John, exiled on what may have been a penal colony island—Patmos, off the west coast of Turkey. Jesus dictates praise and complaints to seven churches located in the geographical center of the Christian world. Some scholars say they wonder if the letters were intended for all churches as general notes of encouragement and warning.

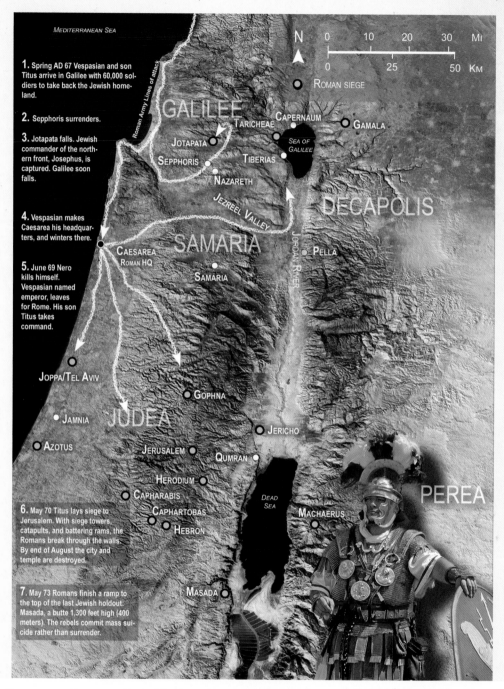

N

0   10   20   30   MI

0   25   50   KM

ROMAN SIEGE

GALILEE

Roman Army Lines of attack

CAPERNAUM

TARICHEAE

GAMALA

JOTAPATA

SEA OF GALILEE

SEPPHORIS

TIBERIAS

NAZARETH

JEZREEL VALLEY

DECAPOLIS

SAMARIA

JORDAN RIVER

PELLA

CAESAREA
ROMAN HQ

SAMARIA

JOPPA/TEL AVIV

GOPHNA

JAMNIA

JUDEA

JERICHO

AZOTUS

JERUSALEM

QUMRAN

HERODIUM

DEAD SEA

PEREA

CAPHARABIS

CAPHARTOBAS

MACHAERUS

HEBRON

MASADA

1. Spring AD 67 Vespasian and son Titus arrive in Galilee with 60,000 soldiers to take back the Jewish homeland.

2. Sepphoris surrenders.

3. Jotapata falls. Jewish commander of the northern front, Josephus, is captured. Galilee soon falls.

4. Vespasian makes Caesarea his headquarters, and winters there.

5. June 69 Nero kills himself. Vespasian named emperor, leaves for Rome. His son Titus takes command.

6. May 70 Titus lays siege to Jerusalem. With siege towers, catapults, and battering rams, the Romans break through the walls. By end of August the city and temple are destroyed.

7. May 73 Romans finish a ramp to the top of the last Jewish holdout. Masada, a butte 1,300 feet high (400 meters). The rebels commit mass suicide rather than surrender.

Romans on the warpath. In AD 66 Jewish rebels manage to run off the few thousand Roman soldiers occupying what is now Israel. But Jewish independence lasts only a year or so. That's how long Rome's top general takes to return with an overpowering force. The army levels Jerusalem and the Jews' only temple. This war changes the way Jews worship God. No more temple. No more priests. No more sacrifices. Forty years earlier, Jesus had predicted this would happen: "Not one stone will be left on top of another...This generation will not pass from the scene until all these things take place" (Matthew 24:2,34).

MEMOS FROM JESUS
COMPLIMENTS AND CRITIQUE OF SEVEN CHURCHES

Jesus is a church critic at the beginning of the end of the Bible.

The Bible ends with the book of Revelation, a collection of visions experienced by a man named John. Many scholars say John probably wrote in the AD 90s, when Emperor Domitian targeted Christians for the afterlife. Domitian was a firm believer in traditional Roman religion with Jupiter as the top god. He had no tolerance for Christians.

John's visions began with Jesus dictating letters to seven leading churches in the heart of the Christian world at a critical time. Generation One was dying. This was the generation of souls who had seen for themselves Jesus and the apostles. If they failed to live the Christian life and to teach it to others, Christianity would die with them.

Some Bible experts say they wonder if John, writing in a highly symbolic genre known as *apocalyptic*, intended Jesus's praise and warnings to serve as a kind of barometer for all churches—a tool for taking stock of what they're doing right and what they're doing wrong.

CHURCH	COMPLIMENT	COMPLAINT
Ephesus	They work hard, show patient endurance, and don't tolerate evil people (2:2).	"You don't love me or each other as you did at first!" (2:4).
Smyrna	Though financially poor, they are spiritually rich (2:9).	No complaints.
Pergamum	They stayed true to Jesus even after one of them was martyred (2:13).	They tolerate two false teachers who commit sex sins (2:14-15).
Thyatira	They love and help each other with patient endurance (2:19).	They tolerate a false prophetess who teaches that sex sins are okay (2:20).
Sardis	At least a few church members "have not soiled their clothes with evil" (3:4).	"You have a reputation for being alive—but you are dead. Wake up!" (3:1-2).
Philadelphia	They have obeyed Jesus and remained loyal to him (3:8).	No complaints.
Laodicea	No compliments.	"You are like lukewarm water…I will spit you out!" (3:16).

12

BIBLE LANDS TODAY

ISRAEL, FAST FACTS

- *Size.* Seven Israels would fit in Florida—8100 square miles (21,000 sq km).

- *Population.* Same as New York City—eight million.

- *Ethnic groups.* Three of four souls are Jewish; most others are Arab.

- *Languages.* Hebrew (official), Arabic (among Arab minority), English (most popular foreign language).

- *Religion.* Out of every 100 souls, 75 are Jewish, 17 are Muslim, 2 are Christian.

- *Natural resources.* Wood, potash (Dead Sea salt with potassium, used in fertilizer), copper, and natural gas.

- *Agriculture.* Citrus, veggies.

- *Industries.* High-tech products, timber, and minerals mined from the Dead Sea.

DISPUTED TERRITORIES

In 1948 the United Nations recommended setting up two ethnic states in what is now called Israel—Arab and Jewish. Arabs would get what are now the West Bank and the Gaza Strip. Jewish leaders agreed. Arabs didn't. War broke out that year. Arabs lost. Israelis captured the West Bank. They added the Gaza Strip and Golan Heights in the 1967 Six-Day War—Israel versus Egypt, Syria, and Jordan.

- *West Bank.* Populated by Palestinians (80 percent) and Israeli settlers. Occupied and patrolled by Israeli army. Governed under Israeli-Palestinian Interim Agreement. Future status: uncertain.

- *Gaza Strip.* Recognized by the UN as part of State of Palestine. Israeli-occupied, though Israel withdrew its settlers and army in 2005. Governed under Israeli-Palestinian Interim Agreement. Future status: uncertain.

SEA OF GALILEE
Saint Peter's fish, a tasty tilapia native to this freshwater lake, is a common dish tourists order when visiting the area. Locals call the lake Kinnereth, Hebrew for Harp because the lake is harp-shaped.

EUROPE
AFRICA

MEDITERREAN SEA

SYRIA
DAMASCUS

MT. HERMON
TYRE
DAN
GOLAN HEIGHTS
Israel captured Golan Heights from Syria in 1967 war
HAZOR RUINS
KORAZIN
CAPERNAUM
HAIFA
SEPPHORIS
TIBERIAS
CANA
SEA OF GALILEE (KINNERETH)
KURSI (GERGESA)
NAZARETH
MT. TABOR
YARMUK
MEGIDDO RUINS
AFULA
CAESAREA
JENIN
MT. GILBOA
NETANYA
RAMAH
SAMARIA NABLUS (SHECHEM)
WEST BANK
TEL AVIV-YAFO (JOPPA)
JOPPA (OLD CITY)
JORDAN RIVER
Population: 2.7 million. About 8 of 10 people in the West Bank are Palestinian Arabs
AMMAN
ASHDOD
JERICHO
GIBEAH
ASHDOD RUINS
JERUSALEM
QUMRAN
ASHKELON
BETHLEHEM
TEKOA
DEAD SEA
GAZA
HEBRON
EIN GEDI
GAZA STRIP
RAFAH
Israel captured Gaza Strip from Egypt in the 1967 Six Days War. Israelis abandoned it to Palestinian locals in 2005. Estimated population: 1.8 million. Size: 139 square miles (360 square km). That's about the size of Atlanta, with four times the population.
BEERSHEBA
ARAD
MASADA
MT. SODOM
SAFI
ISRAEL
JORDAN
NEGEV BADLANDS
WADI AL-ARABAH
PETRA
EGYPT
EILAT
AQABA
CONTESTED, OCCUPIED, OR PALESTINIAN TERRITORIES
10   20 MILES
10   20   30 KM
GULF OF AQABA

JERUSALEM
The Dome of the Rock, a 1300-year-old Muslim shrine, center, dominates the cityscape. It rests on the hilltop where scholars say the Jerusalem temple stood before Romans destroyed it 2,000 years ago.

DEAD SEA
Evaporation pools in the south end of the Dead Sea allow miners to harvest minerals such as salt and postassium (potash) used in fertilizer.

BETHLEHEM
A Palestinian girl searches an Israeli soldier in a reversal of reality. This graffiti decorates a "protective wall" Israelis built around the West Bank city of Bethlehem, where Palestinian Christians and Muslims live. Israeli officials say the wall has reduced terrorist attacks. Bethehem Palestinians call the barrier the "Apartheid Wall," which they say makes the city feel like a prison.

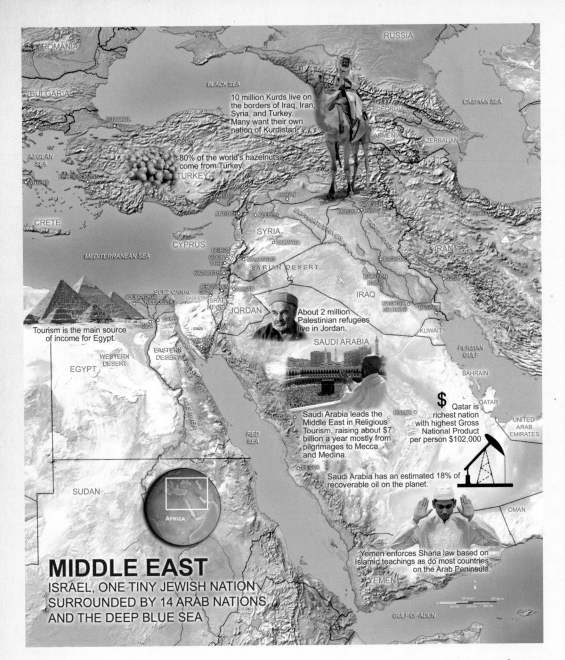

10 million Kurds live on the borders of Iraq, Iran, Syria, and Turkey. Many want their own nation of Kurdistan.

80% of the world's hazelnuts come from Turkey.

About 2 million Palestinian refugees live in Jordan.

Tourism is the main source of income for Egypt.

Saudi Arabia leads the Middle East in Religious Tourism, raising about $7 billion a year mostly from pilgrimages to Mecca and Medina.

Qatar is richest nation with highest Gross National Product per person $102,000

Saudi Arabia has an estimated 18% of recoverable oil on the planet.

Yemen enforces Sharia law based on Islamic teachings as do most countries on the Arab Peninsula.

MIDDLE EAST
ISRAEL, ONE TINY JEWISH NATION SURROUNDED BY 14 ARAB NATIONS AND THE DEEP BLUE SEA

- *Golan Heights.* Former Syrian land lost to Israel in war. It is now occupied by Israelis and monitored by UN peace-keepers. Strategic highland that provides clear view of northern Israel.

- *Jerusalem.* Israel's designated capital since 1950, though not recognized by the United States or other nations, which maintain embassies in Tel Aviv-Yafo. UN leaders have said Jerusalem must be the shared capital of both Israel and Palestine if peace is ever to be achieved.

INDEX OF ILLUSTRATIONS

Phil Hearing/flickr/CC2; Sebleouf/Château de Saint-Priest, dans le département du Rhône/WM/CC3; sculpture of king by Nicolas Cordier/WM; Matson Photo Service/LC; painting by Ludwik Wiesiołowski/WM; **85.** SMM/NASA, (insets) JS; **86.** Ian W. Scott/flickr/CC2; **87.** Justin Ennis/Flickr/CC2; **88.** (maps) SMM/NASA, (insets from left) Painting by Nicolas Poussin/WM, painting by Frederick Arthur Bridgman/ErgSap/flickr/CC2, Ernst Josephson/WM; **89.** Chad Rosenthal/flickr/CC2; **91.** Albert Weisgerber/WM; **93.** BB; **94.** SMM/NASA; **95.** (map) SMM/NASA/Tom Patterson, Natural Earth, (inset chariot) WM, (insets clockwise from horse) José Reynaldo da Fonseca/WM/CC2.5, Howcheng/Fennel seed/WM/CC3, Szaaman/WM, William Scot/WM/CC2.5, Rennett Stowe/WM/CC2, Deror avi/WM; **97.** Edward Poynter/WM; **98.** LC

7. ONE NATION DIVIDED

99. (from left) Frank X. Leyendecker/LC, JS, Edwin Austin Abbey/WM; **100.** SMM/ Rani Calvo/Geological Survey of Israel, (inset bulls) Walters Art Museum/WM, (Ark of Covenant) Lancastermerrin88/WM/CC1; **101.** BMM; **102.** BMM; **103.** SMM/NASA, (inset top heads) Adrian Scottow/WM/CC2, (inset bottom head) Motacilla/Rodbourne Cheney St. Mary Headstop King/WM/CC3; **104,** Olaf Tausch/Relief in the Karnak Temple showing Thutmosis III slaying Canaanite captives from the Battle of Megiddo, 15th Century BC/WM/CC3; **105.** Frederic Leighton/WM; **107.** John Byam Liston Shaw/WM; **108,** SMM/NASA, (insets from top) Edwin Austin Abbey/WM, JS; **109.** SMM/British Museum

8. JEWS EVICTED FROM ISRAEL

111. (from left) BM, SMM/British Museum, David Castor/WM; JS; **112,** SM/NASA, (insets) LC; **113,** John Frederick Lewis/WM; **115,** SMM/British Museum; **116,** (maps) SMM/NASA, (insets from top), BMM, SMM, SMM; **117.** David Castor/WM; **118.** BB; **119.** Aime Nicolas Morot/WM; **120,** (both) SMM; **121,** SMM/NASA, (insets from top) SMM, JS; **123,** Brian Morley; **124.** SMM/NASA/Tom Patterson, Natural Earth; **125,** SMM; **126.** (map) SMM/NASA, (inset) JS, (stone) SMM; **127.** Painting by Egon Schiele, photo by Ondrej Havala; **128.** (maps) SMM/NASA, (inserts from top) SMM, LC, Rembrandt/WM; **129,** (photo) BMM, painting by Arthur Hacker/WM

9. REBUILDING FROM A ROCK PILE

131. Prioryman/Cyrus Cylinder front/WM/CC3, (Roman) JS, (Alexander) WM; **132.** SM/NASA, (inset) WM/PD; **133.** (top) Rembrand/WM/National Gallery, (bottom) Philip Maiwald/WM/CC1; **134.** LC, **135.** Prioryman/Cyrus Cylinder front/WM/CC3; **136.** (maps) SMM/NASA, (insets from top) David Roberts/LC, John Frederick Lewis/WM; **138.** SMM/NASA, (inset) Berthold Werner/WM; **139.** BB; **140.** (top) David Roberts/LC, (bottom) Matson Collection/LC; **142.** Edwin Long/WM; **143.** SMM/NASA, (insets) JS; **145.** Matson Collection/LC; **146.** Seier and Seier/flickr/CC2; **147.** Marcel Masferrer Pascual/flickr/CC2; **148.** 5thCentury monk/WM

10. JESUS ON A MISSION

149. (from the left) BMM, Mihály Munkácsy/WM, Ondrej Havala; **150.** SMM/NASA, (insets from top left clockwise) Reconstruction

proposal of an ancient Roman-Egyptian battle galley - Sven Littkowski/Forum Navis Romana//Terra Romana (Navis.TerraRomana.org), WM, JS; **151.** (top) photo illustration by SMM, photo of city model by Daniel Ventura/WM/CC1, (bottom) Kleuske/Via appia/WM/ CC3; **152.** (top) BB; (bottom) WM; **154.** Painting by John Waterhouse, photo by Athansia Sqouris/Flickr/CC2; **155.** SMM/NASA, (insets from top) LC, LC, Georges de la Tour/WM, James Tissot/WM; **157.** Marcus Cyron/WM/CC2; **159.** Photo illustration by SMM, (sky) Hans-Peter Scholz/WM, (Jerusalem) Hynek Moravec/Jerusalem night 7088/WM/CC3; **160.** SMM/ Rani Calvo/Geological Survey of Israel, (inset) Jastrow/WM; **161.** painting by Henri Regnault/Metropolitan Museum of Art/ photo by Dmadeo/flickr/CC2; **162.** (maps) SMM/ Rani Calvo/Geological Survey of Israel, (insets) man seated by Vasily Polenov/WM, photo by Wolfgang Moroder/Painting of Christ Handing the Keys to St. Peter attributed to Eduard Burgauner in the Parish church of Kastelruth around 1899/WM/CC3, jar by TeresaLarkHeintzman/WM; **163.** Andrey Mironov/Parable of the carpenter by Terje Hartberg; **164.** Israel Tourism/flickr/CC2; **165.** Dan Lunberg/flickr/CC2; **167.** SMM; **169.** WolfgangRieger/WM; **170.** AM/Christ and the sinner/WM/CC3; **172.** SMM/NASA, (insets from top right clockwise) pig by WM, AM/Christ and the pauper/WM/CC3, AM/Last Supper/WM/CC3, Lazarus resurrection by Lippo Memmi/WM, William Bouguereau/WM, WM, woman portrait by Franz Xaver Kosler/WM; **174.** AM/Carrying the Cross/WM/CC3; **175.** BB; **178.** Fedor Bronnikov/WM; **179.** AM/Christ's appearance to the apostles/WM/CC3; **180.** (all) AM/WM/CC3: Expulsion of the merchants from the temple, Where are you going, Lord? Parable of the Unjust Steward; **181.** (all) AM/WM/CC3: Last Supper, This is the Man!

11. THE CHURCH IS BORN

183. (top) David Friel/WM, (bottom from left) Lucas Cranach/WM, Aleks G/The executioner, Peter & Paul Fortress, St.-Petersburg, Russia/WM/CC3, Francesco Hayez/WM; **184.** El Greco/WM; **185.** Ralf Roletschek/WM; **186.** SMM/NASA/Tom Patterson, Natural Earth; **187.** Adam Eisheimer; **188.** AM/Apostle Peter in prison/WM/CC3; **189.** Caravaggio/WM; **190.** (maps) SMM/NASA, (ship) Giorces/WM, (Paul) Parmigianino; **191.** Isidor Kaufmann/WM; **193.** LKA NRW/WM/CC2; **194.** SMM/NASA; **196.** SMM/NASA, (inset) NASA; **198.** SMM/NASA, (inset) Lyn Gateley/flickr/CC2; **199.** Marie-Lan Nguyen/Naples National Archaeological Museum/WM/CC2.5; **200.** Vasily Surikov/WM; **201.** José de Ribera/Museum of Art of Ponce/WM, (inset) Wolfgang Sauber/WM/CC1; **203.** SMM/NASA, (inset) Jean-Leon Gerome/WM; **205.** SMM/NASA; **206.** SMM/NASA, (inset) Luc Viatour/WM/CC1; **210.** (maps) SMM/NASA, (insets from top left clockwise) Etan Tal/Tilapia zilli/WM/CC3, Godot13/Sunset aerial view of the Temple Mount/WM/CC3, Staff Sgt. Jim Greenhill/flickr, Pawel Ryszawa/WM/CC1; **211.** (maps) SMM/NASA, (nuts) Fir0002/Hazelnuts/WM/CC3, (camel rider) Robert Couse-Baker/flickr, (man with hat) Trocaire/flickr/CC2, (crowd) Ali Mansuri/WM/CC2.5, (oil well) NeoRetro/WM, (man praying) Muhammad Mahdi Karim/CC1, (pyramids) WM

GENERAL INDEX

KEY TO INDEX
bold numbers: featured
regular numbers: mentioned
color numbers: image
green numbers: location on map

Aram (Arameans), 107

ark (Noah's boat), 16, 17

ark of the covenant, 59, 67, 100, 101
  holds Commandments, 59, 66
  crossing Jordan River, **56-57**
  captured by Philistines, **66-67**
  possibly stolen by Babylonian invaders, 125

Artaxerxes, 139, 141

Aruru, 13

Ashdod, 67, 77, 83, 210

Ashkelon, 66, 77, 83, 118, 210

Asher, 65, 74

Asherah, 106

Ashurnasirpal, 115, 116

Assyria (Assyrian Empire), 109, **111**, **115-122**, 116, 120, 124
  attack route in Israel, 121
  vicious reputation, 121, 134
  conquers Israel, **118-119**
  destroys 46 Jewish cities, **120-122**
  defeated by Babylonians, 124

Athens, 150, 196, 197, 198, 205

Attalia, 194, 205

Augustus, 150

Azekah, 86, 123, 126

B

Baal, 43, 106, **109**, 120

Babylon (Babylonian Empire), 124, 128, **129**
  invasion into Judah, 126
  destroys Judah, Jerusalem, **123-127**, 147
  exiles the Jews, 128, 133

Babylon (city), 12, 13, 20, 121, 124, 136, 143, 211

Balaam, 54,

baptism (*see also* John the Baptist)

of Jesus, 161, 164
  with Holy Spirit, 185
  of Paul, 191

Barak, 70, 71

Barnabas, 193, 195, 196

Bashan, 52

Beatitudes, 165

Bedouin, 98

Beersheba, 26, 27, 31, 38, 51, 210

Beirut, 211

Belshazzar, 133

Benjamin (son of Jacob), 37, 38

Benjamin (tribe), 65, 90, 101

Berea, 196, 198, 205

Bethany, 155, 170, 172

Bethel, 31, 35, 63, 68, 68, 70, 100, 155

Bethlehem, 4, 69, 83, 155, 155, 210
  hometown of David, 81, 83, 89, 90
  birthplace of prophesied Messiah, 156
  birthplace of Jesus, **155-159**, 172
  star of, 159
  slaughter of boys in, 150
  "protective wall," 210

Bethsaida, 162, 163, 171, 172

Bible, 147,
  first translation, **148**

Bilhah, 32, 34

Black Sea, 211

blessing, 22, 30, 32, 54, 114

blind, 90
  elderly Isaac, 30
  Samson, 78
  elderly Eli,
  healed, 168, **169**
  Saul on road to Damascus, 189, 190, 191

blood, 35

Jesus's sacrifice atones for sin, 27, 165, 176

boat, 4, 153

Bosphorus Strait, 18

bread, 48, 86, 104, 105
  unleavened, 176
  at Lord's Supper, 176

brickmaking, 59

bubonic plague, 66, 67

bull, 100, 101, 106

burial, 141
  of Aaron, 53
  of Moses, **53**
  of Jesus, 175, 179

burning bush, 41, 112

C

Caesar, 146, 202

Caesarea, 152, 153, 172, 190, 196, 198, 201, 206

Caiaphas, 177

Caleb, 50

Calvary, 174

Camel, 72, 134, 136

Cana, 162
  wedding at, 163

Canaan (Canaanites), 22, 38, 46, 52, 134
  cutaway map with elevations, 4
  destination of Abraham, 19, 21
  Promised Land for the Jews, 22

Capernaum, 162, 163, 171, 172, 205, 206
  Jesus's ministry headquarters, 162

Carchemish, 22, 124, 124

carpenter, 158, 162, 163

Carthage, 150

Caspian Sea, 211

Catholic, Roman, 148

cedars of Lebanon, 93

census, 155, 157
    by Romans in Bethlehem, 158

chariot, 43, 70,71, 94, 121

Chebar Riber, 129, 128

Chemosh, 76

child sacrifice (*see* sacrifice)

Christ (*see* Messiah)

Christianity (Christians), 27, 186
    where name comes from, 184
    conversion of first Roman
        official, 195
    persecution of, 186, **186-188**,
        189, 192, 202
    legalized by Romans, 158, 175
    ancient church, 175, 191, 196

church (*see* Christianity)

Church of the Holy Sepulchre,
    175

Church of the Nativity, 157, 158

circumcision, 22, 192, 201

cities of refuge, 65

City of David, 90

Claudius Caesar, 166

Clement of Rome, 205

Colosse, 205

communion (*see* Lord's Supper)

conversion of Paul, **189-191**

Corinth, 150, 194, 196, **197** 198,
    205
    church conflict, **197**

covenant (agreement) of God,
    176
    with Abraham and descen-
        dants, 22, 23, 114, 128
    new, 165, 176, 195

creation, 13, 17
    God's creation temple, **15**
    other creation stories, 33, 42

Crete, 203, 204

crucifixion, **178**

of Jesus, 4, 149, 165, **166**, 174,
    175, 177, **178-179**

curse, **54**, 171, 195

Cush, 13

Cyrus, 132, 134-136

Cyrus cylinder, 131, 135

Cyprus, 192, 194, 194, 195, 196,
    198, 203

Elah, Valley of, 83, 85, 86

Eliab, 83

Elon, 68, 69

Eltekeh, Battle of, 121

Ehud, 68, 69

Elam (Elamites), 25

Elijah, 105, **105-106**, 107, 112, 113
  defeats Baal prophets on Mount Carmel, 106

Elisha, 107, 112, 113

En-gedi, 83, 88, 89, 210

Ephesus, 196, 198, 198, **199**, 207, 205, 211
  riot during Paul's visit, 198
  Revelation letter to, 207

Ephraim, 65, 68, 69, 70, 74, 92

Epic of Gilgamesh, 13, 33

Esau, 30, **30-32**, 52, 53

Essenes, 145

Esther (queen), **142**

Ethiopia, 13

Eucharist (*see* Lord's Supper)

Euphrates River, 12, **13-15**, 18, 20, 21, 54, 82, 95, 115, 116, 128, 129, 137, 141, 211

Eusebius, 205

Eve, 12

exodus out of Egypt, **43-54**

exorcism (*see* demons)

Ezekiel (prophet), 112, 114, 115, 125

Ezion-Geber, 52

Ezra (priest), **136**, 140
  condemns mixed marriages, 142
  route to Jerusalem, 136

F

Fair Havens, 203, 204

faith, 113

of Abraham, 22
for healing, **169**

Felix, 200, 202

Fertile Crescent, 12, 12-13, 14, 17, 115

Festus, 202, 203

fishing, 210

Flood (Noah's), **15-18**

fortune-teller, 196

G

Gad (tribe), 54, 65

Galilee, 160, 161, 162, **162-164**, 164, 206
  farming center, **164**

Garden of Eden, 12, **12-15**

Garden tomb, 175, 179, 181

Garstang, John, 58

Gath, 66, 77, 87, 89, 121, 121

Gaulantis, 160, 162

Gaza, 77, 78, 155, 205, 210, 211

Gaza Strip, 65, 78, 83, 160, 209, 210, 211

Gennesaret, 162

Gentile, 170-173, 200
  Paul's target audience, 195, 200, 201

Gerasene (Gergesa), 162, 172, 210

Geshur, 92

Gethsemane, Garden of, 181

Gezer, 95, 104

Gibeah, 83, 88, 210

Gibeon, 9, 60, **60-61**, 63, 83, 88

Gideon, 68, 69, **72-74**
  battle, 73

Gihon river, 12, 13, 15

Gilead, 35, 75, 76, 107, 108

Gilgal, 57, 59, 61, 63, 66

God

Creator, 12-13, 15

sends flood, 17

holiness of, 18

destroys Sodom and Gomorrah, **28-29**

makes contract with Abraham, 22, 23

tests Abraham, 26-27

sends plagues on Egypt, **41-42**

creates system of sacrifice and priesthood, 27

sentences Jewish nation to years, 50

brings Jews home from exile, 134

sacrifices his Son, 27, 155, 174

Golan Heights, 65, 161, 210, 211

golden calf, 100, **101**

Goliath, 81, **85-87**

Gomorrah, 24, **28-29**, 29

Good Samaritan, **119**, 167

Goshen, 35, 38, 44, 155

Gospels, **156**
  Isaiah as fifth, 163

grapes, 11

Great Bitter Lake, 44

H

Habakkuk (prophet), 112, 113

Hagar, 24

Haggai (prophet), 112, 113, 141
  ministry, 112

hail
  plagues in Egypt, 42
  during Joshua's battle, 61

Haman, 142

Hamath, 117, 31

Hanukkah, 145

Hapi, 42

Hasmonean, 146, 154

Hathor, 42

Mari, 21, 21, 22

Mark (*see* John Mark)

Martha, 170

Mary (mother of Jesus), 158, 185
    pregnant and unmarried, 155
    virgin, 156
    visited by angel, 156

Mary (sister of Martha, Lazarus), 170

Mary Magdalene, 179

martyrs, 186, 187

Masada, 206, 210

Mattathias, 146

Matthew, 165, 166

Medes (Media), 119

Mediterranean Sea, 116, 117, 150, 159, 186

Megiddo, 70, 94, 124, 126, 155, 210

Memphis, 205

Meshach, 125

Mesopotamia, 14, 12, 14, 20

Messiah, 168, 191
    Jewish expectations of, 176
    Jesus as, 156-157, 174, 176, 177, 184, 185, 188

Micah (prophet), 112, 113

Middle East, 211

Midianites (Midian), 41, **72-74**, 52
    camel riders, 72

Miletus, 205

Miller, Stephen, 74

Min, 42

miracles of Jesus
    healing the sick, **168**, **169**, 171
    exorcizing demons, 171
    calming storm, 4
    feeding thousands, 168
    raising Lazarus, 172, 174

Miriam, 70

Miriamne, 154, 161

Mizpah, 75, 128

Moab (Moabites) , 52, 54, 82, 102, 138

Moabite Stone, 102, 111

Moreh, hill of, 73

Moses, **39-54**, 44, 64, 112, 123, 165
    birth and childhood, 40
    plagues in Egypt, **41-42**
    parting the sea, **43-44**
    sends scouts to Canaan, **50-51**
    death, **53**

Mount Ararat, 16, 18, 211

Mount of Beatitudes, 162, 165

Mount Carmel, 70, 106, 108, 153

Mount Gilboa, 210

Mount Hermon, 27, 29, 51, 57, 64, 65, 210

Mount Hor, 52

Mount Moriah, 26, 27

Mount Nebo, 52, 53

Mount of Olives, 151, 175, 176

Mount Sinai, 46, 106, 191, 211

Mount Sodom, 210

Mount Tabor, 68, 70, 162, 164, 210

Mount Zion (*see* Jerusalem)

music, 75, 84, 88, 129

Nefertiti, 55

Negev, 62, 63, 210

Nehemiah (prophet), 112

Nehemiah, 131, 140-142

Nero, 192, 202, 205, 206

Nile River, 23, 40, 42, 45, 116, 211

Nineveh, 22, 93, 119, 122, 124, 128, 136, 143, 144, 211

Noah, **16-18**, 18

O

oasis (*see also* Kadesh oasis), 12, 58, 89

Obadiah (prophet), 112, 113

olive oil, 48, 80, 83, 84, 95

olives, 176

Omri, 102, 104

Othniel, 68, 69

P

Palestine (Palestinians), 78, 210

Paphos, 194, 195, 205

papyrus, 148

parables, 166, **167**
    Good Samaritan, 119, 167

Paran, Wilderness of, 50, 51

Passover,
    first Passover, 49
    Jewish festival, 173, 174, 176, 177

Patmos, 205, 205

Paul (Saul), **189-205**, 193, 200, 201
    early years, 190
    missionary trips, 194, 196, 198
    trip to trial in Rome, 203
    timeline, **192**
    stoning of Stephen, 187
    conversion, 189
    tentmaker, 197

associate minister in Antioch, 193

ministry to Gentiles, 200-201

arrested and imprisoned, 200, **200-205**

voyage to Rome, 203, **203-205**

Penuel, 31

Pentecost, 184-185, 185

Perea, 160, 160, 206

perfection (spiritual), 168

Perga, 194, 195, 205

Pergamum, 150, 205, 207

Persia (Persian Empire) ,132, 133

defeats Babylon, 131

frees Jews, 134-135

warriors, 14, 143

defeated by Alexander, **143-144**

Persian Gulf, 12, 13, 14, 15, 132, 211

Persepolis, 143, 144

Peter, Simon (apostle), 184

House and family in Capernaum, 162

invited to become disciple, 165

not scholarly, 165

denies knowing Jesus, 184

preaches Jerusalem sermon, **184-185**

arrested, 187, 188

Pharaoh, 33, 37-38, 43, 44

Pharisees, 168, 173, 189, 191, 201

Philadelphia, 205, 207

Philip, King, 143

Philippi, 194, **196**, 196, 198, 202, 205

Philistines (Philistia), 45, 53, 55, 64, 66, 68, 81, 85, 85-87

Samson fights, **77-78**

capture ark of covenant, 66, **66-67**

Goliath battles David, **85-87**

Phoenicia (Lebanon), 79, 95, 102, 104

Pisces, 159

Pishon, 12, 13, 15

Pilate, 4-5, 149, 160, 166, 179

trial, execution of Jesus, 177, 181

Pisgah Peak, 53

Pithom, 38

plagues,

Egyptian, **41-42**

Philistine, 67

Pliny, 145, 169

Plutarch, 178

Pompeii (city), 169, 205

Pompey (Roman general), 146, 150

Potiphar, **36**

priests (Jewish priesthood), 64, 66 , 145

condemning interracial marriage, 142

bypassing injured Samaritan, 167

Priscilla, 166

Promised Land, 45, 53-54, **55-65**, 123, 128

tribes, 65, 82

prophecies, 132

fall of Judah and Jerusalem, **123-127**, 128, 141

Messiah, Jesus, 156-157, 176

prophets, Jewish, **112-114,** 112

chart of, **113-114**

killed by Jezebel, 106

women, 70, 71

Psalms, 148

Ptah (Peth, Peteh), 42

Ptolemy, 143, 143

punishment,

of Jews, 69, 72, 126, 141

cities of refuge, 65

Jews exiled from homeland, **128-129**, **133**

Punon, 52

Purim, 142

Puteoli, 205

Q

quail, 47, 48, **48-49**

Qarqar, Battle of, 117

Quirinius, 158

Qumran, 88, 206

R

Ra, 41, 42

rabbi, 136, 165, 166, 173, 191, 192

teachings of, 166

Rachel, 31, 32, 34

Rahab, 59

Ramah, 68, 70

Rameses (city) , 35, 39, 44, 46, 155

Rameses (pharaoh), 39, 42

Ramoth, 31, 65, 107, 108, 108

rape, 36

Amnon and Tamar, 91-92

Rebekah, 32,

Reed Sea, 44

Red Sea, 43, 44, 45, 46, 47, 52, 53, 97, 97, 211

Israelites cross, **43-44**

refuge, cities of, 65

Rehoboam, 100, 101

resurrection, 197, 201

of Lazarus, 172

of Jesus, 165, **179**, 188, 195

Reuben (tribe), 54, 64, 65

Rhodes, 196, 198

Rome (city), 146, 150, 150, 151, 203, 205

founded, 150